PEOPLE OF GOD
THE HISTORY OF
CATHOLIC CHRISTIANITY

ANTHONY E. GILLES

ST. ANTHONY MESSENGER PRESS

Cincinnati, Ohio

Pages i-208:

Nihil Obstat: Rev. Lawrence Landini, O.F.M.
                      Rev. Ralph Lawrence
                      April 4, 2000

Imprimi Potest: Rev. Fred Link, O.F.M.
                      Provincial

Imprimatur: +Most Rev. Carl K. Moeddel, V.G.
                      Archdiocese of Cincinnati
                      April 6, 2000

Pages 209-250:

Nihil Obstat: Rev. Hilarion Kistner, O.F.M.
                      Rev. John J. Jennings

Imprimi Potest: Rev. Jeremy Harrington, O.F.M.
                      Provincial

Imprimatur: +James H. Garland, V.G.
                      Archdiocese of Cincinnati
                      January 9, 1985

The *nihil obstat* and *imprimatur* are a declaration that a book or pamphlet is considered to be free from doctrinal or moral error. It is not implied that those who have granted the *nihil obstat* and *imprimatur* agree with the contents, opinions or statements expressed.

Scripture citations are taken from the *New Revised Standard Version Bible*, copyright ©1989 by the Division of Christian Education of the National Council of Churches of Christ in the U.S.A. and used by permission.

Excerpts from *A History of Christian Thought* by Justo Gonzalez, copyright ©1983, are used by permission of Abingdon Press.

The excerpt from *The Ratzinger Report* by Cardinal Joseph Ratzinger, with Vittorio Messori, copyright ©1985, reprinted by permission of Ignatius Press.

Cover design by Mark Sullivan
Cover image © www.istockphoto.com/Roberto A. Sanchez
Book design by Constance Wolfer

ISBN-13 978-0-86716-363-6
ISBN-10 0-86716-363-1

Published by St. Anthony Messenger Press
28 W. Liberty St.
Cincinnati, OH 45202
www.SAMPBooks.org
Printed in the U.S.A.

08 09 10 9 8 7 6

TABLE OF CONTENTS

PREFACE

WHAT IS CHURCH HISTORY? What is it not? To some extent, the answer to that question is in the eye of the beholder. But not entirely.

A VOYAGE TO THE DEPTHS

Suppose we were oceanographers examining the wreck of the *Titanic* through the lenses of "Alvin," Dr. Robert Ballard's deep-water submarine that was the first human instrument to explore the sunken ship after it had lain undetected for seventy-four years. What would grab our attention as we curled our way up and around the grand staircase, or cruised carefully over the deck toward the bridge? Would we engage in a hunt for missing jewels? Would we wonder how the musicians of the chamber ensemble managed to stand courageously and play their final piece as the frigid water rushed over their feet and ankles?

Would we grow angry at the cowardice of the White Star Line's owner, Bruce Ismay, as he shoved his way into a lifeboat ahead of the other passengers? Would we wonder why the *California* ignored Captain Smith's distress signals and sailed away without coming to the drowning ship's rescue? Once we had returned to the deck of our mother ship on the surface and faced the media's questions, what memories from the depths would be the most urgent for us to share?

Naturally our answers would differ if we were actually a scientist like Dr. Ballard, as opposed to a moviegoer who sat tearfully through the film *Titanic*, mourning the fate of the young lovers, Jack and Rose, who were separated by death as the floating behemoth sank beneath the North Atlantic on April 14, 1912. The scientist in us might have remembered only technical details, such as the angle at which the two parts of the huge hull had split apart. The Romantic in us might have thought only of the scene on the prow, where the two young lovers had stood breathlessly facing the wind, sailing toward a new life of freedom and bliss.

As I approached this book, I struggled with that part of me that is scientist and that part which is romantic, trying to mediate between the two, hoping that by doing so I could maintain a viewpoint that would bring to the surface the essence of Church[1] history. Naturally I could not scoop up everything that the great treasure of the Church's history holds and examine it for you the reader. I had to take a certain stance.

My stance is this. Judging from what is most important in the life of the Church, from our vantage point today, what stands out as having been most significant during our twenty-century existence? It seems to me that what stands out most noticeably, and with greatest effect on our life as Church today, is the relationship which the Church has had with the world. Hence this book is principally about the love-hate, up-and-down, tumultuous, perplexing, vexing, paradoxical struggle we the Church have been engaged in for twenty centuries to define our self-image and mission while having to relate to a value system that does not share our vision of reality. For that, after all, is what I mean by "world," *i.e.,* a system of values that is opposed to the gospel, as in the Scripture passage which proclaims that Jesus' disciples do not "belong to the world any more than I belong to the world" (John 17:16).

Somewhat along the lines of Mel Brooks's *History of the World, Part One*, a short synopsis of this Church-world story might be rendered as follows:

HISTORY OF THE CHURCH
RECITED WHILE STANDING ON ONE LEG

We the Church start out as the world's hated enemy. The world tries to eliminate us. But we turn the tables on the world and convert its leaders to our cause. These leaders, however, don't fully understand what the Church's mission is, and attempt to substitute their earthly power for the Church's spiritual authority. Things go downhill from there, and the world turns the tables on us. The world converts our leaders to its cause, and we become too worldly to proclaim the gospel with much credibility. Schisms, revolts, breakaways within the Church follow. Then, we the Church, realizing that the Church-world relationship is too hot to handle, decide to withdraw from the affair altogether. We climb behind the walls of our fortress and simply condemn anything that looks like the world. This goes on until a short, pudgy Pope named John XXIII decides to open a window on the world in order to see if we can start the dance again—on our own terms, but with respect for the good that the world has to offer. Next comes the enthralling chapter called, "Who's Really a Catholic?", wherein everyone tries to decide what Vatican II means and just how much Church-world dialogue and contact there ought to be. That's about it. You'll have to read the book for the exciting details. Take my word for it, you'll love it.

---

[1] I capitalize the word "Church" in this book because I use it in two senses that I think call for capitalization: (1) in the sense of a title with the words "Roman Catholic" missing, as in the proper name, Roman Catholic Church; (2) in the sense of an abstract entity or set of relationships that exists, in whatever form, to symbolize the community of believers who see themselves, however described or defined, as the followers of Jesus Christ and seekers after the Gospels' Kingdom of God.

INTERNAL VERSUS EXTERNAL FOCUS

I couldn't tell the story of the Church-world relationship without some reference to what was going on *within* the Church. So, there is much here that has to do with "internal affairs" only. Actually, until we get to Vatican II, we the Church don't really tackle head-on the issue of our relationship with the world. We either assume the world will go away and leave us alone or that we will dominate it with threats and denunciations or that we will just glide along in partnership with the world. It isn't until Vatican II that we the Church say, "Listen up, people! We've got to face this issue. The world isn't going away. We've gotten the internal issues satisfactorily argued about and defined to the *n*th degree. We know which labels to put on each other, who's orthodox and who's not, so now let's figure out how we bring the gospel into play in the Church-world dance."

Vatican II itself, as is now obvious, had an impact not only on the Church-world relationship, but on our own quest to understand and define ourselves aside and apart from the world. Thus, one can never really get away from internal affairs while exploring the Church-world relationship. However, in this book, there are certain internal matters about which the reader might want to know more and upon which I do not focus much attention. For example, while I do touch on the subject, I don't explore in much detail the history of the liturgy, even though an historical understanding of the liturgy is vital to understanding who we are as Church in the Church-world relationship. I don't discuss miraculous events or stories of the saints. And while I couldn't ignore the papacy in a book on Church-world interactions, I don't believe that the history of the Church is the same thing as a history of the popes. Nor do I enter beyond a superficial way into the realm of spiritual devotions. For instance, I don't talk about the apparitions of the Virgin Mary, or how the First Friday and First Saturday observances got started, or discuss petitions to have Padre Pio or Mother Teresa canonized.

KNOW YOUR AUTHOR

Since so many people today are playing "Who's Really a Catholic?"—with such dreadful seriousness—perhaps I should say more about my own perspective on today's Church-world relationship. First, I don't particularly care for the world's values. For example, I can't stand to watch the average TV show. In 1998 a popular show called *Seinfeld* went off the air, and I didn't even know who Mr. Seinfeld was. To show how out of touch with the world's popular culture I am, when Princess Di and her lover, Dodi, died in 1997, I committed the unpardonable offense of asking if Dodi was the Princess's grandmother. ("Dodi" sounded like a grandmother's name to me.) Yet, as turned off as I am by the world's pursuit of icons, I do have my own saints and heroes who have come from the world rather than from the Church: Einstein, Gandhi, Churchill and Jung, for example.

I was raised in the pre-Vatican II Church and had to learn how to be "updated" like everyone else of my generation. As with Churchill's observation about Russia, the post-Vatican II Church is for me something of "a riddle wrapped in a mystery inside an enigma." But so be it. I prefer mystery stories to *Mechanics Illustrated*.

Yet, I do not believe that because I am in touch with a mystery, that I am confused[2] about where we have been and where we are going. I believe that as we the Church have marched forward on our two-millennium (and now three-millennium) pilgrimage into the post-Vatican II era, we have not been engaged, as some would conceive of it, in a quest for the brave, new world. As always, and more than ever, we are still called to be a "people set apart" (cf. 1 Peter 2:9) from the world and its ways.

Nothing I say as a criticism of the Church in the pages that follow is intended to suggest that I wish we would do away with the Church and merge with the world. Nor am I suggesting that sin is a thing of the past. The great error of the world today, as it has embraced the New Age gospel and the cult of the victimized, narcissistic self, is to suppose that Nature, undisturbed by human beings, is benign, loving and wonderful. I don't believe that. There is good and there is evil, and both exist in our world today. An historical critique of the Church's errors does not imply that I buy into the world's values or that I am recommending abolishing the Church's historic mission of building a kingdom different from that of the world.

---

[2] A mystery is not a phenomenon that leads to confusion; instead, it leads to a deeper awareness of one's own inability to know perfectly that which inspires the sense of mystery. Much of the confusion in the Church today stems from people's unwillingness to face the challenge that contacting a mystery brings with it.

CHAPTER ONE

INTRODUCING THE EARLY CHURCH

IMAGINE FOR A MOMENT that you are living in the ancient city of Ephesus in today's Turkey, about the year A.D. 95. In your childhood you were baptized into the new Christian faith, and you are now struggling to live that faith in the face of opposition from your friends and threats of arrest by the authorities. The local police are suspicious of you and your family because you will not participate in the official Roman religion, which is based on worship of the emperor. The man who is emperor now, Domitian, has decreed that he is to be called "Our Lord and our God" by his subjects, but you and your family refuse to use this title.

You, your family and other Christians in Ephesus, make up a small minority of the population, less than five percent. You meet frequently in each others' homes to pray together and to study writings which are carried to Ephesus by Christian teachers who travel back and forth across the Empire, from Jerusalem to Rome. On "the day named for the sun," you gather and worship together by breaking bread in the name of and in memory of Jesus Christ. You believe that Jesus was the Son of God, and that he died for your sins and rose from the dead to become Lord of the universe.

CHURCH AUTHORITY AFTER THE APOSTLES

Aside from the scorn of the non-Christian townspeople and the constant threat of being arrested for practicing your faith, you also are concerned about how your little *ekklesia* (Greek, "assembly" or "church") is to be run and organized. Your parents and other founders of your local Church are getting up in years. They never knew Jesus personally. Instead, they knew a man named Paul, who traveled to Ephesus and instructed them in the faith. Paul had known apostles like Peter as well as other direct disciples of Jesus. But Paul and Peter are dead, and thus you can't rely on the guidance of such men. Some members of your Church urge you to compromise with the Romans by performing the rituals of the state religion—burning incense to images of the

Emperor, for example. Others are opposed to this, arguing that no compromise is possible.

How are you and your fellow Christians going to resolve this issue and others like it? It's bad enough having to worry about whether the authorities are even going to allow you to *be* a Christian, without also having to contend with controversy within the body of believers. Gradually a solution begins to present itself. One thing you and the other Christians in Ephesus agree on is the need to stay in close touch with those who authentically represent what Jesus taught. Thus, you always have respected the writings of Paul, for example, and other writings about Jesus' life written down by men who knew Jesus personally or who studied with one of his apostles. This respect for authentic teaching is at the core of what you believe. You don't feel comfortable branching out on your own into doctrines and theories about Jesus that are not taught by authoritative representatives of the "Good News."

As a result, you and the other Christians in town have agreed to submit to the leadership of a man whom you have chosen and designated as your *episkopos*, or bishop. He is someone whose reputation for authentic faith in Jesus is well respected. The congregation in turn has chosen assistants to help the bishop guide the Church and teach the faith. Some of these assistants are named *presbuteros* or priest, and others *diakonos* or deacon. The priests administer the all-important rite of initiation called Baptism, especially in outlying areas that are too far from town for the bishop to visit. The deacons assist the bishop in practical matters, such as collecting money from the faithful and distributing it to widows in the Church.

WHAT DOES 'CHURCH' MEAN TO YOU?

But there is more to your understanding of "Church" than just the community of Christians in Ephesus. You and your fellow believers consider yourselves part of a universal body. You regularly offer hospitality to Christians who travel through town, and eagerly listen to their account of how the faith is being practiced in other cities. You give a great deal of weight to the teachings of bishops who reside in places where the Christian faith is strongly rooted—especially the cities of Jerusalem, Antioch, Alexandria and Rome. These four cities are regarded by Christians everywhere as "Mother Churches" of the Empire. The bishops of these cities often write letters to smaller Churches, in order to encourage the faithful and to explain fine points of doctrine. Just last week, for example, your bishop in Ephesus read your congregation a letter written by Bishop Clement of Rome. Along with the letters of Paul and the Gospel stories about Jesus, the letters written by bishops from the Mother Churches of the Empire help you to grow in knowledge of your faith.

You first came to understand this faith from your parents, who taught you the key Christian doctrines which they had learned from Paul. These key doctrines are now capsuled in the form of questions asked of people who are preparing for Baptism. Thus when people who have been studying the faith, who are called *catechumens*,[1] present themselves for Baptism, they must first give a public answer to such questions as the following:

> Do you believe in God the Father almighty?
> Do you believe in Jesus Christ, the Son of God?
> Do you believe that the Son of God was born by the Spirit and power of
>   God the Father made flesh in Mary's womb and born of her?
> Do you believe that he was crucified under Pontius Pilate, that he died,
>   that on the third day he rose from the dead and ascended into heaven,
>   that he sat down at the right hand of God the Father and will come to
>   judge the living and the dead?
> Do you believe in the Holy Spirit and in holy Church?

When the catechumens satisfactorily answer these questions in the presence of the entire congregation, they are considered ready to be baptized. Baptism usually takes place early in the morning on Easter,[2] but exceptions are made for people who are sick, elderly or dying, and thus baptisms are performed throughout the rest of the year as well. Young children and infants who cannot answer questions about their knowledge of the faith are baptized with their parents, who answer the questions for them.

Once catechumens have been baptized, they are permitted to participate fully in the congregation's worship services. For example, they are now allowed to recite the Our Father with the congregation and to eat the bread of the *Eucharist*. The Eucharist, a word which in Greek means "thanksgiving," is the symbolic ritual by which Christians most deeply sense and share the ongoing presence of the Lord Jesus among themselves because the bread and wine have become His Body and Blood. Many of the sermons given in your Church by traveling Christian teachers stress the importance of the Eucharist and emphasize the proper decorum which Christians are to observe when participating in the Eucharistic service.

CHRISTIAN IDENTITY: THE CHURCH'S SELF-IMAGE

This brief sketch gives us a taste of what life was like for Christians in the days of the early Church shortly after the age of the apostles. From our imaginary visit, we have learned what was important to the early Christians: such things as leadership and teaching authority, forming loving relationships in a committed community, teaching one another what the gospel means, practicing one's faith under the threat of persecution. All of these concerns had to do with the issue of *Christian identity*, or with the Church's self-image. For the

---

[1] The catechumenate becomes a structured institution beginning in the second century.
[2] Before the fourth century, Easter was not universally reserved as the time for Baptism.

early Christians it was crucial to answer the question, "What is the Church, and how does a Christian live the gospel in the world?"

Of course, these are still crucial questions. In our own day, for example, Pope John Paul II has written that Vatican II can be thought of as a "question" which the Holy Spirit was asking the Church. The question is, "Church, who are you and what do you say of yourself?" This is a question which we will constantly be asking ourselves as we study Church history. For those of us living two thousand years after Jesus, answering this question usually does not involve a life-or-death decision, as often was the case for the early Christians.

THE AGE OF PERSECUTION

Living in the Roman Empire as a Christian during the last decades of the first century and until about the year A.D. 311 was a dangerous enterprise. As early as A.D. 64, when the Emperor Nero covered Christians with pitch and then burned them alive as human torches to light the streets of Rome, followers of Jesus were engaged in a deadly serious effort to survive in a world that considered them dangerous to the Empire and the human race.

Christians were despised principally because they refused to accept Caesar as the supreme authority over their lives. Instead, they proclaimed their allegiance to an obscure Jewish rabbi named Jesus, about whom most people knew nothing, and who was put to death in the Roman province of Judea for allegedly trying to become "king of the Jews." Thus, Christians, in addition to practicing a religion that was offensive to the Romans, were looked upon as traitors to the state for following someone who had tried to usurp Roman authority. Christians were said to have been "atheists," for not worshiping the pagan gods, and they were regarded as anti-social for avoiding civil rituals, theater, games, etc.

The persecutions ebbed and flowed in intensity until A.D. 311. Until that time some emperors didn't concern themselves about the Christians, believing them to be harmless fanatics. Other emperors, however, rightly concluded that the quickly spreading new faith was a serious threat to imperial control of the State religion. Some emperors tried to eradicate Christianity root and branch. Emperor Trajan (99-117), for example, made it illegal just to be a Christian. He had Christians transported to Rome where they were taken into the packed Circus Maximus and torn apart and eaten by wild animals.

Within a century, however, there were getting to be too many Christians to kill in this way, and so Emperor Severus (197-211) made it illegal to *convert* to Christianity. He hoped that the Church would die out for lack of new members. But this didn't work either. Emperor Decius (249-251) ordered all people in the Empire to sacrifice publicly to the Roman gods. Some Christians, even some bishops, renounced their faith and complied with the emperor's decree. Many other Christians remained faithful, earning the title *martyrs* ("witnesses"), by dying for the faith. Still others, called *confessors*, spoke out heroically for the faith, but were not put to death.

The height of the persecutions was reached under Emperor Diocletian (284-305). He destroyed churches, burned Bibles and other sacred books, and tortured and executed as many bishops and priests as he could get his hands on. Things got so bad that many Christians fled to deserts or other isolated places, living by themselves in caves or in small communities away from the world. Many of these communities continued to flourish after Christianity became respectable. This type of life came to be called *monasticism*, which is the living of Christian life away from the world and focusing on God alone. (Monasticism was not just a response to persecution. See page 34 ff.)

WHY THE CHURCH SURVIVED AND FLOURISHED

Finally, the persecutions stopped. In A.D. 311, Emperor Galerius issued an edict tolerating the Christians. Why did Galerius do this? For several reasons. First of all, it had become obvious to the Roman authorities that persecution was counterproductive. Instead of squelching the Christians, persecution made them stronger. As the Christian writer, Tertullian (160-225), observed, "The blood of the martyrs is seed for the Church."

Second, by Galerius' time the Roman Empire was in serious trouble. It had spread itself too thin, was internally corrupt, constantly operated at an economic deficit, and was besieged on all its frontiers by barbarian peoples who wanted to plunder its riches. Thus it simply no longer made sense to persecute Christians, especially when more and more Roman citizens were becoming Christians. Rome needed all the talent it could get to solve its problems.

But the principal reason why the persecutions stopped was that Christianity had won the minds and hearts of great numbers of people to the gospel. Aside from the appeal of the gospel message itself, the *life-style* of Christians played an important role in attracting converts. The biblical account in Acts reflects the actual historical situation in many places: prayer, study, discipline, sharing of possessions and communal service. "[N]one claimed private ownership of any possessions, but everything they owned was held in common.... There was not a needy person among them, for as many as owned lands or houses sold them and brought the proceeds of what was sold" (Acts 4:32, 34).

A contemporary historian described this Christian life-style by writing, "See how these Christians love one another!" As the Romans compared their own deteriorating morality, with its tolerance of abortion, infanticide, sexual perversity and violence, to that of the Christians, it became obvious that the Christians actually practiced the ethical conduct that Roman philosophy only preached.

At first it was principally the poorer classes and slaves who converted to Christianity, largely because in the Gospels Jesus openly sided with the poor, downtrodden and oppressed. In Luke's Gospel, for example, Jesus is depicted as beginning his public ministry in order "to bring glad tidings to the poor"

(Luke 4:18). The preached gospel appealed to the poor, especially in a society marked by discrimination, injustice and economic oppression.

Eventually, however, more members of the upper classes were won to the gospel. On occasion, rumors circulated that this or that emperor was secretly a Christian. It was often even less of a secret that emperors' wives or daughters attended Christian meetings. During periods of lull in the persecutions, some Roman senators converted to Christianity. Noted intellectuals began to espouse Christian doctrine. With all of this happening, Christianity's success was inevitable.

AN EMPEROR BECOMES CHRISTIAN

The greatest boost to Christian fortunes took place beginning in the year A.D. 312, when Emperor Constantine defeated his rival to the imperial throne in the famous Battle of the Milvian Bridge. The night before the battle, Constantine had a dream in which he saw a Christian symbol and heard the words, "By this, conquer." He inscribed the symbol, a sort of bent cross known as the *labarum*, on his soldiers' shields, and prevailed in battle. From that time on, with Constantine's enthusiastic support, Christianity became the favored religion of the Empire. It was not until A.D. 380, however, under Emperor Theodosius, that Christianity became the "official" religion of the Empire.

HOW CONSTANTINE'S CONVERSION AFFECTED CHURCH AUTHORITY

Constantine's conversion to Christianity in 312 (he was not actually baptized until his death in 337) brought mixed blessings to the Church. Although Christians could now practice their faith openly, they lost much of the independence they had possessed in earlier times when they had to fend for themselves. For the first time, the Church had to deal with the issues of political power and wealth. As we shall see, the Church did not always resolve such issues wisely. Then, too, Constantine once described himself as "a bishop of God," and on several occasions issued orders to the actual bishops as if they were his underlings. Naturally, many of the bishops resisted Constantine's efforts to control the Church. Some bishops were more successful in doing this than others.

In the Eastern half of the Empire (see Focus 1, page 8), where Constantine had moved his capital, and where he could keep a closer eye on the Eastern bishops, the Church gradually came more and more under the thumb of the imperial bureaucracy. In the Western Church, on the other hand, where Roman law and order were deteriorating rapidly, and where Constantine wasn't present to control things, bishops remained relatively independent from imperial control. Gradually, the bishops of Rome (in place of the emperors) came to be seen as preservers of the old *Pax Romana*, or "Roman Peace." These bishops of Rome assumed more and more control over the Western Church's institutional structure.

Although all bishops in the early Church were known as *pappas*, the Greek word for "Daddy," it was the bishops of Rome who gradually came to bear this name exclusively, thereby becoming known as "popes." In the East, however, in Constantine's new capital city of Constantinople, the *patriarchs* (Greek and Latin = "Father"), or chief bishops of the capital, saw themselves as heads of their own Churches, independent from the pope's authority.

The question of the pope's authority versus that of the Eastern bishops was never answered to everyone's satisfaction, as we shall see later in our study of Church history. The main point to remember for the moment is that in the East, Church authority came more and more under State control, while in the West the opposite was taking place, with the popes in Rome stepping into a leadership vacuum and asserting more and more authority over both the Church and Western society. Bishops such as Ambrose of Milan (339-97) successfully defied imperial authority.

OTHER CHANGES IN THE CHURCH AFTER CONSTANTINE'S CONVERSION

Before Constantine, the differences between clergy and laity in the Church were not as pronounced as after his conversion.[1] Many priests and bishops before Constantine's reign did not serve the Church full-time, but worked for a living in other occupations to support themselves. Most of them were married men with families. They dressed like everyone else and lived in the same fashion as other Christians.

With Constantine, however, the clergy, being among the most educated and skilled people in the empire, were drawn into the service of the State. They were given titles like "most illustrious," the forerunner of today's "reverend" or "excellency." They began to dress like imperial officials. For example, the bishop's tall, cylindrical hat, or *miter*, was patterned after the hats worn by imperial officials, who thought that by wearing tall hats they "stood above" everyone else.

This process by which the clergy came to be seen as separate and *implicitly* of more importance than the laity, had a tremendous impact on how the Church thought of itself. We could perhaps conceive of the first-century Church as a closely knit family, which we can imagine holding hands together and standing in a circle. After Constantine, the Church came to be thought of as a pyramid, with popes, bishops, priests, and eventually all sorts of other ranks, placed at the top, and the laity placed at the bottom. After Constantine's con-

---

[1] A work called *Apostolic Tradition*, written about the year 215, describes in great detail the differences between the various ranks of the clergy.

version, the Church's identity—its self-image—was changed drastically.

This change in the Church's self-image is something we will notice often in our study of Church history. In actuality, there is no one, fixed image of what the Church is. The Church, by its very nature, constantly changes. The question is, does our changing self-image as Church match the gospel's vision of Church, or is it at odds with that vision? In the pages ahead, we will return often to this theme of how the Church's image of itself changed in response to changes in the world in which the Church lived.

FOCUS 1

THE EARLY CHURCH: WHERE GEOGRAPHY MADE HISTORY

In the map at right, notice the line separating the eastern and western halves of the Roman Empire. This line corresponds roughly to the division of the Empire made by Emperor Diocletian in the year 286. The dividing line also marks off the two different "worlds" of the early Church. The Eastern Church, centered in Constantinople, was largely Greek in language and thought. The Western Church, centered in Rome, was principally Latin in orientation. This meant that Eastern Christians tended to approach their faith more conceptually, wanting to understand abstract doctrines like the Trinity. Western Christians tended to be more *practical*, focusing on issues like Church authority and organization. As time went on, the gap between East and West widened, and each side of the Christian world tended to look down its nose at the other. Greeks often spoke of the Latins as "superficial" and "ignorant," while some Latins thought of the Greeks as "effeminate" and "daydreamers." We will follow closely in the pages ahead this difference in outlook between East and West and observe how it eventually led to a major *schism*, or split, between the two halves of the Church.

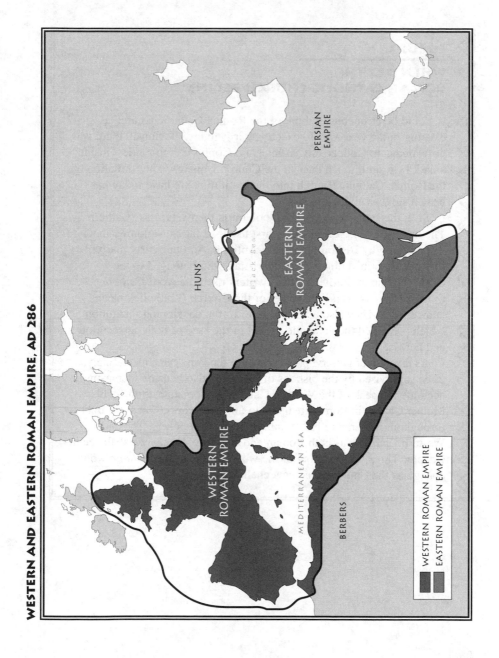

WESTERN AND EASTERN ROMAN EMPIRE, AD 286

WESTERN ROMAN EMPIRE
EASTERN ROMAN EMPIRE

PERSIAN EMPIRE

HUNS

Black Sea

EASTERN ROMAN EMPIRE

WESTERN ROMAN EMPIRE

MEDITERRANEAN SEA

BERBERS

WESTERN ROMAN EMPIRE
EASTERN ROMAN EMPIRE

FOCUS 2

WHEN DID THE ROMAN CATHOLIC CHURCH BEGIN?

It would be erroneous to think of the Roman Catholic Church as existing in the year A.D. 30 exactly as it is today. Obviously there was no Vatican, no College of Cardinals, no Confession to a priest inside a dark box, until much later in the Church's history. The formation of the Roman Catholic Church into the institution we have today has been a slow, evolving process.

Still, the early Christians did look upon themselves as "Catholic." The name *Catholic Church* was first used, so far as we know, about the year 105 by Bishop Ignatius of Antioch. And one early martyr, Pionius, described himself as a Christian who belonged to the Catholic Church. Early Christian writers used the word *Catholic* to refer to the universal character of the Church ("catholic" means "universal"). They also used it to refer to the developing institution which preserved the authentic gospel in the face of both persecution and heresy.

As this task of preserving the gospel in the West came increasingly to be supervised by the bishops of Rome, it also became increasingly accurate to speak of the Western Church as Roman Catholic. This Mother Church in Rome attempted to unite the various local Churches throughout the Empire into a unified body of believers. The early Western Church was both Roman and Catholic. But as we shall see in Chapter Three, the meaning of the words *Roman* and *Catholic* would change as the Church faced new challenges.

CHAPTER TWO

THE EARLY CHURCH DEFINES ORTHODOX CHRISTIANITY

MARY ANN DONALDSON walks toward her CCD classroom lost in thought. "These tenth-graders ask the *darndest* questions. After last week's class on marriage and sexuality, I felt lucky just to have gotten home in one piece! Surely this week will be easier. After all, I'd much rather tell these little know-it-alls about the Profession of Faith than explain to them why pre-marital sex is a sin."

Mary Ann opens the door to her classroom to find the usual chaotic scene—thirty teenagers draped over desks, chasing each other around the classroom or otherwise demonstrating that religious education was the farthest thing from their minds. "Good evening, everyone," Mary Ann shouts. After a few half-hearted responses of, "Good evening, Mrs. Donaldson," the class comes to a state of semi-order. Mary Ann leads the class in prayer and a period of silent meditation, and then announces, "Tonight we're going to discuss the Profession of Faith. Who wants to tell me what it is?"

"That's that thing we say after the sermon," Tommy Riordan answers.

"Very good," Mary Ann says. "And just to show you that I do *my* homework, too, I've written the whole 'thing,' as Tommy calls it, on this piece of poster paper."

Mary Ann attaches to the blackboard her handwritten version of the Profession of Faith which she has copied from the Sunday missalette. "OK," she says to the class, "let's go over each line together, and then talk about what it means." The class reads the Profession of Faith out loud, and then Mary Ann leads a discussion. Roseanne Medina raises her hand. "What is this 'One in being with the Father' stuff all about? Does that mean Jesus and the Father are the same?"

"Well, no, they're not the *same*, Roseanne, but they are both divine."

Judy Walsh quits snapping her chewing gum long enough to say, "That doesn't make sense! If the Father 'begot' Jesus, than Jesus can't be God just like the Father is."

"That's right," Eddie Lynskey says. "How can Jesus and the Father both be God at the same time?"

"Well, it's hard for us to understand," Mary Ann answers half-heartedly. "We just have to accept some things on faith."

The class is not impressed with her answer. Bobby Hoffstedter, the noted chess whiz and math genius, adjusts his glasses and asks, "How do we know that Jesus was God, Mrs. Donaldson? Does it say anywhere in the Bible, 'Jesus Christ is God' or 'Jesus Christ is one in being with the Father'?"

"Yeah," half the class replies. "Does it?"

Mary Ann wishes she had signed up for aerobics class as she had originally planned instead of accepting Father Growers' invitation to teach CCD. "Well, no, I don't think it specifically says anywhere in the Bible 'Jesus is God' or that he was one in being with the Father. That's why we have the Profession of Faith."

Rudy Johnson, the two-hundred-pound fullback, asks, "Well, why should we believe *that*?"

The class erupts in chaos. "Yeah, how do we know Jesus was God? Maybe Jesus was just like any other man. And how'd we get the Profession of Faith in the first place?"

Mary Ann looks hopefully at the clock and thinks, "How did I ever get myself into this mess!" Aloud she announces, "All right, all right, we'll talk about all those things next week. But time is up for tonight."

What will Mary Ann do? Her task is not unlike that of her predecessors in faith who lived in the first three centuries of the early Church. Like Mary Ann, today's imagined religious education teacher, they, too, believed that Jesus was the Son of God and the Savior of the world. Like her, they had a lot of beliefs which they couldn't explain and perhaps some which seemed hazy or unclear to them.

RELIGIOUS EDUCATION QUESTIONS IN THE EARLY CHURCH

It was the special task of the Christians living in the first three centuries to answer the very questions which Mary Ann's students are asking today, such questions as, "Was Jesus truly God? Wasn't he perhaps 'less of a God' than the Father? Isn't it possible that the Father just gave Jesus some share of his divinity at a later point in Jesus' life, such as when Jesus was baptized in the Jordan?[1] And even if Jesus was truly God, surely he wasn't an actual human being like all the rest of us, was he? Isn't it possible that he just looked and acted human?"

The early Church's answer to such questions was of vital importance to the way in which Christianity was to develop. Was Christianity truly the unique religion it proclaimed itself to be in which the eternal God entered fully into the human condition by becoming a man in the person of Jesus? Or was Christianity just another version of the ancient religious myths, about which people in the Roman Empire had speculated for centuries.

---

[1] An early heresy, *Adoptionism*, taught this doctrine.

GNOSTICISM: THE CHURCH CONFRONTS HERESY

Consider, for example, the Gnostics. The Gnostics were people who believed that they possessed a special version of secret knowledge about life (Greek *gnosis*, "knowledge") reserved only for an elite few. There were many varieties of Gnostics. Some of them borrowed bits and pieces of their beliefs from Judaism, but they distorted Judaism. They taught that Yahweh, the God of the Old Testament, was in actuality an evil angel who created the earth and human beings.

The Gnostics believed that spiritual realities were of more value than earthly realities. For example, they mistrusted the human body, marriage and all material creation. Many Gnostics acted like some of the hippies did in the 1960's, ignoring moral values and living in communes where group sex was practiced and marriage was scorned as foolish. Other Gnostics, however, were strictly ascetical, remaining celibate for reasons of "purity," and adhering to strict dietary rules so as not to cloud their spiritual perception.

Gnosticism's principal threat to the gospel was its teaching that God had not really become a human being in the person of Jesus. The Gnostics taught either that Jesus was simply a highly enlightened man or that he was an angel or spiritual messenger who only *appeared* to be a man. The latter teaching was the heresy of *docetism*, which comes from the Greek word for "appear." The bishops of the early Church realized the danger which Gnosticism presented and confronted it.

The most skillful foe of Gnosticism was Bishop Irenaeus of Lyons in southern France. Irenaeus lived from about the year 130 to about 200 and wrote a treatise called *Against Heresies*. The thrust of Irenaeus's work was to preserve the main doctrine of Christianity—namely, that God actually had become a man in the person of Jesus. Jesus was not an angel who merely *appeared* to be a man; Jesus truly was a human being while at the same time divine. The eternal Word, the Son of God, really had become human, and really did live among people on earth.

Through the work of bishops like Irenaeus, Gnosticism as such began to diminish in importance. By the year 200 or so, most Christians were capable of distinguishing between Jesus as a divine messenger or angel, as the Gnostics taught, and Jesus as the man who was divine, as Christianity taught. But questions about the nature of Jesus' divinity did not go away. Many people now wondered whether Jesus was of "equal divinity" to the Father. In other words, some Christians asked, was Jesus *fully* divine?

ARIANISM AND THE COUNCIL OF NICEA

Confusion about Jesus' relationship to the Father was especially prominent in the East. In the early fourth century, an Egyptian priest named Arius taught that the Son of God was inferior to the Father. Arius was a skilled preacher

and gained much support for his doctrine, even among bishops. A great controversy began to rage, known to us today as the Arian controversy. Arius's
doctrine is known as *Arianism*, which is the belief that the Son of God was
created in time and is inferior in his divinity to the Father. The debate between
Arian and non-Arian bishops became so heated that Emperor Constantine
himself found it necessary to intervene.

In the year 325, the Emperor convened a council at Nicea, located in today's
Turkey, south of Constantine's capital of Constantinople (named Istanbul
today). Some 318 bishops came to the Council of Nicea, but only five of them
were Western bishops. By and large, it was still Eastern bishops who were
involved in the great theological debates, although of course it was much
easier for Eastern bishops to travel to Nicea than it was for Western bishops.

The leading light at the Council was a young deacon from Alexandria
named Athanasius. Athanasius argued that it would be impossible to overcome Arianism unless the Council arrived at a formula, or *creed*, which
defined just what the relationship was between the Son and the Father.
Athanasius believed that truths in the gospel sometimes need further explanation in order to be made clearer. He thus proposed using a Greek word (see
Focus 3, page 17) not found in Scripture in order to make it clear what
Christians believed about the relationship between Father and Son.

That word is translated in today's Profession of Faith as "one in being," so
that the Son is said to be of equal divinity with the Father. To make this point
clearer, the bishops at the Council of Nicea, in writing their *Nicene Creed*,
added that the Son of God is "eternally begotten of the Father, God from God,
begotten, not made." In other words, the bishops emphasized that the eternal,
pre-existing Son was not created in time as the Arians taught, but had always
co-existed with the Father.

ENTER THE HOLY SPIRIT

Even though Emperor Constantine approved the Nicene Creed and proclaimed
it to be the correct statement of Christian doctrine, not everyone agreed with
it. In fact, it would be accurate to say that during most of the fourth century,
Arianism was often the dominant viewpoint. It took fifty years or so after the
Council of Nicea before the Nicene Creed was fully accepted as orthodox doctrine. Even then, some bishops and priests found something of a loophole in
the Nicene Creed because it had not said much of anything about the Holy
Spirit, other than the bland assertion, "We believe in the Holy Spirit."

Some of these "closet Arians," we could call them, began to say the same
things about the Holy Spirit that it had once been popular to say about Jesus.
They said that the Holy Spirit was merely a divine messenger. Athanasius,
now the Bishop of Alexandria, rejected this doctrine too, teaching that the
Holy Spirit was fully and eternally God.

But it was really three other Christian thinkers in the East who helped Christians better understand the doctrine of the Holy Spirit. These three thinkers were Bishop Basil of Caesarea (known today as "Basil the Great"), Basil's brother, Bishop Gregory of Nyssa, and a monk named Gregory of Nazianzus. All three men flourished in the second half of the fourth century. Because they lived in the Roman province of Cappadocia (today's Turkey, between the Mediterranean and Black Sea), they are commonly known in Church history as "the Cappadocians."

The great contribution of the Cappadocians was to define words precisely and apply those words to that most difficult to comprehend of all Christian doctrines—the Trinity. The Cappadocians cleared away a lot of the confusion surrounding the philosophical concepts of "person," "substance" and "nature," and showed that the Trinity could be understood as three divine persons in one divine substance. Contrary to what others were teaching, God did not have three different natures, but only one nature, a divine nature. Yet this divine nature was shared by three persons—Father, Son and Holy Spirit.

THE COUNCIL OF CONSTANTINOPLE

Despite what Athanasius and the Cappadocians taught, many bishops disagreed about the Holy Spirit. As a result about one hundred fifty bishops, all from the East, met in Constantinople in the year 381 to settle their differences over the Holy Spirit. They drafted another creed. This "Creed of Constantinople" is virtually identical to the Profession of Faith that we have today.[2] The bishops at the Council of Constantinople agreed completely with the Nicene Creed, but they spoke more fully about the Holy Spirit than had the bishops at Nicea, fifty-six years earlier.

They called the Spirit "the Lord and life-giver, Who proceeds from the Father, Who with the Father and the Son is together worshiped and glorified, Who spoke through the prophets. Notice that the bishops did not say, "Who proceeds from the Father and the Son..." as we have it today in the Roman Catholic liturgy. As we shall see, these words were added later by the Western Church and led to an angry debate between Eastern and Western theologians.

ANOTHER CONTROVERSY: 'MOTHER OF GOD' OR 'MOTHER OF JESUS'

One would have thought that two great councils and two creeds would have settled the doctrinal issues in the early Church. Such was not the case. A new

---

[2] Hence it is technically incorrect to refer to the Creed of the Mass as "The Nicene Creed." But it is much easier to pronounce Nicene than Constantinopolitan!

controversy now arose, this one even more heated than the Arian controversy had been. It started about the year 430 when Bishop Nestorius of Constantinople disapproved of the title, "Mother of God," as applied to the Virgin Mary. Nestorius reasoned that if Christians were to call Mary Mother of God, then Jesus would not be thought of as truly human. Nestorius wanted Mary to be called simply Mother of Christ. There was a problem with this. As long as anyone could remember, Mary had been called Mother of God, and the Christians in Constantinople were angry that Bishop Nestorius was trying to change their faith.

Nestorius had overlooked the fact that Christian doctrine is found within the day-to-day life of the Church and its worship as much as it is in the lofty speculations of theologians. Nestorius did not give credit to what Vatican II would later call the *sensus fidei*, or "intuitive sense of the faith" possessed by ordinary believers, who in their prayer, devotions and day-to-day faith arrive at theological truths just as certainly as do bishops and popes. The faithful had long called Mary Mother of God, and it was offensive to them to have intellectuals in the hierarchy suddenly change this ancient title. Because Nestorius was not sensitive to this *sensus fidei*, he set off another bitter conflict—calling for yet another council.

The Council of Ephesus met in the year 431. It was not actually concerned with Mary, but with the person of Jesus. The debate over Mary's title was simply the starting point for the "real" debate. The real debate was about the person of Jesus. Was Jesus human or divine, or both? The Council of Ephesus endorsed Mary's title as Mother of God. It also said that Jesus had both a divine and human nature joined together in one person. Yet, because the two sides at Ephesus were so opposed to each other, the bishops did not write a creed to express in official language what they thought about Jesus' divine and human nature. A later council would do that.

THE COUNCIL OF CHALCEDON

The last of the four great councils of the early Church met in the year 451 in Chalcedon (directly across a narrow sea channel separating the city from Constantinople). The purpose of the council was to issue a creed that would settle matters debated at the Council of Ephesus, twenty years before. More than five hundred bishops attended, including a delegation from the West. These westerners brought with them a theological treatise written by the bishop of Rome, the *Tome*, or "great book," of Pope Leo the Great (440-461).

Pope Leo was a highly skilled theologian in his own right. He sent his *Tome* to Chalcedon as an official statement of doctrine to be adopted by all the bishops in attendance. In other words, Leo proclaimed himself the spiritual leader of the bishops of the Eastern Church as well as of the Western Church. While not all the bishops at Chalcedon agreed that Leo's word was supreme, the majority at the Council nonetheless enthusiastically endorsed Leo's *Tome*, exclaiming, "In Leo, Peter has spoken!"

The Council of Chalcedon followed both what the Council of Ephesus had resolved and what Leo had written in his *Tome*. The bishops at the council said that in Jesus the Son of God, two natures, a human nature and a divine nature, were united in one person. Jesus was thus formally declared by the Church to have been both fully human and fully divine.

After these many years of struggle, the early Church had finally achieved an authoritative doctrinal statement about the person of Jesus. The Creed of Chalcedon was accepted by the majority of Christians in both East and West.

Yet, there were, and still are today, Christians who do not honor the Creed of Chalcedon. Such people insisted that Jesus had only a divine nature and not an authentic human nature. They were called *Monophysites* (from the Greek for "one nature"). Yet, the majority Christian position had become firmly accepted. The early Church had now established, in words that were clear to all, the most basic Christian doctrine: "The Word became flesh and dwelt among us."

FOCUS 3

PHILOSOPHY IN THE SERVICE OF FAITH: 'HOMOOUSIOS'

It would have made things easier if the bishops meeting at the Council of Nicea could simply have turned to a verse in the Bible and said to the Arian bishops, "See, it says right here that the Son of God is one in being with the Father and that the Son was not created in time but eternally begotten." The problem was, however, that the Bible doesn't use such words. What would you have done in such a situation?

Perhaps you would have done what Athanasius did, and argued for a creed which uses a word that clarifies what the Bible says about the Son's relationship to the Father. What word would you use? Since the bishops spoke and wrote in Greek, they had roughly three Greek words to consider in formulating the section of the Nicene Creed referring to the relationship between the Son and the Father. They could have said the Son was *homoiousious*, or *of like substance with* the Father, that the Son was *homoios*, or *like* the Father, or that the Son was *homoousios—of the same substance with* the Father.

In the end, the bishops chose the third alternative. This is a philosophical concept called *homoousios*. It is translated in today's Profession of Faith as "one in being with." No, it is not found in the Bible, but nowhere in the Bible is there a word which so precisely defines the core Christian doctrine of the Son's equal divinity to the Father. This was a case where philosophy came to the assistance of revelation, with the Holy Spirit continuing to clarify Church doctrine well after the Gospels were written.

FOCUS 4

THE POWER BEHIND THE COUNCILS: THE ROLE OF THE HOLY SPIRIT IN FORMULATING DOCTRINE

Is it "historical" to talk about the Holy Spirit's role in shaping the outcome of the great debates over Christian doctrine? "Let's face it," you might say, "didn't the bishops of the early Church often have political or personal interests in the outcome of these debates?" For example, at the Council of Ephesus, Bishop Cyril of Alexandria, who was jealous of his rival, Bishop Nestorius of Constantinople, saw to it that Nestorius was condemned as "the new Judas." Nestorius did not even have a chance to come to the council to defend his theological position. Is that the Holy Spirit at work? And weren't the bishops at Nicea, a century earlier, influenced by the fact that Emperor Constantine's personal theological advisor opposed Arianism?

Such questions are valid, but tend to overlook the way in which the bishops saw themselves undertaking doctrinal debate. The written remembrances of the bishops in attendance at the great councils show that they believed the Holy Spirit helped them make their decisions. The great councils of the early Church were not legislative assemblies like Congress or Parliament. Despite the human factors that may have influenced the decisions of the bishops, the councils were more than just debating societies. The historian is struck by "something more" than just religious argument going on at the councils. In the eyes of faith there is no better explanation for the extraordinary achievement of the great councils than the power of the Holy Spirit at work.

The bishops had a sense that they were trustworthy teachers of the Good News and therefore capable of identifying orthodox doctrine in the midst of controversy—even if that required using non-Scriptural terms like "nature" and "person." The bishops spoke in the sense of Acts 15:28: "It is the decision of the Holy Spirit and ours."

CHAPTER THREE

THE FALL OF ROME AND THE RISE OF THE WESTERN CHURCH

LET'S IMAGINE THAT YOU ARE a Christian living in Ravenna, in northeastern Italy, about the year 410. Let's say that your parents are both alive, that you are a young woman in your late teens, and that you have two brothers and two sisters. Your father is an official in the local government, and your mother is active in teaching other Christians to prepare for baptism. What are the principle concerns that you have as a Christian in this day and age? It has been some thirty years now (A.D. 380) since Emperor Theodosius declared Nicene Christianity[1] to be the official religion of the Empire, and so you have no hesitation about practicing your faith in public.

Yet, for some time you have heard your father speak with fear in his voice about the breakdown of law and order in Ravenna, and in the rest of Italy and the Empire as a whole. He has complained that the emperors and imperial officials are more interested in the cities of the East than they are in the birthplace of the Empire—Rome and the other cities of Italy. "No more do our Roman customs appeal to the imperial family," he has lamented. "If it weren't for our bishop and our Holy Father in Rome, there wouldn't be anything left of the old ways."

Your father senses that a great change is overtaking society, and since your Church is part of society, change is in the air for the Church as well. And then there is the other fear your father talks about—the marauding tribes of people from the North who are constantly battering at the gates of the Empire. Several young men in your Church have gone off to serve in the imperial army and have been killed in battle against strange peoples from distant lands. Like everyone else in your Church, you, too, wonder what is going to happen. Will these non-Christian "barbarians," as they are being called, come to Ravenna and destroy your Church, as they are doing everywhere else?

One day your father returns home breathless and frightened. "Rome has

---

[1] That is, the version of Christian doctrine as set forth in the Creed of Constantinople in 381.

fallen!" he exclaims. "That horrid Visigoth, Alaric!² Everyone knew he would turn on the generals and, sure enough, he has."

"What does this mean, Father?" you ask, trying to hold back the tears.

Your father embraces you and says, "It means, my dear one, that we must leave Ravenna. We must go south, to Sicily. It will be safer there, at least for the time being."

"Dear God!" your mother exclaims. "What will become of our Church? We have nearly forty people who are awaiting Baptism. Who will protect them? Will these savages kill every Christian in Italy?"

"I don't know," your father answers. "I just don't know."

The following morning, you and your family pack your belongings, leave your home and board a ship heading south for Sicily where your father has relatives, and where he hopes to begin work as a fisherman. You are sad to leave your friends behind, and your mother is even sadder to leave behind the little group of catechumens that she has been training. (As a woman, your mother probably was allowed to teach only other women.) What will become of your family? What will become of the Church that you are leaving behind?

. . . .

This imagined scene is not uncommon in fifth-century Italy. This is a time of turmoil and transition in the very land that once served as the impregnable fortress of the mighty Roman Empire. For nearly a thousand years the Romans maintained a civilization that rivaled anything the ancient world had seen. Then it all began to unravel. Decay from within and attack from without gradually wore the Romans down. By the late fourth century, Rome was a shadow of its former greatness.

Already the emperors had moved their power base to the East, to Constantinople. There they hoped to preserve their once-dominant Latin empire in a land of Greek culture and language. As this process took place, the very concept of empire was changed forever. By the late fifth century, it was no longer accurate to refer to the "Roman" Empire, except out of nostalgic reminiscence.

As we shall discuss more fully in Chapter Six, a new Christian state was taking shape in the East, the Byzantine Empire, which would claim to be Rome's heir. Its capital, Constantinople, was said to be the Second Rome.³

---

² Alaric was a mercenary who served the Roman army, but then betrayed his paymasters and sacked the city of Rome in A.D. 410.

³ The "Third Rome" was Moscow with its new Caesars ("Czars"). It succeeded to Constantinople's place after the fall of that city to the Turks in 1453.

THE WESTERN CHURCH DURING THE AGE OF BARBARIAN INVASION

What effect did all this have on Christians living in the West?[4] Obviously, it affected them greatly. The Church is a human institution that lives in a human society. It was as impossible for the Western Church in the fourth and fifth centuries to avoid the effects of the Roman Empire's collapse, as it was for the Catholic Church in America in the days of the great Irish immigrations of the nineteenth century to remain the small, isolated, self-protective Church it had once been.

In both cases, what happened in society as a whole had tremendous effects on the path of Church history. Faith would say that the Holy Spirit always uses the human situation in which the Church finds itself and molds the Church to take on a new identity in order to meet new challenges. Let's see how this process occurred in the Western Church during the period from about the death of Emperor Constantine, to about the time of Pope Gregory the Great, who died in the year 604.

In the Church's first three centuries, the persecutions were the principal external force shaping the Church's self-image. In the next three centuries, the barbarian invasions made the Church reassess its identity. How would the Church react to the influx of an entirely new type of people into the Roman Empire? On the one hand, the barbarians threatened to destroy the very civilization in which the Church had come to life and flourished. On the other hand, the barbarians needed to hear the gospel and be converted by it just as urgently as did the citizens of the Empire.

The Western Church faced two questions: *First*, could it remain Roman, in the sense of preserving all that was good about the Empire, with its order, peace, stability, learning and culture? *Second*, how could the Church, as Roman, also make its appeal *catholic*, or universal, so that *all* peoples, even peoples who had no tradition of stability and order, would be attracted to the gospel? The answer was that the Church had to be both Roman and catholic (universal in its outreach) at the same time.

Thus, even more so than in the first three centuries, the Church had to become both "one" and "many." It had to stay rooted in its ancient Roman origins, and it had to reach out to strange, new peoples who knew nothing about the classical Roman heritage which the Church wanted to preserve. At this point in its history the Church reached another of those moments of crisis. The Church once again had to assess its self-image, and ask itself, "Church, who are you in this day and age?" In Chapter Five, we will see that the Church did not always give a gospel response to this question, particularly when it came to relating to the new barbarian kingdoms that had replaced the Roman emperors.

---

[4] For "West" and "East," see Focus 1, page 8.

For one thing, after Christianity became the official religion of the Empire, many Christians assumed that Roman culture and Christian faith were virtually identical. For many people, to be Roman was to be Christian, and to be Christian was to be Roman.[5]

Now, all of a sudden, here were all these barbarians on the scene. What was the Church to do about such non-Roman people? Would the barbarians have to be turned into Romans before they could be baptized? Would they have to speak Latin and dress, think and act like everyone else? Or could the Church somehow let them keep their tribal customs while at the same time admitting them into the Church on equal footing with everyone else?

These were thorny questions. Christianity does not come wrapped up in one "package." Had the Roman Christians confused their culture with their faith? Had they become Christian simply because Christianity was the official religion and practiced by the emperors? Was Church "unity" confused with social conformity? And what about "converting" the barbarians? Were they to be truly converted to the gospel, or simply brought into Roman life and told to accept the official religion? These were hard questions, and the Church did not always do such a good job answering them. But one thing was sure. The Church would be changed forever by its contact with the new, non-Roman peoples breaking across the frontiers of the Empire.

NEW CHALLENGES IN AN AGE OF CHAOS

In the first three centuries the Church had to learn how to preach the gospel in a way that appealed to educated Romans. Now the Church had to learn how to preach the gospel in a way that would appeal to people who could neither read nor write and who had for centuries practiced crude forms of nature worship.[6] As the Church began to evangelize the barbarian peoples, it had to phrase the Gospel in less "intellectual" language. This was not a dialogue with educated Romans. The Church had to learn how to be more "earthy" in its approach to evangelization. We will see in a later chapter how this worked itself out, especially as we discuss worship and devotion in the medieval Church.

For the moment, consider just one example. Most of the barbarian peoples believed in some form of ancestor worship. The Church could not accept this belief. Yet, in its devotion to the saints, the Church found a means of accommodating the cult of ancestor worship to Christian belief and tradition. In this way, the gospel message was made comprehensible to people who had no other frame of reference by which to understand that message.

---

[5] That is, accustomed to Roman law, culture and institutions, as established in the Mediterranean world for centuries.

[6] Some of the barbarian tribes, particularly in today's Eastern Europe, had already become Arian Christians. Arianism might have converted all of the barbarians had it not been for the acceptance of Catholic Christianity by the King of the Franks, Clovis (466-511).

THE CHURCH AS
PRESERVER OF ORDER AND STABILITY

The barbarian invasions and migrations brought the Church another challenge. By the year 489, a barbarian tribe known as the Ostrogoths had gained the ascendancy in Italy. There was really nothing left of Roman government. The old Western Empire was divided among various barbarian tribes who established new and autonomous kingdoms. In the East, the new Byzantine Empire, with its capital in Constantinople, managed to keep the ancient classical civilization intact. In the West, however, a new society and a new culture had come into existence. Previously, the Empire had provided order and served to unify society. Now there was only one institution left from Roman times which could provide the stability that the Empire had formerly provided, and that institution was the Church.

The Western Church from the late fifth century onward, increasingly took over from the defunct Empire the role of providing society with a stable base. The Church served to bring something of the ancient *Pax Romana* into a disintegrating society. Perhaps the best example of this took place during the papacy of Pope Leo the Great (440-461). A barbarian chieftain named Attila and his tribe of Huns had successfully pushed back a combined Roman-Visigothic army and threatened to capture Rome itself. It was not the emperor or one of his generals who went to negotiate peace with Attila, but Pope Leo the Great. We don't know everything they discussed by we do know that Attila was so impressed with the pope that he promised not to sack the city, and he moved his troops elsewhere.

This story illustrates what was happening frequently in the West. Priests, bishops and popes were stepping into the vacuum created by the collapse of order in cities, towns and rural areas all throughout Western society. This is not to suggest that the Church simply *became* the state, or that the clergy suddenly became political leaders. There was still a secular government which kept society going, separate and apart from the Church. The Church's increasing leadership role within society was not political, but *moral*.

Yet, people increasingly looked to the Church instead of to the state for moral leadership and for guidance in ordering their lives. The emperor's representative lived in Ravenna but increasingly lacked power. As the state was losing its moral force as the preserver of social order, the Church began to assume this role in place. But there were, nonetheless, always two very separate and distinct institutions— Church and state—attempting to guide society through very tumultuous times.

AMBROSE: A BISHOP PROVIDES
SOCIAL ORDER AND STABILITY

Consider one prominent bishop who served during this era, Bishop Ambrose of Milan, who was chosen bishop by the people of Milan in the year 374. Ambrose was unquestionably the most skilled leader of his day. He successfully asserted the independence of those who suffered from poverty and the collapse of order.

Ambrose and strong bishops like him served as focal points of unity in a society that was everywhere in a state of disintegration. But Ambrose nevertheless had to contend with an emperor who attempted to assert control over the churches of Milan. Ambrose fought back, telling the emperor that he had no authority over "the things of God." The emperor backed down, and the Church's independence from state interference was preserved.

From Ambrose's time onward, the Church would constantly find itself locked in a struggle to maintain its freedom and autonomy in the face of attempts by secular rulers to subordinate the Church to the state. Not all Church leaders would be as strong and successful as Ambrose was. Aside from being a strong personality, Ambrose succeeded because the times demanded moral leadership and spiritual discipline. People knew the state could not provide this leadership and discipline, and that the Church could. Consequently, people were willing to side with Ambrose against the emperor. In future times, when the Church grew lax and its moral authority diminished, people were more willing to side with the state when it attempted to control the Church.

THE CONTINUING DEVELOPMENT OF PAPAL AUTHORITY

Gradually, the task of providing moral leadership in a disintegrating society fell increasingly to the bishops of Rome. At first not all Western bishops believed that the bishops of Rome, or the early popes, were superior to the other bishops in authority.

For example, one notable Western bishop, Cyprian of Carthage, who had been martyred in 258, had argued that all the bishops shared equally in the exercise of episcopal authority. Cyprian once disagreed with Bishop Stephen of Rome over the question of whether someone who had renounced the faith had to be rebaptized. Cyprian believed that he could make a decision on this issue by himself, even though the bishop of Rome said otherwise. Cyprian and Stephen never settled their disagreement (though the Church eventually accepted Pope Stephen's position of not rebaptizing).

By the time period we are considering in this chapter, the fourth and fifth centuries, Church unity was a more important concern than episcopal independence. Thus, independent bishops like Cyprian were now in a minority. By the fifth century, when people in the West looked to the Church for moral leadership, there already existed an institution which was fully Roman that could provide this leadership and the sense of unity which society needed— the papacy. By this time in our account, the unifying leadership of the papacy is best seen in the title given to the Bishop of Rome: "Patriarch of the West."

It was thus the papacy that offered the best hope of imposing unity on the unstable diversity caused by the formation of the new barbarian kingdoms.

But this raised another challenge for the Church. How could the papacy respect the differences which existed from place to place within the vast stretches of the growing Christian world?

Or to put it another way, how could a working unity be established among the diverse peoples who lived in far-flung places outside the former borders of the Roman Empire? The papacy was faced with a continual struggle to balance unity with diversity. As we shall see in the pages ahead, sometimes the popes respected a healthy diversity among Christians, and sometimes they demanded conformity. The Church would often learn with difficulty that conformity and unity are not the same things.

WORKING OUT A THEORY
OF PAPAL PRIMACY

How did the papacy as an institution develop during the fourth and fifth centuries? From ancient times, Christians had paid respect to the city where Saint Peter, the first among equals in the apostolic body, had preached. In addition, the Christian emperors themselves gave a boost to the theory of papal primacy. They regulated the appointment of men to the bishopric of Rome and treated their appointees as superior in authority to the other bishops.

But by the time of Pope Leo the Great (440-461), the popes were vigorously asserting their independence from imperial control (what little of it there was left). They were also formulating their own theories of papal primacy.[7] Leo, for example, wrote that episcopal authority had been conferred first and foremost on Peter the Rock. The bishops of Rome were thus heirs to Peter's authority and his primacy over the other apostles.

The greatest exponent of papal primacy was Pope Gregory the Great (590-604). Gregory came from a prominent Roman family and had pursued a career in government before deciding to become a monk. This was typical in Gregory's day. Talented men often left secular positions and took their skills to the Church. Gregory dropped the popes' previous title of "universal bishop" and adopted the less imperious "servant of the servants of God." Still, Gregory wrote that leadership of the Church had been entrusted by Jesus to Peter, "the prince of all apostles." On Peter's death, Gregory said, leadership passed from Peter to Peter's successors, the bishops of Rome.

From Gregory's time onward, the Western Church came to be organized more and more around the papacy as the focal point of authority and leadership. And since the Church was the greatest moral force of the age, the papacy became the greatest moral institution of the age. It is little wonder that the

---

[7] "Primacy" simply means "the state of being first," that is, preeminent. It does not connote "the only," or "the sole." The popes were not the *sole* authority; they were the "first." The question became: Were the popes right because they were first, or first because they were right? Around the answer to this question revolved much later conflict between Christians.

future course of Church history would revolve around the competition between state and Church. These two competed constantly for moral authority over the minds and hearts of peoples in the newly forming barbarian kingdoms.

By Gregory's time, however, one thing was clear, the Western Church had become decisively Roman and Catholic. It was Roman in its role as preserver of the classical tradition of law, stability, order and wholeness. It was Catholic in its openness to the Holy Spirit's work among the barbarian nations. In attempting to be both Roman and Catholic, the Church would find itself faced with constant challenges. Sometimes it responded to these challenges in the spirit of the gospel, and sometimes it responded in the ways of the world. As we follow this story in the pages ahead, let's continue to consider the question that the Spirit repeatedly asks: "Church, who are you and what do you say of yourself?"

FOCUS 5

TROUBLE FOR THE FUTURE: THE ORIGINS OF THE DONATIST CONTROVERSY

When the persecutions stopped and Constantine became emperor, the Church was faced with a thorny problem. What do we do about all those people who gave in to the threat of persecution and renounced their faith? Now that it's permissible to be a Christian, do we exclude those who betrayed the gospel, or do we let them back into the Church? And what about bishops and priests who renounced their faith? Do they still have the authority to serve as valid ministers of the sacraments? This question rose to the level of a heated controversy in the Church of North Africa.

When Bishop Caecilian (311-345) was consecrated bishop of Carthage, one of the bishops consecrating Caecilian had earlier renounced the faith by turning sacred books over to the Roman secret police for burning. Several other bishops in North Africa said that this betrayer bishop had lost the power to consecrate other bishops. They reacted angrily by consecrating their own bishop to serve as bishop of Carthage. Their spokesman was a man named Donatus. Thus the controversy became known as the *Donatist* controversy.

Emperor Constantine supported Caecilian, and so the other bishops remained in the minority. Yet, their ideas and their movement spread. They eventually became a rival Church in North Africa. At times they were even the majority Church. They were suppressed only later in the fifth century after bitter debate and intervention on the part of the emperor. We will discuss the later stages of the Donatist controversy in the next chapter, as we take up the career of Saint Augustine.

FOCUS 6

THE EARLY CHURCH'S MOST FAMOUS 'CHARACTER' GIVES CHRISTIANITY THE BIBLE: SAINT JEROME AND THE VULGATE

Perhaps the funniest and most eccentric character in the early Church was the scholar Jerome (374-419). Despite the fact that he was a saint (perhaps *because* of this fact), Jerome never gained control over his temper and his sharp tongue. One never had to guess what Jerome thought of a person he disliked. He would begin letters with such colorful salutations as, "To So-and-so, not a man, but a dog that returns to its own vomit, Greetings!" Jerome once made a pest of himself by telling everyone who would listen that he thought Pope Siricius had been a terrible choice for pope. And who did Jerome think was actually qualified to be pope? Jerome himself, of course.

Jerome dedicated himself wholeheartedly to his life's love—the translation of the sacred Scriptures into Latin, or the "vulgar," popular tongue. (Greek was considered to be the language of the upper-crust, educated classes.)

Although his was not the first Latin translation of the Bible, Jerome's version proved most influential because of his skill in translating Hebrew and Greek. Jerome's translation came to be known as the *Vulgate*, and was used as the standard Bible by all Christians for over a thousand years, and by Catholics until just recently. When one considers the tremendous obstacles Jerome had to overcome to make his translation—the scarcity of ancient manuscripts (scholars today have more than Jerome had), the chaos in society, the lack of communications, the lack of technical equipment—faith would say that the very human Jerome had a lot of help from the divine Spirit.

Through Jerome, the Catholic Church made the Bible available to the people. (Vulgate can also mean "of the people.") After Jerome, educated Christians became "Bible Christians," as they read, pondered and meditated on the truths of the faith as presented in Scripture. The Church became the great preserver and teacher of Scripture. Especially among the educated, Christian piety was first and foremost biblical piety. In later centuries, with the breakdown of culture and education, the Bible became less common in Christian society, but never less popular, thanks largely to Jerome.

CHAPTER FOUR

CONCLUDING THE AGE OF THE CHURCH FATHERS

ONE OF THE DISTINCTIVE FEATURES of Catholicism is that its doctrine and practice are founded not only on the Bible and the teachings of the apostles, but also on the writings and teachings of intellectuals in the early Church who helped to elaborate upon the Bible and apostolic teaching. We have seen an example of such an elaboration in the case of Athanasius' refutation of Arianism. These early Christian intellectuals—men who developed and speculated on Christian doctrine until about the start of the seventh century— are called *Fathers of the Church*.[1] We owe them an incalculable debt. (See Focus 7, on page 37 for more on the meaning of the term *Church Fathers*.)

We could not hope adequately to discuss the writings of the Fathers in this chapter, or even in this book. Their writings fill several hundred volumes in both Greek and Latin, as there were both Greek Fathers and Latin Fathers, that is, Fathers who lived principally in the East and wrote in Greek, and Fathers who lived principally in the West and wrote in Latin. In this chapter, we will discuss the life and work of the man who is perhaps the most influential of all the Fathers— Saint Augustine. Then we will discuss developments in Christian life during and after Augustine's time, as we close out this period of the Fathers.

Augustine was unquestionably the greatest person of his time in many respects. His writings were the greatest in the sense that they leave us a better portrait of the inner journey of an early Christian Father than any other writings we have. His mind was the greatest in the sense that he decisively settled major issues, both theoretical and practical. His opinions affected the future course of Christianity in a way that no one in the early Church was able to match. His influence was also the greatest. No significant Christian thinker until modern times, when discussing a theological proposition, departed from Augustine's conclusions.

---

[1] Any dating of an era is tenuous, but we can safely adhere to the usual understanding by saying the Age of the Fathers began with the letter written by Bishop Clement of Rome in A.D. 95, and that it ended with the death of Isidore of Seville in 636.

Who was this man on whom so much of the later course of Christianity depended? He was born in 354 in North Africa of a pagan father and Christian mother, Patrick and Monica. He was not a healthy child and was probably small of stature, even for his day. Yet, he was extroverted and vivacious, and possessed a keen intellect. He studied the classics from boyhood, and had a slight familiarity as well with some of the Christian writings, which he rejected as being intellectually inferior to pagan works. From adolescence on, he was caught up in the lustful, sensual life-style that characterized the ancient world. By his day, Christian morality had not yet replaced Roman immorality as the predominant value system. Augustine succumbed in particular to sexual promiscuity, and he fathered an illegitimate child. By the age of twenty-nine Augustine was cynical and jaded, not knowing what he wanted to do with his life.

On the recommendation of friends, he traveled to Milan to listen to the preaching of Bishop Ambrose, whose reputation for persuasive rhetoric and oratory was widely known. Ambrose stunned Augustine with his masterful presentation of the gospel. Augustine felt himself unable to contradict Ambrose's eloquent words. Yet, although his mind was convinced of the truth of the gospel, Augustine did not have the will to resist sin. One day Augustine found himself in a friend's garden and experienced a conversion that changed both his life and that of the Church. While he was praying, he heard a child's voice coming to him over the wall of the garden, repeating the words, "Take and read, take and read...." On impulse, Augustine turned the pages of a nearby Bible and found Saint Paul's admonition in Romans 13:14, "[P]ut on the Lord Jesus Christ, and make no provision for the flesh, to gratify its desires." Augustine felt deep in his soul that these words had been written for him. In his later spiritual autobiography, entitled *Confessions*, Augustine felt "all the gloom and doubt" of his life "vanish away."

He returned to North Africa, determined to live as a monk, and actually founded a monastic community. At age thirty-seven, however, he made the fateful decision to travel to the North African city of Hippo. When the Christians of Hippo asked him to stay on as a priest in their Church, Augustine reluctantly agreed. Four years later, he was consecrated bishop of Hippo, an office he would hold until his death in 430. Augustine achieved so much as a Church Father (see Focus 7, page 37) because he lived, preached and wrote as a pastor and not as a theoretician cut off from day-to-day issues. He brought his intellectual gifts to bear upon the practical problems which his flock faced in their everyday struggle to live the gospel. Augustine saw himself as a shepherd, first, and a theologian, second. As a result, we can still hear Augustine speaking to us today in our own struggles, even if those struggles aren't the same as those faced by the Christians of Hippo. In order to get some idea of how influential Augustine's teaching was, let's consider two doctrinal controversies that would reappear in the Reformation of the sixteenth century. In that century both Catholic and Protestant theologians relied explicitly on Augustine for their respective positions.

In the last chapter (see Focus 5, page 26) we discussed Donatism. By the time Augustine became bishop, the Donatists were no longer just a noisy minority. They had become a rival Church possessing as many if not more members in North Africa than the Roman Catholic Church. Their principle disagreement with the Catholic Church was this: The Catholic Church taught that the sacraments were validly administered by any priest who was authentically ordained and in good standing with his bishop. The Donatists disagreed. They argued that only a priest who was in the state of grace, or free from mortal sin, could validly administer the sacraments.

Augustine wrote and preached eloquently in support of the Catholic position. To his way of thinking, *subjective* standards such as the spiritual condition of the priest who administered a sacrament were impossible to judge. Moreover, anyone who doubted the holiness of a particular priest would have to reject the sacraments he administered. After all, how could someone really know whether a given priest was in a state of grace when he administered the sacraments? Augustine argued that God wanted the sacraments to be available to all people at all times. Thus, the only accurate standard which could be applied to judge the validity of a sacrament was the *objective* standard of the priest's valid ordination and good standing in the Church. Everyone could know this fact—whether the priest was in a state of grace or not.

In a series of conferences, or *synods*, with Donatist bishops, Augustine showed to nearly everyone's satisfaction that the Catholic position was correct and the Donatist position incorrect. Emperor Honorius backed the Catholics and condemned the Donatists. He ordered them to turn over their church buildings in North Africa to the Catholics. Some of the Donatists resisted. The emperor imposed a solution by force—the first time that force was used to settle a religious *schism,* or internal division, within the Church.

Augustine at first disapproved of this use of force. Then he read a parable in Luke's Gospel, where the master of the banquet tells his agents "to force" his guests to come to the banquet (Luke 14:23). After that, Augustine accepted the use of force in resolving the Donatist controversy. The issue was settled for the moment—but only for the moment. Some Protestant reformers in the sixteenth century raised the same challenge to the validity of the sacraments as the Donatists had.

PELAGIUS'S CHALLENGE: GRACE VERSUS FREE WILL

Another sticky problem arose when a wandering Irish priest named Pelagius openly disagreed with Augustine on the subject of grace. Augustine taught that the human will was incapable of responding to God's gift of salvation unless God first gave the sinner grace to say "yes" to God. Without grace, Augustine taught, human beings lack the power to be saved and to do good.

Pelagius, on the other hand, taught that the first impulse toward salvation comes from human beings, rather than from God. For Pelagius, human beings possessed a good will and the capacity to perform good actions even without God. They had the *natural* ability to move toward salvation without God's grace. At a synod in Carthage in 418, the North African bishops condemned Pelagius's teachings on grace. They also rejected his related teaching that Baptism was just a "blessing," and not actually necessary for salvation. Pelagius's view of Baptism would resurface in certain strands of Protestant thought during the Reformation.

As Augustine was pressed to respond to Pelagius, he formulated his theory of predestination. That teaching has been variously interpreted and misinterpreted ever since. Both Martin Luther and John Calvin relied on it during the Reformation. The principal issue in the debate with Pelagius over grace naturally evolved into an issue of free will. If it's up to God who gets saved and who doesn't get saved, as Augustine taught, then are we human beings really free to choose salvation or reject it? Are we free to do good or to do evil? Augustine responded by saying that there is such a thing as free will. But he said that free will can only function in the direction of good in a soul that has been graced by God toward salvation. If God withholds the grace of salvation from a person, Augustine argued, who are we to criticize God?

In his later years, Augustine showed that he was not really teaching that God wants some people to be damned and some to be saved, as, for example, John Calvin would teach during the Reformation. Instead, he really meant that God gives everyone the *capacity* to do good and be saved. Nevertheless, it is only God who can enable people to *develop* this capacity. God does this through the means of grace, a free gift.

Not everyone in the Catholic Church was satisfied with Augustine's explanation. After his death, a great debate arose over this question of grace versus free will. At the Synod of Orange (in France) in 529, the bishops of southern France agreed with Augustine's teaching that human beings cannot be saved without God's grace. Nevertheless, the bishops declared that God wants no one to be damned. If people are damned, the bishops said, it is *their* doing and not God's. It was this interpretation of Augustine which the Catholic Church generally accepted from that time on. But, as noted, the Protestant Reformers would interpret Augustine differently than did the Catholic Church.

ORDINARY CATHOLIC LIFE IN THE AGE OF AUGUSTINE

Augustine's teachings on such issues as sacramental validity and free will went a long way toward helping the Church achieve its medieval Catholic identity, to be formed in the centuries ahead. Let's look for a moment at that evolving Catholic identity as it is reflected in the life of the Church to about the time of Pope Gregory's death in 604, where we left off in the last chapter.

The first thing we notice is that the Church's sacramental life has become more fully defined. Baptism and the Eucharist are still the principal sacraments, but the Sacrament of Penance now has also become more important in the life of the Church. Baptism, which now was performed more and more frequently, owing to the increase in converts, ceased to be administered principally at the cathedral and during the Easter vigil as before. Baptism was now regularly administered in parish churches throughout the year. And since whole households were not baptized as frequently as in the first three centuries,[2] newborn infants now were assigned "godparents," in the place of their actual parents. The godparents recited baptismal promises for the infants.

As for the celebration of the Eucharist, by Augustine's time a standardized form of celebration known as the "Roman rite" (or ceremonial form) was becoming the norm in most places. It had been developed by the Church in Rome. And as the Bible came to be consolidated into Old and New Testaments, Scripture readings were added to the Eucharistic celebration. The Roman rite is preserved today virtually identical to its fourth-century form. It is the first of four options found in Catholic *missals* which a priest can use in praying the prayers of the Mass. This rite was first written in Greek, but by the late fourth century it was translated into Latin. Latin came to be the usual language in which "Mass" was celebrated.

The word *Mass* comes from the Latin word for "send." The name refers to the practice by which the celebrant would send the people out into the world after the liturgy to live and proclaim the Gospel. Today, the priest frequently says, "Go forth to love and serve the Lord and one another." Again, the emphasis is on the congregation's being sent forth as messengers of the gospel. The Mass, then was principally a *sending forth*. For the early Christians, what happened at Mass was not something that was to be kept in the church building. In addition to Mass, Christians attended public prayer services, such as morning *lauds* and evening *vespers* and *compline*.

The Sacrament of Penance underwent a steady evolution in the days of the early Church. At first, Christians believed that once a baptized member of the Church committed a serious sin, he or she could only be readmitted into the body of the faithful *once*. That readmission took place only by making a *public* confession of serious sin, which was defined in most places as murder, adultery or apostasy. After confession, the sinner then had to complete a penance usually consisting of a prolonged period of fasting combined with almsgiving. Only then did the entire congregation give its *public* absolution and allow the sinner to return to the Eucharistic celebration.

---

[2] That is, it now was becoming common for infants to be born of Christian parents. Thus, the Church now baptized infants alone, rather than as part of a household that had converted to Christianity.

After Constantine's conversion, however, more and more people came forward with serious sins. Of course, there were then more Christians to commit sins. Gradually the Church allowed confession of sins to be made in private and on more than one occasion. The nature of the penance assigned to the sinner likewise changed, with prayers being added to fasting. In some cases prayers alone were given as penance. Finally, by the time of Pope Gregory the Great, absolution was everywhere being given by priests in private, rather than by the entire congregation in public.

DEVOTION TO MARY AND THE SAINTS

Popular piety during this era revolved around the Eucharist, listening to stories about Jesus from the Gospels, shared prayer in homes and devotion to the saints. The latter devotion started in the first century. The first Christians believed that holy men and women who had died in God's grace could intervene before God for those on earth.

We find evidence of this in writings on the walls of the *catacombs*, or underground burial chambers from the first century. There Christians scrawled such prayers on the walls as "Vincent, you are in Christ, pray for Phoebe. Paul and Peter, pray for Victor. Sentianus, in your prayers, pray for us, for we know you are in Christ." Prayers to the saints were incorporated into the Roman rite of the Mass and thus became part of the official liturgy[3] of the Church.

The greatest of the saints in the early Church was the Virgin Mary. The early Christians understood Mary to have been specially privileged by God in ways that the rest of the saints were not. For example, we find early church buildings named after the honors God had bestowed on Mary, such as "the church of Mary's Assumption." This illustrates something we noticed in Chapter Two. The faithful in their devotions and everyday sense of the faith also contribute to the Church's belief, just as do intellectuals like Augustine. The doctrines of the Immaculate Conception and the Assumption were not declared infallible doctrines of the Catholic faith until 1848 and 1950, respectively. Nonetheless, the Church long ago authorized devotions pointing toward these doctrines as they were expressed by the faithful in everyday worship and piety.

MONASTICISM: THE LAITY STARTS A MOVEMENT

The most significant development in Christian spirituality during the days of the early Church was monasticism. We alluded to the origins of monasticism in Chapter One (see page 5). Many Christians had fled to the desert and other isolated places to avoid persecution. Yet this is not the whole story of how monasticism got started.

---

[3] *Liturgy* means "people's work."

The father of monasticism was an Egyptian, Anthony of the Desert (250-355). He went to live alone in the desert, not because he feared persecution, but because he felt that God had called him to live away from the world. He wanted to spend his entire life in prayer and fasting for the salvation of others. Anthony came to this conclusion after hearing the Gospel passage read in which Christ admonished the rich young man to sell all that he had, give the proceeds to the poor, and "come follow me" (Matthew 19:16-21). Anthony and the other founders of monasticism believed that following after Jesus meant single-hearted, all-or-nothing commitment to a life in isolated places where prayer, fasting and manual labor filled their day.

Monasticism was first and foremost a *lay* movement. The first monks were not priests and had no desire to become priests. This obviously applied to the first monastic nuns as well. It was only later in Church history that monks became priests and were drawn into the hierarchical pyramid of Church ranks. Anthony's hermetical style of monasticism (living alone as a *hermit*) attracted many followers, but another style of monasticism also developed. In the *cenobitic*, or *communal* life-style, a number of men lived clustered around a common church building to share work, meals and prayer.

This communal style of monasticism became popular in the West thanks to Benedict of Nursia (480-550). Saint Benedict founded some twelve monasteries from his hermit's cave in Subiaco, Italy. Later, he started a larger monastery at Monte Cassino. Monte Cassino became the founding headquarters of the Benedictine movement, which we shall encounter again in our study.

Benedict's, sister, Scholastica, founded a monastic community of Benedictine nuns. The women's branch of monasticism, like the men's branch, traces its origins back to the East. Two Roman women, Melania the Elder and Paula the Elder, had traveled east to found communities of nuns during Jerome's time, and were in fact Jerome's friends. Paula is notable for the fact that she was the mother of five children. When her husband died and her children were grown, Paula heeded the call of the gospel to leave everything and follow after the Lord.

LEAVING THE ERA OF THE FATHERS: A CHURCH IN TRANSITION

In later chapters, as we continue to explore how the Church defined and redefined its identity throughout its history, we will again study the everyday spiritual life of Christians. But let us leave the early Church now, and turn toward the Church of the Middle Ages. We leave a Church founded on a stable footing—on the blood of the martyrs, on the creeds of the great councils, on the Roman Catholic institution, on the achievement of Augustine and the other Church Fathers and on the faith of the ordinary believer.

We also leave a Church that changed greatly after the first three centuries. The sacramental life of the Church has become more organized and developed. It has adapted to meet the needs of a growing Christian population. In the cities, most priests are now becoming full-time ministers, rather than working part-time at other occupations as Saint Paul did. Small community meetings of Christians are being replaced by large congregations meeting together in large buildings.[4] Fewer bishops know their flocks by name.

Ministries are changing, too. In the first three centuries, unordained people, men and women,[5] took an active part in training others for life as a Christian. Now, Christian education and formation is being taken over by ordained men. Further, doctrine is becoming highly formalized, and it is being taught more and more by ordained men chosen by bishops, rather than by lay men and women chosen by local congregations. Dioceses led by bishops are replacing small congregations led by hometown pastors. And bishops themselves are now being *appointed*, rather than chosen by the faithful. Sometimes bishops are chosen by other bishops, sometimes they are appointed by the emperor. And while the people of Rome selected their bishop until the mid-fourth century, now the popes are being selected by the emperors or chosen by the priests of the Roman diocese.

The roles of women in the Church are likewise changing. In the early Church women served as "deaconesses." Now only men may be ordained as deacons. And while priests in the early Church were frequently married, there is now a growing movement to make priests remain celibate. All in all, the Church is growing toward a more formal structure. It is becoming less of a family and more of an institution. As with all changes in the Church, something is lost and something gained with the changes we find at the end of the era of the Fathers.

In the next chapters, we will continue to follow the evolution and development of the Church's self-image. And we will continue to judge whether these changes in the Church's self-image have been good or bad. We will also strive to learn how the Church's experience during these times affects our lives as Christians today.

---

[4] Although in large cities like Rome, basilicas had replaced house churches as early as the second century.
[5] While women served as "deaconesses" in the first century (and we cannot be sure what was meant by that title), after that time their ministry was restricted to working as catechists to other women and as "ordinary laborers."

FOCUS 7

LEAVING THE AGE OF THE FATHERS—
AND MOTHERS—OF THE EARLY CHURCH

The period of Church history through the first six centuries is some-times called the *patristic period*, after the Latin, *pater*, for "father." This term refers to the fact that by about the time of Pope Gregory the Great's death in 604 the Church's doctrine had been essentially settled by the Fathers of the Church. The Fathers of the Church taught in the form of writings. Pope Gregory was one of these Western Fathers, as were Augustine, Athanasius, Jerome, Ambrose and Irenaeus. We have discussed all of these in preceding pages. All are regarded as saints of the Church.

But, there were saints who were not Fathers. Consider Scholastica, for example, the founder of the women Benedictines. This raises another important point. Since women in the society in which the early Church was situated were not generally given as much education as men, the founding Mothers of the Church did not leave writings behind as men did.

This fact should not keep us from acknowledging the historical fact that women made enormous contributions to the formation of the early Church. Consider Augustine's mother, Monica, for example, who prayed for years that her son would be converted. Without her we would never have had a Saint Augustine. We don't know the names of the early Christian women as well as we do the names of the men. Yet, this should not deter us from referring to the first six centuries of the early Church as the age of the Fathers—and the Mothers—of Christianity.

FOCUS 8

ARE WE PELAGIAN TODAY, YEARS AFTER THE EARLY CHURCH CONDEMNED PELAGIANISM?

The part of Augustine's teaching which modern people find most offensive today is his teaching on grace and free will. In today's world Pelagius would be more accepted than Augustine. Why? We moderns tend to believe that we control our own destinies or that we make ourselves according to our own talents and efforts. This attitude often extends into our spiritual lives. We think that the more we try, the more progress we make. Consider, for example, the hundreds of self-development courses and techniques being offered today by which people can seek to gain inner peace, happiness, fulfillment or enlightenment—all through their own efforts. This frantic "New Age" quest to achieve spiritual wholeness is purely and simply Pelagianism. It is the belief that human nature can heal and perfect itself through its own power.

In place of this, Augustine, and Christian teaching as a whole, emphasize that salvation and happiness are not achieved through human effort. Rather they are achieved through human *surrender*—surrender to God's grace. In the Christian tradition, thanks in large part to Augustine, God is seen as the source of all the good that we achieve. God, and not our own human effort, is what brings us to fulfillment. This is something to think about in a Pelagian age like ours, where the "self-made" individual is our standard for success and happiness. But where is the happiness that all of our self-improvement efforts are supposed to bring us? Perhaps Augustine still has something to say to our age after all.

CHAPTER FIVE

PAPACY AND EMPIRE VIE FOR CONTROL OF THE CHURCH

YOU MAY WONDER, upon reading the title to this chapter, if we are regressing in time. Are we going back to the days when the Roman emperors attempted to control the bishops of the early Church by telling them how to conduct Church affairs? Haven't we already discussed that era in Church history? In Chapter Three, for example, we considered how the Roman Empire declined and how the early popes gained a certain measure of independence from imperial control, becoming the moral leaders of Western society. Why go back and discuss this again?

In actuality, we have not entered into a science fiction "time warp." The issue that was so important in the days of the early Church was how to maintain Church autonomy in the face of attempts by strong emperors to control the Church. This struggle resurfaced in the time period which we will discuss in this chapter, that is, from about the year 600 to about the year 1150.

The difference is that in the present chapter we will not be talking about the same "empire" as before. Let's first say a word or two about this "other empire." The Western empire (the classical Roman Empire) disintegrated in the fifth century, as we saw in Chapter Three. The power vacuum left by the fall of Rome was filled by various barbarian tribes. Two tribes in particular rose to prominence: the Lombards in Italy and the Franks in today's France and Germany.

The Lombards proved particularly troublesome to the papacy. The Lombard kings acted much like some Roman emperors had acted by attempting to control the popes and regulate Church life. Pope Gregory the Great (d. 604) was a strong enough personality to keep the Lombards from subjugating the Church, but popes after Gregory were not so strong. When some of these popes found themselves at the mercy of Lombard kings, they sought help. They turned first to the new Byzantine state in Constantinople. But relations between the Latin and Greek Churches were steadily deteriorating, owing to several theological arguments which we will discuss in the next chapter.

(Pope Martin I [649-655] was even arrested by a Byzantine official and taken to the East, where he died captive.)

Notice that in turning to the Byzantines for protection, the popes acted more like threatened secular rulers than like the spiritual leaders they were. They sought protection from the Lombards by appealing to the power of the Byzantine state rather than to the power of the gospel. The popes did not turn their troubles over to God and simply not worry about what would happen to their possessions. Instead, the popes wanted to keep both their worldly power and their possessions intact. This was a bad omen. The Church was entering into a period when it started acting like another secular state. As that happened, the Church's spiritual and moral authority eventually went into a tailspin.

As we take a look in this chapter at some rough truths about our history, let's keep in mind the following. The gospel is always the standard by which the Church's actions should be judged, and we should never be afraid to make that judgment. The Church is always undergoing reform, growth and change, until it becomes the perfect bride of Christ that it is meant to be (Ephesians 5:22-33).

ENTER THE FRANKS

The deteriorating relationship between the popes in Rome and the patriarchs (chief bishops) in Constantinople had many implications. Most important, the popes turned elsewhere for help in asserting their independence from the Lombards. The popes thus chose the only other major power on the scene, and that was the Franks.

And so, in the year 753, Pope Stephen II traveled to Germany to implore the Frankish king, Pepin, to come to the Church's rescue.[1] Again, we see that the pope chose a worldly solution rather than a gospel solution. Instead of becoming poor and humble, the pope turned to Pepin in order to protect his religious and secular power.

The pope's request for protection greatly impressed this barbarian king. Like all barbarians, he saw the popes as the heirs of the ancient Roman dignity. We might imagine a scene in our own day where Queen Elizabeth of England would travel to Canada and ask the Canadians for assistance. The Queen has no actual authority over the Canadians, who are an independent nation. Nonetheless, many Canadians have great respect for the Queen and all that she represents, and thus would probably respond favorably to her request.

At any rate, Pepin leapt at the chance to help the pope. Pepin took his army to Italy and defeated the Lombard king, Aistulf. After his victory, Pepin restored certain lands to the pope that the papacy had claimed as its own. Pepin also gave the pope new lands. These lands came to be known as the *Papal Estates*. To formalize this real estate transfer, King Pepin issued a docu-

---

[1] The Franks were already Catholic. King Clovis (466-511) already had accepted Catholic Christianity on behalf of his people. Clovis's conversion ended the possibility that future barbarian kingdoms would be Arian.

ment which was something like a deed, later called *The Donation of Pepin.*

We might ask today how it was that Pepin thought he had the right to give the pope someone else's land, but Pepin didn't think in our terms. Actually, the Byzantines asked the same question we ask, because they had conquered part of the land in question. They claimed that *they* owned the land which Pepin donated. This led to yet another cause for conflict between the Western and Eastern Churches. During the period we will cover in this chapter, we will see how the Church often acted just as the world acts.

This fact was damaging to the Church's self-image. For the *Donation of Pepin* caused still another problem. If a king gives someone a large chunk of land, there are bound to be strings attached. Pepin's donation was no exception. He and his descendants as Frankish kings believed that by becoming papal protectors they gained the right to tell the popes how the Church should be governed. Because they acted like secular rulers, the popes would be treated accordingly.

WHO CONTROLS THE CHURCH— KING OR POPE?

Thus the papacy found that by inviting the Franks to come to their rescue they were in much the same situation as the Arab who allowed a camel to stick his nose into the tent. The camel liked the tent so much that he was not content to stick just his nose inside. He wanted to bring the rest of his body inside as well. In the end, the camel was sleeping in the Arab's bed.

Gradually, as the Franks grew stronger, the papacy relied more and more on their protection. The climax to this process was reached on Christmas Day in the year 800, when Pope Leo III crowned the Frankish king, Charlemagne,[2] "Holy Roman Emperor." This title delighted the Franks. To them it meant that now they had been given divine approval to succeed to the dignity and prestige of the former Roman Empire. Thus, not more than four hundred years after the collapse of the *old* Western empire, a *new* one came to birth—the Holy Roman Empire.

As Voltaire (1694-1778) later observed, this new state was neither holy, Roman, nor an empire. Nevertheless, people in the early Middle Ages wanted so desperately to regain the lost concept of empire, with all that it stood for, that they gladly accepted the new title as a reality. And that is how the Church found itself confronting an entirely new struggle for independence with an entirely new empire. Let's now look at how Church history evolved once Charlemagne became emperor.

---

[2] This is his French name, which has come down to us through the French and then English chroniclers. He called himself Karl der Grosse, "Charles the Great."

CHARLEMAGNE: A NEW CONSTANTINE TRIES TO CONTROL THE CHURCH

Charlemagne ("Charles the Great") was like his predecessor Constantine in several respects. Both men's names began with a C. Both were large of stature and devout but under-educated in spiritual matters. And both thought that God had called them personally to supervise the Church for the Church's own good. And of course, by seeking the Franks' help, the popes gave Charlemagne every reason to think that the popes *wanted* him to run the Church.

It was foolish to expect a barbarian king untrained in Roman customs to think anything else. Charlemagne could not distinguish between God's law and civil law. In *Teutonic* law, or in the *Germanic* conception of law, Charlemagne was both chief of his tribe and chief priest of his people. This meant that he saw himself as called by God to provide guidance and supervision to the Church. This, of course, was actually a function reserved to the bishops. Charlemagne, to say the least, had little appreciation for the concept of hierarchical spiritual authority presented by Saint Paul in his epistles.

Charlemagne looked at Church and state as if they were virtually one entity. Thus, distorted Church-state relations were the root of a long and protracted struggle between medieval popes and emperors all through the period we are considering in this chapter. The Church's main struggle in this era involved a life-or-death struggle for autonomy.

A key question here is, why did the Church have to be involved in such a struggle? Why did the Church need worldly power? Did the popes and bishops need to own land and wealth to shepherd their flocks? In the age of Charlemagne, an entirely new image of the Church emerged.

THE CHURCH 'GOES TO THE DOGS'[3] (THE FIRST TIME)

One of the principal results of the Church-state struggle was the deterioration of Church discipline, leading to a decline in competence and morality among the clergy. The clergy in Charlemagne's empire, for example, were usually uneducated men appointed by the imperial court or by bishops who themselves had been appointed by the imperial court. Many priests didn't really want to be priests—and they lived a life-style to prove it.

Many, if not most bishops and priests during this time were married and had large families. Their interest in a Church office was often political rather than spiritual. Under Teutonic law, the man who owned the land on which the church was located was also seen as the owner of the church and supervisor of its affairs. Sometimes this landowner was the bishop himself. In that case,

---

[3] Gilbert Keith Chesterton (1874-1936) observed, "Five times the Catholic Church has gone to the dogs, and each time the dog died."

the bishop often did not consider himself called to a uniquely spiritual office. Rather, he saw himself as part warrior, part landowner, part imperial servant—and, oh yes, part bishop.[4]

Such men wanted more than anything to protect their own interests. They saw to it that their churches were bequeathed to their sons. This often led to scandalous fights between rival claimants to a deceased bishop's office—brother against brother, nephew against son, etc. Then, too, families often would compete with one another *to buy* a vacant episcopal chair. One can point to numerous illustrations of this sin[5] of *simony*—buying and selling of Church offices. One notorious nobleman, for example, outbid an abbot for a vacant bishop's seat, paying today's equivalent of over ten million dollars for the office and then giving it to his ten-year-old son, making his ten-year-old son bishop.

LAY INVESTITURE

All of this was completely at odds with the Church's official teaching emanating from Rome. But by carrying on like worldly rulers, the popes had become either too weak to correct the situation or too implicated in corruption to make a convincing protest. Powerful Italian families now started to act in Italy like the Frankish nobility to the north. They fought with each other or bid against each other to put their own family's candidate into the papacy. The worst problem of all was a practice known as *lay investiture*.

Lay investiture was a procedure by which laymen—princes, counts, dukes, or other powerful lords—would invest bishops and abbots with their insignia of office. Imagine today, for example, a new bishop being installed, not by his brother bishops, but by the mayor of Boston or the governor of New York. Such a procedure obviously contradicts what is actually taking place—the passing of *spiritual* authority from one bishop to another. Lay investiture was a public statement to the effect that the state had the authority to regulate the Church's life.

But the Church itself already had signaled its acceptance of the worldly transfer of power. In the first three centuries, bishops and popes had been chosen by the faithful. Eventually, however, when popes and bishops first started allowing emperors to appoint them to office, they opened the door for state control of episcopal appointments.

Then, too, by centralizing all Church authority into the hands of ordained men, the Church was acting just like the imperial bureaucracy. In a sense, the Church was now reaping the fruit of its own harvesting. Whether an emperor appointed a bishop or the pope appointed a bishop, the Church was still oper-

---

[4] This situation arose principally because of the mixing of ancient Germanic concepts of law with the principally Mediterranean concept of Roman law that the Western Church had adopted.

[5] The church officially and doctrinally condemned simony, but was powerless to stop it.

ating from the premise of a worldly system. It was still prince appointing prince, rather than we the Church, as a whole, choosing our shepherds.

We see how bad this situation had become when we consider what happened after the Frankish dynasty came to an end and a new dynasty succeeded to imperial office in 962. This new dynasty was called the *Saxon* (or *Ottonian*) dynasty, after the region in Germany where the new emperors came from—Saxony. The first of these new emperors, Otto I, went to Rome in 963. There he threw Pope John XII out of office and installed his own Pope Leo VIII.

For the next few decades only the weakest, most pliable men were made popes, so that the emperors could easily control them. For example, Emperor Otto III went to Rome in 983 and arrested Pope John XVI, who had been installed by an Italian faction hostile to Otto. Otto tortured and mutilated the pope and then led him through the streets of Rome in order to emphasize the pope's subservience.

When the Saxon dynasty ended, the new *Salian* dynasty of emperors came to power. They proved that they, too, intended to control the Church. At one point, as if to emphasize how completely the emperors dominated the Church, the Salians made a twelve-year-old boy pope, Benedict IX (1033-45).

THE DOG DIES (THE FIRST TIME)

At this point in the story, one could easily conclude that the Church had lost all contact with its spiritual origins and completely forsaken its calling to serve as Christ's body on earth. But such was not the case. Even during those times when the Church has publicly aired its dirtiest linen, there are nonetheless believers who hold fast to the gospel. Sooner or later, authentic followers of the gospel rise to the surface to reform the Church. Actually, reform belongs to the very nature of the Church; The Church is both "reformer and reforming" at all times. The Church constantly seeks to cleanse itself of nongospel elements. Thus, it should not surprise us to find reform coming from within the ranks of the Church itself.

PHASE ONE: CLUNY

During the period covered by this chapter there were two waves of reform. The first of these began in monasteries affiliated with a large Benedictine monastery in Cluny, France. The monks of the monastery at Cluny had initially been given the right by their lay founder (a duke) to select their own abbot. This meant that Cluny was independent from the system of secular control which crippled Church autonomy elsewhere.

A large number of monasteries, perhaps as many as a thousand, joined ranks with Cluny and submitted to its authority. Thus a powerful spiritual force was now opposed to the continuation of lay investiture. Eventually, the Cluniac monasteries came under the direct supervision of the papacy. With that, the papacy had a means of spreading reform over the heads, or perhaps, under the noses, of bishops and abbots who owed their offices to secular rulers.

The Cluniac reformers insisted on ending two abuses—simony and the lack of gospel life-styles within the clergy. Actually, both abuses were part and parcel of the same phenomenon—a married clergy which fought to perpetuate its own family's control over Church offices. This, in turn, was based on a *distortion* of Church offices—associating Church offices with power, prestige and possessions—rather than with service of the flock. Thus the Church moved toward a universal policy of obligatory celibacy, or prohibiting the clergy from marrying and having families.

THE ORIGINS OF PRIESTLY CELIBACY

The origins of celibacy go farther back than the period under consideration here. Originally, most priests were married. Thus, the Spanish Synod of Elvira, meeting in 306, had to content itself with requiring *married* clergy not to engage in sexual relations with their wives. Pope Damasus (366-384) taught that spiritual fatherhood was more important that biological fatherhood, and thus prohibited priests in Rome from marrying. Pope Damasus spoke of preserving priests' "cultic purity." He thought that sexual intercourse made a man unclean and unsuited for priestly service. (The Hebrew Scriptures, too, taught that temporary uncleanness made one unfit to offer sacrifice.)

This attitude was a distortion of the gospel's teaching that both the body and the soul are good. In actuality, in promoting celibacy, the Church was in many ways enforcing a gnostic way of looking at the world. Recall that gnosticism stood for the proposition that spiritual realities were of more value than material realities, or that spirit was nobler than flesh.

Gnostic dualism was completely contrary to the gospel, which was based on the idea that God had become man. The Incarnation meant that the body was just as good as the soul. Thus, to say that sexual intercourse in marriage interferes with someone's holiness is not a Christian idea. Nevertheless, at the Fourth Council of Toledo in Spain in 633, bishops and priests were required to take a vow of chastity, that is, renouncing all sexual activity for life. But these requirements were never rigidly kept—or they were kept in some places more strictly than in others. It was not until the year 1139 that the Second Lateran Council definitively settled the question of celibacy in the Western Church. The Council declared any marriage of the clergy invalid as a matter of Church law.

THE CARDINALS

Even before the Second Lateran Council, Pope Leo IX (1049-54), greatly influenced by Cluny, had started to champion reform by insisting on celibacy for the clergy. Leo also started another policy which helped to continue the reform efforts of Cluny. He chose certain bishops to be his "cardinal" bishops, or "first-line" bishops, we might say. These cardinals often stayed in Rome or accompanied Leo on his many trips around the empire. In this way they showed that they were independent of imperial control. When they did return to their own dioceses, they made it clear that they submitted to the pope's authority in spiritual matters and not to the emperor's.

Soon the cardinals were considered clergy of Rome and the election of the bishop of Rome was reserved to them. This College of Cardinals served as the pope's first line of defense against imperial control of the Church in lands where the popes previously had to submit to the will of powerful princes and their hand-picked bishops. Had the popes once again chosen a worldly solution to their problems? "Cardinal" was an imperial term signifying a powerful civil official. The cardinals came to be looked upon not as spiritual shepherds, but as temporal princes.[6]

PHASE TWO: THE GREGORIAN REFORM

Leo's reform of the papal office and his reinstitution of clerical discipline was continued, and reached its peak, under Pope Gregory VII (1073-85). Gregory's reform effort is often called the *Gregorian Reform*. Along with the Cluniac Reform, the Gregorian Reform virtually eliminated the abuses we have discussed above, but not before Pope Gregory himself went through a very painful personal defeat.

Gregory was first and foremost a monk, and even wore his monk's cowl while he served as pope. He thought the best way to assure the Church's independence from imperial control was to "force the issue" on lay investiture, by challenging the emperor's right to install bishops.

In Emperor Henry IV, Gregory met someone who gladly accepted the pope's challenge. Henry insisted on his right to control the Church, and proved his point by investing his choice for bishop of Milan with the episcopal insignia of office. Gregory's opposition to Henry was made all the more difficult because Henry's German bishops openly sided with the Emperor against the pope. These bishops weren't the least bit interested in Church unity. Instead they wanted to keep their large land holdings intact and to maintain their power at the imperial court. The bishops could play politics as well as the pope could.

Henry threatened to depose Gregory, and Gregory excommunicated Henry. Politics in Germany came to Gregory's rescue. Along with the German bishops' desire to be independent from the pope, German *barons* likewise wanted to be independent from their emperor. They saw the pope as an ally in their struggle to weaken the power of rich German bishops and of the emperor. Thus, these barons sided with Gregory in the controversy.

Henry realized that without his barons he had little chance of continuing

---

[6] To this day some people still refer to Cardinals as "princes of the Church."

his domination of the Church. Henry decided to ask Gregory to forgive him. He traveled to meet the pope at a small town in northern Italy named Canossa. Henry stood outside in the snow for three days dressed in rags until the pope absolved him and rescinded the decree of excommunication. But Henry's repentance was short-lived. As soon as his own fortunes improved, he schemed to drive Gregory from the papal office. Playing on the fickle nature of Italian politics, Henry won thirteen cardinals to his side and persuaded powerful Roman families to help him drive Gregory out. Fearing for his life, Gregory fled to southern Italy, dying some four years later. On his deathbed he mourned, "I have loved justice and hated iniquity, and thus I die in exile."

THE TIDE TURNS IN FAVOR OF THE POPES

Yet, the tide turned once again. As emperor, Henry did not have the same power that Charlemagne had. The political fortunes of emperors had deteriorated since the ninth century. By Henry's time, powerful kings and princes, especially the new kings of England and France, strongly resisted the idea of empire. They made life difficult for "emperors" like Henry.

Two events helped the papacy to regain its long-lost independence. First, the papacy made an agreement with King Louis VI of France to end lay investiture in France. Second, the German barons revolted against Henry's successor to the imperial throne. The end came for the emperors at a little German town named Worms in the year 1122. In a document entitled *The Concordat of Worms*, Emperor Henry V gave up the right of lay investiture. He promised to allow the Church to select its bishops, and swore to help eliminate simony.

It was an impressive victory for the papacy, which had struggled long and hard to win the Church's independence from the state. Yet, in the wake of the papacy's triumph, one issue got lost. The popes were now victorious, but victorious as what? As worldly rulers or spiritual shepherds? At Canossa the Church won a great victory for its own independence, but who was now to lead the Church—prophets or princes? As we enter the next phase of Church history, we shall see that while the Church may have gained in worldly power and prestige, it had lost much of its spiritual and moral authority.

Yet, thanks to the sacrifices of people like Pope Gregory VII and the monks of the Cluniac reform, the Western Church had largely cleaned up its house. It could now enter into what many feel was to be its most influential era. In Chapter Seven, we will discuss the history of that era. But before we do so, we must first go back and recover some of the loose threads of Eastern Church history that have been left dangling from earlier chapters.

FOCUS 9

THE CATHOLIC WORLD IN CHARLEMAGNE'S DAY: WHO WERE OUR ANCESTORS IN THE FAITH?

Charlemagne's empire was very different geographically and racially than the old Roman Empire. For one thing, the center of gravity in the Christian world had shifted from the sunny, Mediterranean, Greek-speaking culture which Saint Paul knew, to the colder, multi-lingual climate of the North. For example, Charlemagne made his capital in Aachen, not far from today's Netherlands. Then, too, the peoples in Charlemagne's empire were of a completely different stock than the Latins, Semites, Africans and Persians that populated the early Church.

Who were these people, who would eventually be called French, German, English, Irish, Spanish Christians? Perhaps their names strike us as foreign-sounding. They came from regions, rather than countries such as Aquitaine, Burgundy, Austrasia, Nesutria, Serbia and the Asturias. (See the map on page 49 for assistance in locating these areas.) As for their language, they spoke mostly regional dialects, nothing like the modern European languages we have today. Most people couldn't understand anyone who lived even a hundred miles away from them. Not that it made any difference, because most people never traveled more than a few miles from the spot where they were born.

Keep in mind also that Charlemagne's empire was hardly Christian at first. As we shall see in the next chapter, most of Spain was Muslim. Vast portions of Charlemagne's Eastern empire—today's Hungary and Czechoslovakia—were wild, untamed frontiers. Charlemagne spent a good portion of his time converting peoples in these regions to Christianity. His method was to defeat pagan tribes in battle, and then line up entire tribes for Baptism. One of his bishops would walk among the people and splash them with holy water sprayed from a large broom. Those who resisted were often put to death. Needless to say, this hardly made for enthusiastic conversions. Yet, to the barbarian mind, this was the way things worked. If your tribe was beaten in battle, it meant that your victor's god was more powerful than your own, and thus you accepted that new god. But was this a true conversion of hearts and minds to the gospel? It was a far cry from the way Saint Paul evangelized people.

What is our attitude toward evangelization today? Do we try to win people to the gospel because our culture is more powerful in war or finance than that of the people to whom we preach the gospel? Or do we make ourselves all things to all people, like Saint Paul did, in order to win their hearts and minds to the gospel?

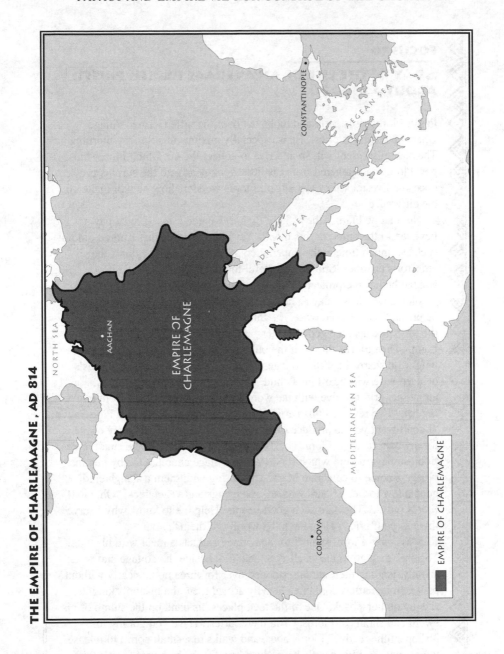

THE EMPIRE OF CHARLEMAGNE, AD 814

CONSTANTINOPLE

AEGEAN SEA

ADRIATIC SEA

NORTH SEA

AACHAN

EMPIRE OF CHARLEMAGNE

MEDITERRANEAN SEA

CORDOVA

EMPIRE OF CHARLEMAGNE

FOCUS 10

A DAY IN THE LIFE OF AN AVERAGE PARISH PRIEST, ABOUT A.D. 1000

Pastor Florus rises early and looks out over the little German village where he serves as priest. He is especially anxious this Sunday morning. The bishop's knight will soon arrive to collect the tax which Florus must pay. Florus has gathered from his little flock nearly all the surplus produce and livestock they can afford. Florus wonders how he will make up the difference.

Not that he blames the bishop. Bishop Konrad himself must pay a large tax to the emperor this month. Yet Florus wishes that Konrad did not spend so much time at the imperial court, or off fighting against the emperor's enemies. Still he is grateful that in serving under Bishop Konrad he has the protection of one of the noblest warriors of the realm.

Florus wonders today as he often does why Konrad ever chose him to be priest. "I can't even write," he thinks. "I can only read the prayers of the Mass because the good brothers at the monastery patiently taught me Latin." Then Florus thinks of the other problem he has. His common-law wife, who shares his little cottage with him, is pregnant. Soon, Florus's beloved wife will bear him a child. Konrad, who has a large family, allows his priest to live with the woman, but prohibits Florus from marrying her. "I've reserved this parish for my son," Konrad has told Florus. "I don't want you to produce offspring that would get in the way of plans for my own family." Florus kneels to pray before Mass in the small, bare-floor, stone structure which serves as the village church. One by one the villagers come to celebrate Mass. They bring with them a slaughtered goat, a few loaves of barley bread, some eggs and vegetables. "Oh, God!" Florus prays. "They are such good people. Help me to know why I serve them as your priest. Help me to be worthy of them."

Mass over, Florus returns to the cottage and has a meal with his wife. Together they go to the small vegetable plot beside the cottage and work silently, tending their garden, stooped over for three hours nearly without pause. In late afternoon, three heavily armed men, the bishop's knights, ride up on horseback. One of the men places his hand on the stump of his sword and shouts at Florus. "You there, priest! Have you got my lord bishop's tithe ready?" Florus nods, and walks to a small corral to release the animals that his people have given him for the bishop. Florus's wife goes inside the cottage to retrieve bread and produce which she has already placed in sacks. The men grunt in satisfaction, and then ride off. Florus crosses himself and sighs. "Dear Lord, give me strength," he prays.

CHAPTER SIX

CATHOLICS, BYZANTINES AND MUSLIMS

REMEMBER THE FAMILY we met at the beginning of Chapter Three? During the time that Rome was collapsing, this family set out from Ravenna in northern Italy, for Sicily in the south. They were escaping the barbarian invasions in the West. It so happens that both Ravenna and Sicily were to become strongholds of the new "Byzantine Empire." The Byzantine Empire was the successor to the old Roman Empire in the East, with its capital in Constantinople. The Byzantine Empire was to the Christian (Greek) East what the Holy Roman Empire was to the Christian (Latin) West—namely, the Christian inheritor of the Roman Empire's dignity and prestige.

The Byzantines wanted to reclaim from the barbarians the former Italian lands of the Western Roman emperors. Ravenna, in Italy, even became the capital in the West of Byzantine emperors seeking to reassert the ancient, universal Roman dignity. Travelers to Ravenna today can still see traces of Byzantine architecture in the city's ancient buildings.

Our family from Chapter Three, with their roots in Ravenna and their new home in Sicily, found themselves attracted to the Byzantine culture. They also greatly appreciated the protection offered by Byzantine soldiers stationed in the West. As time went on, some members of this family traveled to Constantinople (in modern Turkey) and settled there. Let's take up the story of a later generation of our imagined family as it attempts to make the transition from being Western and Roman Catholic, to being Eastern and Byzantine Christian (at this point in history, they were not yet called "Greek Orthodox").

Let's say it's about the year 800. Charlemagne is just becoming Holy Roman Emperor in the West. You are living in Byzantium (Constantinople), far from Charlemagne and his Western empire. You are also far from Roman Catholicism and the Western Church. You now live in Byzantium, or the Eastern Christian empire, where the Greek language and culture predominate. Your grandparents, who live in Constantinople with you, often speak in the Italian dialect of their youth. You can make out only a few words of that

51

strange language. You likewise have difficulty understanding your grandparents' Western religious devotions.

Some of your friends question whether your grandparents are really Christian. You sometimes wonder the same thing. Their ways are different in many respects from the Christian ways which you have learned here in the East. Are your friends right? Are your grandparents followers of the "barbarian" Christianity that the Westerners are said to practice? Let's look at how their ways differ from yours.

One thing that annoys you is your grandparents' attitude toward the priests in your Church. Your grandmother constantly chides the priests for being married and raising families. In Rome, she often reminds you, the priests don't marry, keeping themselves free to serve only the Church. This strikes you as silly, and it makes some of your priests furious. One day, one of your priests angrily scolds your grandmother for airing her opinions on this subject, telling her that it is ridiculous not to let priests marry.

Your grandmother gets angry herself and tells your priest that he shouldn't be administering the Sacrament of Confirmation. Only bishops are supposed to administer that sacrament, as is the custom in the West. You look on hopelessly, wondering what you can do to reconcile two people whom you love and respect. But the argument continues.

Your grandmother is mad because she can receive the bread of the Eucharist only on Sundays. "In my childhood," she says, "we could receive the Lord's Body *every* day." Your priest doesn't help matters by responding, "That's just what I would expect those barbarian Christians in the West to do. We *orthodox* Christians celebrate the Lord's Supper as it was meant to be celebrated, only on Sundays." And so it goes—one argument after another with no apparent prospect for resolution.

That night, your grandmother is in tears. "I miss the old ways," she cries. "Why can't I do things the way we used to do them when I was a girl living in Italy?"

You place your arm around the old woman's shoulder. "I know, Grandmother, I know. I'm sure it's very hard for you, but couldn't you just *try* to do things the way they are done here?" You think of one of the little things that infuriates your grandmother. "Look," you say, making the Sign of the Cross. "Does it make any difference that I make the Sign of the Cross with three fingers and you make it with four? Do you think the Lord cares how we do it?"

Your grandmother looks at you through her tears, struggling to understand you and accept what you are saying. "But these churches here are so strange!" she exclaims. "All that incense! And everywhere you look, icons and pictures! We had pictures and statues in my church when I was a little girl, but nothing like they have here. And when I go to Communion, they hand me a clump of brown bread to eat, instead of the fine, unleavened bread we received in my day. It seems sacrilegious to me! Shouldn't the Lord's Body be given to us pure and white, instead of like something right out of the baker's shop?

"And the creed we say on Sunday! Isn't it blasphemous to say that the Holy Spirit proceeds only from the Father, and not from the Father and the

Son, as we said in Italy? Who changed all that anyway? And another thing! I don't like the way the priests here show disrespect to the Holy Father in Rome. To me he's the head of the Church. The priests here say he's just another bishop. Oh, I don't know what to think. It seems to me that things were better in the West before Papa brought us here."

You don't know what to say to your grandmother. You just hold her while she cries. You think to yourself, "Oh, poor Grandmother, what am I going to do with you?"

CONSTANTINOPLE: THE SPLENDOR OF THE CHRISTIAN WORLD

What is life like for you in this strange and wonderful city of Constantinople? Let's start with the city itself. Compare magnificent Constantinople with, let's say, Charlemagne's paltry little capital at Aachen, far away to the West. No wonder that Eastern Christians consider their ways superior to those of the West. Constantinople is much more vibrant than any Western city. There are libraries, museums, bookstores! And on every street corner people gather to debate theology, as if every Christian were a skilled theologian.

In the West, on the other hand, few Christians can read or write, much less understand abstract religious issues. Increasingly, the clergy in the West is becoming a separate caste. It's becoming common in the West to think of the priests as practicing Christianity *for* the people. In the East, the ordinary Christian is much closer to the day-to-day practice of the faith.

Constantinople has dozens of beautifully adorned churches. There, scores of priests lead marvelous liturgical celebrations in which the whole congregation sings, processes and prays in unison with the celebrants at the altar. In the West, things are different. Increasingly, the congregation stands silently and watches what goes on at the altar. The much smaller size[1] and the geographical location of the *Byzantine Empire*, as it is called, make for a more compact, closely integrated Christian community. In the West, the Church is spread out over thousand of miles, encompassing peoples of many different languages and customs. In Byzantium, however, the Church is mostly Greek in orientation. It is restrained by the seas which surround it on three sides and by the ancient frontiers of the Roman Empire to the north. The Byzantine Church is better organized, like everything else in Byzantium, and for good reason.

---

[1] The size of the Byzantine Empire grew and diminished according to the Byzantines' success or failure in keeping the Muslims at bay. Sometimes it occupied all of Turkey and parts of Greece. Toward the end (1453), it barely occupied the city of Constantinople.

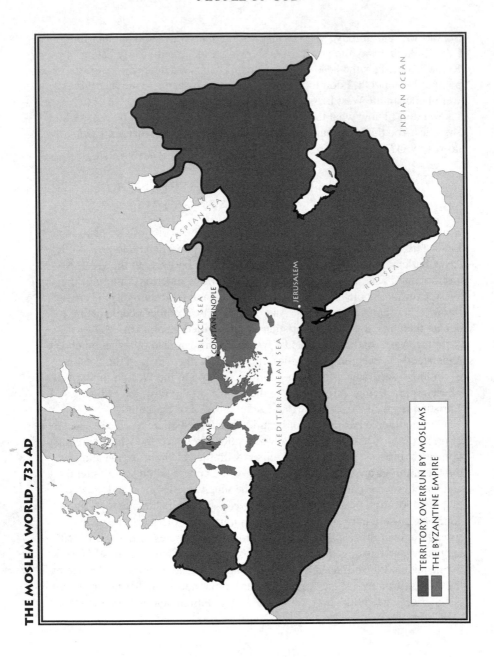

THE MOSLEM WORLD, 732 AD

TERRITORY OVERRUN BY MOSLEMS
THE BYZANTINE EMPIRE

INDIAN OCEAN

CASPIAN SEA

BLACK SEA

CONSTANTINOPLE

ROME

MEDITERRANEAN SEA

JERUSALEM

RED SEA

ISLAM: A NEW FAITH COMES TO BIRTH IN THE EAST

In the seventh century, a new religion came to birth in the East—Islam or Muhammadanism. *Islam*, which means "submission," was founded in 612 by the Arab prophet, Muhammad. Muhammad had studied both Judaism and Christianity. He believed that God had revealed truths to him which required a new religion, a religion that superceded both Judaism and Christianity and perfected them.

The Muslims believed in aggressive conversion of non-Muslims. In the lands of the Middle East, Persia and Syria, which had once been strongholds of Christianity, the Muslims made holy war against Christians. Many Christian families became Muslim. By the year 700, Islam threatened to become the sole religion of the former Christian East.

The Muslims pinned down the Byzantines in a narrow stretch of territory in today's western Turkey. They overran former Christian North Africa and conquered all of Spain and parts of today's southern France. A quick glance at the map on page 54 shows just how successful the Muslims were in winning the early Middle Ages to Islam. If it hadn't been for Charlemagne's grandfather, Charles Martel, Roman Catholicism might have been completely eradicated from Europe, and Islam established in its place. Charles Martel defeated the Muslims in a famous battle at the French town of Tours in 732.

If Islam had dominated, perhaps the only form of Christianity anyone would know about today would be Byzantine Christianity. The Byzantines successfully defended themselves from the Muslims until the year 1453. In that year, Seljuk Turks, a Muslim dynasty that arose much later in history, captured Constantinople. They changed its name to Istanbul and made Islam the majority religion in the former Byzantine capital. In the time period of the present chapter, however, Byzantium served as Christianity's eastern outpost and most ardent defender against the Muslim onslaught. That condition existed from about the time of Rome's collapse in the late fifth century, to about the time of the great schism between the Western and Eastern Churches in the year 1054 (discussed below).

Because of this constant threat from the Muslims, Byzantium was better organized than the Western empire. In the West, anything like the unified Byzantine state was prevented from arising because of greater numbers of people, greater distances, and vastly different cultures and ethnic groups. Let's take a quick look at how Byzantine Church and society developed during the time period from about 500 to about 1054.

INTERNAL AFFAIRS IN BYZANTIUM

The first true Byzantine emperor in his own right was Justinian the Great (483-565). Justinian wanted to regain the lands lost to the old Roman Empire.

Thus, he spent a good part of his years as emperor fighting the barbarians in the West. Remember that this was before Muhammad had been born and before there existed any Muslim threat.

As the map on page 54 shows, Justinian succeeded in winning for the Byzantines large chunks of land in Italy, Sardinia, Sicily and all along the coast of the Adriatic sea. During Justinian's time, then, it was accurate to think of the Byzantine Empire as a true empire. Yet, later Byzantine emperors lost most of their Western holdings. This incursion by the Byzantines into the West and the later loss of the Byzantines' lands to Western kings (see p. 54) contributed to the suspicion and dislike which Western and Eastern Christians had for one another. Remember that it was Western Christian rulers, like the Frankish king Pepin (see p. 40 ff.), who were involved in taking over the Byzantines' Western land.

THE ICONOCLAST CONTROVERSY: WHAT ROLE DO IMAGES PLAY IN PRACTICING THE FAITH?

We get some idea of how seriously the Byzantines took their day-to-day practice of their faith when we consider the infamous *iconoclast controversy*. This conflict roared on for over a century. Icons are pictures and images of Jesus, his mother and the saints. They were an important part of Byzantine piety— much more important than in the West. No Byzantine home was without its icons. The whole family usually started its day by praying in front of its favorite icons. To take away a Byzantine Christian's icons would be the same thing as preventing a Bible-belt Christian in our own day from reading or owning a Bible.

Emperor Leo III (717-741) attempted to suppress icons. Leo was convinced that an excessive reliance on icons by Christians would make it difficult to attract Jews and Muslims into the Church. Neither Jews nor Muslims tolerated religious art. Further, monks in Byzantine society controlled the trade in icons, and Leo thought the monks as a group had become too powerful. Leo's troops went around publicly destroying many of the icons in churches. They were called *iconoclasts*, or people who "break" or destroy icons. Byzantine Christians reacted so violently to Leo's policy of *iconoclasm* that they revolted. At one point, Leo was almost thrown out of office. With a mob about to enter his palace, his wife came to his rescue and helped him sneak away to consolidate his forces and regain power.

The Byzantine emperors during this period were able to stay in power solely because the army remained loyal to the imperial throne. So, too, did many bishops, although other bishops supported the masses and preached against iconoclasm.

From 725 to 842, the iconoclast controversy completely disrupted Byzantine society. The Muslims were initially successful in conquering

Byzantine territory in the East partially because the Byzantines were at each others' throats over the iconoclast issue.

Empress Irene (780-802) recognized the threat to imperial security which this internal dissension posed. She convened the *Second Council of Nicea*, which met in 787. This council condemned iconoclasm as a heresy and authorized the restoration of the previous use of icons in Byzantine religious life. As with the controversy over "Mother of God" (see page 15), the Church found itself following the common sense of the ordinary believer, basing its doctrine not so much on abstract theological principles as on the everyday prayer life of the faithful.

The significance of the iconoclast controversy is that it helped pave the way for the split between the Roman Catholic and Byzantine Churches. Westerners feared that Byzantines were closet Monophysites (see page 17), *i.e.,* they feared that Eastern Christians, while formally accepting the Creed of Chalcedon, in reality tended to doubt that Christ had possessed a human nature like everyone else. Westerners saw iconoclasm as an effort by the Byzantine emperors to enforce Monophysitism on the Church. By prohibiting the use of icons, it was thought the emperor was saying, in effect, remove anything tangible, earthly or fleshly from your piety and focus instead only on that which is heavenly and transcendent.

Then, paradoxically, when the Second Council of Nicea restored the veneration of icons, more suspicion arose in the West. The acts of the council were circulated in the Frankish lands as translations from the Greek. The translations were of very poor quality, and when the Frankish bishops read them, they concluded that the council had gone to the other extreme by decreeing that icons were as worthy of veneration as the Trinity! Thus the Synod of Frankfurt (794) condemned the Second Council of Nicea. Eventually, at the prodding of the popes, the Frankish bishops were persuaded that they had misread the acts of the Council of Nicea and they withdrew their opposition to that council.

But in the West the most bothersome aspect of iconoclasm was that the Byzantine emperors got away with imposing doctrinal decisions on the Byzantine bishops. As we saw in the last chapter, the Western Church had its own struggle to endure insofar as domination by the state was concerned. Yet, in the West, emperors and barons did not set the Church's doctrinal agenda for it. In the East, however, *caesaropapism* (state control of the Church's doctrine) was different; it meant that the Eastern bishops could not even exercise their episcopal authority once they were installed as bishops. The Western Church saw the iconoclast controversy, with its fellow-traveler, caesaropapism, as a cancer that had to be kept from spreading west.

THE BYZANTINES QUARREL WITH THE ROMAN CATHOLIC CHURCH

By the mid-ninth century the iconoclast controversy was largely resolved. Byzantine society turned its attention to more important matters, such as fighting the Muslims and arguing with Christians in the West (who loved to reciprocate by starting arguments with the Byzantines). Let's look at some of the doctrinal issues dividing Roman Catholics and Byzantine Christians.

First was the question of Church leadership and authority. The popes in Rome continued to insist that they were superior in spiritual authority to the patriarchs (chief bishops) of Constantinople. The latter were equally insistent that authority in the Church should be shared by bishops of the "Pentarchy" or five major *sees* (episcopal cities) of the early Church—Rome, Antioch, Jerusalem, Alexandria and Constantinople. Rome argued that the early Church had always accepted the teachings of the bishops of Rome as final and supreme. Consider, for example, the effect which Pope Leo and his *Tome* had on the Eastern bishops at the Council of Chalcedon (see Chapter Two).

This argument for the popes' reliability in teaching orthodox doctrine lost much of its weight when Pope Honorius I (625-638) was perceived to be supporting Monotheletism[2] because of his failure to clearly distinguish between the unity of purpose or synergism between the two wills in Christ and the doctrinal issue as to whether or not there are in fact two distinct wills in Christ. The heresy of Monotheletism meant that the man Jesus did not possess both a human will and a divine will, but only a divine will. It didn't matter to the Byzantines that Honorius's successors, Popes Severinus, John IV and Leo II, all condemned Honorius's teaching, accusing Honorius of treachery. The damage had been done. Eastern bishops now had a clear example to point to of how popes could err. Popes, they said, patently were not infallible. In 681, at the Third Council of Constantinople, the Byzantine bishops anathematized the pope ("cut him off" from the Church). Consequently, by the start of the eighth century, the argument for papal primacy had lost much of its effect in the Byzantine Church.

DIFFERENCES IN EVERYDAY PIETY FROM EAST TO WEST

Further, as we saw in our imagined scene at the start of this chapter, Byzantine Christians worshiped and practiced their faith differently than did Roman Catholics. In the Byzantine tradition, married men with families could be ordained priests, though not made bishops. Byzantine priests administered

---

[2] It is unclear whether Honorius knowingly supported the doctrine, or whether he endorsed a formula, "one will," carelessly and without understanding its implications. At any rate, the pope did not promulgate this doctrine, but, in some fashion sanctioned it.

the Sacrament of Confirmation, whereas in the West only bishops could do so. In the East, the Eucharist was usually celebrated only on Sundays, while in the West it was becoming common for Mass to be celebrated daily.

There were other differences regarding the Eucharist. The word "Mass" was commonly used only in the West. And in the West the bread of the Eucharist was given to the faithful in its unleavened form, without yeast, similar to what the Jews had done in their own liturgical practices. In the East, on the other hand, Christians received the bread of the Eucharist with yeast in it. It looked and tasted like ordinary bread. Byzantine Christians thought the Westerners' use of unleavened bread was "too Jewish." They wanted a clear break with Old Testament doctrine in favor of the New Testament.

Perhaps the greatest offense in the eyes of the Byzantines occurred in the late sixth century. In the sixth century, the Western Church added the words *"and the son"* to the creed adopted at Constantinople in 381. (See page 15 and Focus 12, page 61.) In Latin this doctrine came to be known as the *filioque*. That word simply means, in Latin, *"and the Son."* The Byzantines were horrified at this tampering with the ancient creed. Originally the creed had said that the Holy Spirit proceeded from the Father (only) and not from the Father and the Son, as Western versions of the creed started to read. Westerners added *"and the Son"* to the creed in order to emphasize the Bible's teaching in John's Gospel that Jesus, along with the Father, sent the Holy Spirit into the Church (John 15:26). Nonetheless, the Byzantine Church detested this addition to the creed.

SCHISM: TWO CHURCHES INSTEAD OF ONE

The official break between Roman Catholics and Byzantine Christians came on July 16, 1054. A delegation of boorish and tactless Westerners from Rome, led by Cardinal-Bishop Humbert, excommunicated the patriarch of Constantinople in the patriarch's own city. It was as if the Ayatollah of Iran had marched into Congress and condemned Americans for not practicing democracy. Humbert and his abrasive entourage also declared many Byzantine beliefs to be heretical. The patriarch responded in kind, excommunicating Humbert and his companions. But he did not excommunicate the pope. In doing this, the patriarch extended a hand of possible reconciliation, but Rome did not grasp it.

This East-West schism[3] in the Church dates from this event. Thereafter, it would no longer be accurate to speak of one, unified, Western and Eastern Church, but of two separate Churches, one Roman Catholic, and one Byzantine. The latter would eventually come to be known as the Greek Orthodox Church.

---

[3] From the Greek word, *schisma*, meaning "tear." In the West, the Donatists likewise were schismatic (see Focus 5).

FOCUS 11

MUSLIMS VERSUS CHRISTIANS: OVERCOMING FALSE STEREOTYPES

It would be highly inaccurate to impose on the early Muslims the image of the bigoted, murderous ayatollahs that we know in our own day. Muhammad himself was tolerant of both Jews and Christians and had many friends of both faiths. He had been a traveling merchant in his early days and learned much about Judaism and Christianity from his customers.

The basis of the religion Muhammad founded was monotheism, or the belief that there is one God, a doctrine which Jews and Christians likewise profess. Further, Muhammad's successors, the *caliphs*, who carried out *jihad* (holy war) against Christians in the East, were not any more vicious or intolerant than Christian warlords. Consider, for example, how Charlemagne converted the pagans in his own empire (see Focus 10). Religious tolerance was largely unknown in the ancient world.

Another point to keep in mind is the beneficial effect which the Muslim conquests had on Western society. The Muslims established a civilization in North Africa and Spain, for example, far superior to that which barbarian Christian kings were able to provide. They brought education, health care, art and architecture, horticulture and stable political rule to areas that had known only war and ruin for three centuries.

The Muslims were hardly unwanted conquerors. In southern Spain, for example, when Christian kings began to win back territory from the Muslims, Spanish Muslims, whose families had at first been Christian, often had to be forcibly reconverted to Christianity. One of the tragedies of the early Middle Ages was the Christians' inability to appreciate the good which the Muslims had to offer. Instead, Christians looked upon them solely as messengers of a false and threatening religion. Such an attitude was the origin of the crusades, which we will discuss in the next chapter. This attitude was also the origin of much of today's continuing hostility between Muslims and Christians.

FOCUS 12

THE *FILIOQUE* CONTROVERSY: PROCEEDING VERSUS SENDING

One of the enduring controversies separating Roman Catholics and Greek Orthodox Christians to this day involves three little words— "and the Son" (in Latin, *filioque*). The original creed of 381 declared that the Holy Spirit proceeds from the Father—period. Western bishops at the Third Council of Toledo in 589 added "and the son" to the original version of the creed. Therefore, the Catholic Profession of Faith reads today, "proceeds from the Father and the Son." Scripture is clear that Jesus *sends* the Holy Spirit into the Church. In John 16:7, for example, Jesus says unequivocally, "I will send him [the Holy Spirit] to you." The Greek Christians agreed with this, but they argued that sending and proceeding are not the same thing. To them, the word *proceed* was equivalent to the word *begot*, as in the verse in the creed which refers to the Son as begotten of the Father. Greek Christians argued that only the Father could beget, and thus both the Son and the Spirit had to proceed from the Father. Pope Gregory the Great argued against this interpretation, teaching that the Spirit's *proceeding* and the Spirit's being *sent* were the same thing.

In John 15:26, Jesus speaks of the Spirit as *coming* from the Father. At the same time Jesus says, "I myself will send [the Spirit] from the Father." One could read this passage and argue both ways— either that the Spirit proceeds from the Father and the Son or that the Spirit proceeds only from the Father. The West's acceptance of *filioque* owed much to Augustine's understanding of the third person of the Trinity as being the love between the Father and the Son, manifested as an entirely unique person.

CHAPTER SEVEN

THE VANISHING DREAM OF CATHOLIC CHRISTENDOM

HAS CHRISTIANITY EVER HAD a "golden age?" The question is filled with difficulties. The concept of a golden age suggests a static time of perfection in which no further change or growth is needed. "If things had just stayed the way they were in the golden age," some people think, "then we wouldn't be in the mess we're in now." If that is what "golden age" means, then Christianity never had a golden age and never *should* have had one.

Christianity always points ahead, to the Second Coming of Christ and the goal of history. Thus, to suggest that there has been one moment in Church history in which things were "golden" is to distort Christianity's purpose and thrust. Christianity should always be on the move, always seeking to bring the Reign of God into reality. That requires constant death to things we hold dear and constant adaptation to change and growth.

Yet, some Church historians have attempted to describe the era we are about to enter as the golden age of Christianity. One Church historian years ago wrote a popular book entitled, *The Thirteenth: Greatest of Centuries*. In it, he glowingly described the great achievements of the Church in this epoch. This was the age of Gothic cathedrals, the unification of the Church under the leadership of a strong and well-organized papacy, monastic spirituality, the foundation of the Franciscan and Dominican orders by two of the Church's greatest saints, the brilliant writings of Thomas Aquinas and a list of other accomplishments of which the Church can truly be proud.

The thirteenth century and the decades immediately before and after it (from about 1150 to about 1350) were truly a time of great achievement. We can't hope to do this period justice in one chapter, and so we will look in this chapter only at the external events of Church history. In the next two chapters we will focus on the Church's intellectual and spiritual life during these "High Middle Ages," as this era is frequently called.

THE CONCEPT OF 'CHRISTENDOM'

There is a catch-all word which has come to be associated with this epoch of Church history, and that is *Christendom*. In one sense, the word simply means that area of the world where Christianity is the principal religion. In addition, however, the word has come to mean the entire domination of Western life, culture and society by the Christian faith. It is this latter sense which we will give to the word in this chapter and the next two. The term "Byzantium," has a somewhat parallel meaning for the Christian domination of the East.

How did the concept of *Christendom* come about, and how did it become so popular? To answer the question, let's start by taking up where we left off at the end of Chapter Five. Recall that with the Concordat of Worms in 1122, the papacy, by regaining for the Church the right to conduct its own affairs, had won a decisive victory over the Holy Roman Emperors.

As the popes became more independent of imperial control, stronger and more capable men became popes. No longer did the Church have to witness the shameful spectacle of German politicians coming to Rome to install their favorites on Saint Peter's throne. Further, as the emperors themselves found their power limited by strong national monarchies, Christians in these new nation-states looked to the popes instead of to the emperors as symbols of a united Christian world.

"World" meant for Westerners, of course, only the Roman Catholic West. Europeans didn't bother with the fact that the entire Orient, the Byzantine Empire and the Muslim lands didn't share their view that Rome was the center of the universe.

POPE INNOCENT III:
A POWERFUL KING IN THE PAPAL OFFICE

The man who did more than anyone else to spread the idea of a universal Christendom was Pope Innocent III (1198-1216). Innocent was a strong pope who inspired Christians by his sanctity. He was also a strong political ruler, reigning over the Church as a king. Innocent and his advisors thought a monarchical papacy was the best protection from state domination of the Church.

Like his predecessors, Innocent never asked whether he should act like a king in the first place. He didn't seem to realize that there was a different way to serve as pope than to try to outdo kings in wealth, power and prestige. But Innocent was a man of his times. For too long the popes had considered themselves secular as well as spiritual rulers. Innocent was not about to change things. Innocent even went his predecessors one better. They *acted* like kings. He really *was* a king.

He turned the Papal Estates in Italy into an independent political unit, running this territory as any king would have run it. It seemed to him that the best means of keeping the Church independent was to make the papacy a strong secular power.

Innocent wanted to make it absolutely clear that, from now on, the Church was supreme in spiritual matters. It could tell secular governments what to do insofar as spiritual matters were concerned. In the thirteenth century, supremacy in spiritual matters carried with it at least the *appearance* of supremacy in political matters. Kings thought they should run both Church and State in their kingdoms. Innocent's attitude, while in keeping with the times, was quite a threat to other kings' ambitions.

Consider how Innocent treated the secular rulers of his day—and how he got away with it. In England, for example, King John (of Robin Hood fame) installed his own man as archbishop of Canterbury. Innocent immediately excommunicated the king and forbade bishops and priests in England from administering the sacraments to anyone until King John relented. The technical term for this action is *interdict*, that is, the pope "imposed an interdict" on England. The English people sided with the pope against their king, and thus John had to back down. Innocent installed Stephen Langton as Archbishop of Canterbury and exacted from King John an oath of loyalty to the new archbishop. John meekly submitted, and proclaimed England to be the pope's vassal state.

Innocent was just as successful with both the German emperor and the king of France. The pope excommunicated Emperor Otto IV when the latter invaded Sicily. At the same time, the pope saw to it that his own favorite, Frederick of Sicily, became king in Germany. Innocent also excommunicated King Phillip II of France when the king divorced his wife. When the French people supported the pope against their king, all Europe realized that the papacy had become the leading power of the day, at least in spiritual matters. And in an age when politics and religion were inseparably united, the pope's leadership in spiritual matters meant that he was also a major force in the secular realm.

But the story would not end with the papacy in firm control of European politics. By the end of this chapter, we shall see how the tables were soon turned.

THE CRUSADES

The most pressing issue in the High Middle Ages was the Muslim threat. It was similar in urgency to our own anxiety over the possibility of nuclear war. In what sense was it a "threat?" Christians everywhere feared that the Church was losing the competition for the minds and hearts of people who sought after God. The Muslims spread their faith in all directions, becoming true universal evangelists of the Muslim gospel, as revealed in the Muslim "Bible," the *Koran*.

Despite growing Christian victories over the Muslims, Christian rulers feared the spread of Muslim political power. The Muslims were now being driven out of Spain. The Mediterranean was being reclaimed as a Christian sea. Nevertheless, the Muslims controlled that part of the world most sacred to Christian memory, Palestine, or, as it came to be called, the Holy Land.

The Byzantines still clung tenaciously to their ever-shrinking Empire in the

East, but Western kings and princes wondered if Byzantium could hold out much longer. They knew that if Byzantium was captured by the Muslims, the Christian West would soon be fighting the Muslims on the West's own doorstep.

Thus it was that Western Christians conceived of the crusades, or a holy war, to combat the Muslim's own holy war of conversion and conquest. The name "Crusade" perhaps comes from the Spanish *cruzada* or "crossed," since the crusaders wore crosses on their garments. There were some eight or nine separate military crusades in the East. The First Crusade lasted four years, from 1095 to 1099. Some twenty thousand peasants tramped idealistically eastward. When this vanguard of starving marauders reached Muslim-controlled Turkey, they were slaughtered to the last man, woman and child.

This disaster didn't dissuade a group of French nobles, who had organized an army of thirty thousand. They marched on Jerusalem. Acting out of vengeance, they killed the entire Muslim population. And, as if to celebrate their good fortune, they burned the city's Jews alive after locking them in their synagogue. Four powerful Western noblemen then divided the Holy Land into four territories, which they ruled as their own kingdoms.

It should have occurred to someone that the crusades had gotten off on the wrong foot, and that there was nothing "holy" about this Christian holy war. Yet, the West embarked on the Second Crusade. In 1148, at Damascus in Syria, the Saracens (as the Muslims were then called) annihilated a Christian army led by both King Louis VII of France and the Holy Roman Emperor, Conrad III. The crusades had turned into a debacle. A Third Crusade (1191-1192) was moderately successful, leaving Muslims and Christians each with their own occupied territories to guard in the Holy Land.

The Fourth Crusade, which took place during the papacy of Pope Innocent III, proved to be the most brutal of them all. Innocent hoped for one, final and daring strike at the Muslims. Thus he assumed the leadership of yet another call to arms. What Innocent got, however, was more greed and stupidity on the part of the nobles who led the crusade. Financed by the merchants of Venice, four French war lords led an army east, hoping to make a fortune for themselves and their investors.

When the lords reached Christian Constantinople, they were greatly impressed by the wealth and culture achieved by their Byzantine brothers in Christ. They were so impressed that they decided to plunder Constantinople before proceeding on to loot the Holy Land. From 1204 to 1261, Western princes took over the Byzantine capital and ran it to their own interests. Their realm was called "The Latin Kingdom of Constantinople."

THE CRUSADES' EFFECT ON THE CHURCH'S SELF-IMAGE

Needless to say, the Fourth Crusade further alienated Byzantine Christians from the West. It also infuriated Pope Innocent III, who realized that even the prestige of the papal office could not thwart the political ambitions of Catholic princes intent on making their own fortunes. Thus, one result of the crusades was to disillusion Western Christians about the prospect of establishing a universal Christendom, ruled over by the pope and winning all non-Christians to the gospel.

Instead, Christians now realized that the Muslims were here to stay. It was also evident that supposedly Christian princes were more interested in power and wealth than they were in converting infidels. A third conclusion was that the pope possessed no supernatural power to make the world operate according to Christian principles. In other words, the crusades debunked the myth of a universal and holy Christendom proving its moral superiority to the non-Christian world through force of arms. What Christians came to see instead was that the Muslims were every bit as strong in their faith as Christians were supposed to be, and perhaps even stronger militarily. That realization gave Christians the uncomfortable feeling that perhaps God was on the Muslims' side instead of the Christians'.

As a result, the idea of the papacy as the one, invincible, unifying force of Christendom began to lose its hold on people's minds. Instead, many people began to think that the Church, by attempting to wield power like any other monarchy, had lost its spiritual authority. People began to demand that Church leaders return to the gospel ideal of poverty and forsake the struggle for worldly power and wealth. Once again, the Church's self-image was in crisis. Many Christians began to look back on the simple life of the early Church as the ideal Christian existence.

THE LAITY'S IMPULSE TOWARD GOSPEL SIMPLICITY SOMETIMES LEADS TO EXTREMISM

Consequently, small numbers of lay Christians throughout Europe began to live in communes where poverty and common sharing of possessions were practiced. Many of these groups led exemplary Christian lives. Others became fanatically gnostic (see Chapter Two). They denounced both marriage and ownership of worldly possessions. Such groups condemned the clergy for its wealth. They emphasized the universal priesthood of all believers, proclaiming that every Christian could administer the sacraments.

These communes became especially popular in southern France, where they settled in and around the town of Albi. Hence they came to be known as *Albigensians*. By Pope Innocent III's day they had become openly scornful of Church authority. They started to preach their own radical doctrines of poverty, group marriage and rejection of the sacraments. They also resurrected the old gnostic belief that Jesus had not really been a man. They taught instead that Jesus was an angel who imparted secret knowledge to the chosen few, enabling them to reach heaven.

The mainstream Church acknowledged that the Albigensians were heretics. The question was what to do about them. In the age of the crusades, the easy answer was "Make war on them." And thus the crusading effort to conquer the infidels in the East took on an internal dimension. Now the Church sought to eradicate heresy in its own backyard.

When preaching and persuasion failed to convert the Albigensians, Pope Innocent asked the king of France to undertake a full-scale military campaign against them. The king declined, but the powerful Count Simon de Montfort obliged. He committed numerous atrocities in forcing the heretics to return to the Church. Many did return. But many others didn't, never reconciling themselves with the Church. Such groups became a smoldering seed-bed of resentment and bitterness which burst to life three centuries later during the Protestant Reformation.

FRANCIS AND DOMINIC

Inspired by the new demand for poverty and simplicity on the part of many lay people, Francis of Assisi (1181-1226) and Dominic Guzman (1170-1221) founded religious orders that were neither monastic nor priestly, but *mendicant*. Mendicancy was a lifestyle in which *"friars,"* not monks, took the traditional religious vows of poverty, chastity and obedience. They did not pledge to live in any particular place. (In contrast to *friars*, *monks* were committed to a monastery and most *priests* to a diocese.) Instead, the mendicant friars walked from place to place and preached the simple gospel lived by Francis and Dominic. The new Franciscans and Dominicans were successful in winning to the Church both heretics like the Albigensians, and Christians who believed that the gospel demanded a simple life-style.

Yet, neither Franciscans nor Dominicans could escape the fear and paranoia of the times. Shortly after Francis and Dominic died, men from both orders abandoned the peacefulness and simplicity upon which their founders had insisted. On the positive side, they became the Church's new breed of intellectuals, taking over prestigious chairs of learning in universities. On the negative side, they frequently served as prosecutors in inquisitions. (See Focuses 13 and 14.)

POPE BONIFACE VIII:
THE CHURCH BLUNDERS ITS WAY BACK INTO DOMINATION BY THE STATE

At the beginning of the "golden" thirteenth century, Pope Innocent III symbolized the high point of papal prestige. A century later, Pope Boniface VIII (1294-1303) symbolized less than the best the Church had to offer. Boniface served as pope in a different Europe than the one which Innocent had known.

Innocent could count on most Christians in Europe to support him when he struggled against kings. In contrast, Boniface found that the new force of nationalism had firmly taken hold of people's allegiance. Christians now backed their king against the pope, instead of the other way around.

Boniface got into a fight with Kings Philip IV of France and Edward I of England, both of whom wanted to reassert control over the Church in their kingdoms. Boniface wrote a papal *bull* (an official document sealed in a red *bulla* or wax seal) in which he said that popes were supreme over kings, both in spiritual matters *and* in secular matters. When King Philip responded with a counter-treatise, Boniface wrote another bull, the infamous *Unam Sanctam* (1302). In this he proclaimed that anyone disobeying the pope would go to hell. Enraged, King Philip determined to make the papacy back down.

After Boniface died, Philip engineered the papal election of his own French candidate, Clement V. Clement moved the papal office to Avignon in France. That was the beginning of a sixty-eight-year absence of the popes from Rome. A famous poet of the day, Petrarch (1304-1374), named this voluntary exile the "Babylonian Captivity." The title has remained to this day.

We will take up the story of the externals of Church history again in Chapter Ten, by discussing the aftermath of this Babylonian Captivity of the papacy. But before doing that, let's take a deeper look at the Catholic High Middle Ages, by considering the intellectual and spiritual life of the Church during this turbulent era.

FOCUS 13

THE SOUL OF AN AGE: SAINT FRANCIS OF ASSISI

As if to provide a counterweight to the bloodshed and violence of the century into which he was born, Francesco Bernardone (1181-1226) dedicated his life to simplicity, poverty and peace. Francis was born to a comfortable life as the son of an upper-middle-class merchant. He stood to become wealthy himself. At first, Francis had been like most other young men of his day, and had gone off to war. Disillusioned by what he saw on the field of battle, he turned inward, to examine his own soul, and outward, to find God in nature.

Converted to the gospel by the many small beauties he found in God's creation, Francis renounced his inheritance in order to become one with the poor and to preach the gospel as the poor lived it. Most people know the rest of the story. Francis talked to the birds and to savage beasts. He helped his friend Clare of Assisi (1194-1253) set up a more democratic monastic life. He established the Secular Franciscan Order to help lay people (single and married) and diocesan clergy live the Good News within their chosen vocations. His preaching and miracles mirrored those of Jesus. The poet Dante said that Francis "burst on the world like the sun."

Should we consider Francis simply a saint surrounded by pious legends? Or was he truly a figure who had an impact on history? Today there is no doubt. Despite the enormous differences in communications between Francis' day and our own, nearly everyone in Europe had heard about Francis while he was still alive. People from every country wanted to join forces with him. He epitomized in his person the medieval Christian's hunger to live the gospel of poverty and simplicity.

Like Gandhi or Martin Luther King, Jr., in our own century, Francis inspired a whole generation to work for justice. Francis wanted simply to be simple. The force of his simplicity stirred everyone in his age, from the most powerful to the poorest, to seek their own soul in the gospel. Francis influenced his time as surely as did popes, kings and crusaders. He was an authentic historical figure who stood as the conscience and the soul of his age.

FOCUS 14

YOUR 'DAY IN COURT' BEFORE THE INQUISITION

"Bring the accused in," shouts one of the three priests seated at the table in the Duke's throne room. You are thrust before the men, your arms chained behind you.

"On your knees," your guard grunts, throwing you to the slate floor.

"Speak!" your inquisitors demand. "Are you ready to confess your crimes before this holy tribunal?"

"But, but, Your Reverence," you stammer. "What have I done?"

The Duke's bailiff answers. "Come, come, don't try to deny it. You were seen in the company of that mob of heretics we arrested last week. Do you deny that you are one of them?"

"But, Your Grace, I was only listening to what the men said. I didn't know they were heretics. They read from the Gospels and talked about the poor as God's chosen ones. I thought they were holy priests, perhaps followers of Blessed Francis."

"Silence!" one of the priests screams. "Do you dare place our holy father Francis in the company of heretics?"

"But, Your Reverence, I am a simple man who cannot read or write. How was I to know who these men were?"

The members of the tribunal whisper among themselves. One of them turns to you and says, "Very well, wretch, we will set you free—for the moment—but see to it that you keep watch over the company you keep. Should you return to us, you could well lose your tongue—or worse. Do you understand?"

"Yes, Your Reverence," you answer, bowing deeply before turning to leave the room. In the courtyard you are met by your family. Your wife cries in gratitude for your release, and your children hug you. "Oh, dear God!" you whisper. "What has come over the Church that it treats us so?"

CHAPTER EIGHT

THE CHURCH'S INTELLECTUAL LIFE

THE PHRASE "CHURCH HISTORY" means much more than a study of the activities of popes and emperors. If we were to leave the Catholic Middle Ages behind, having looked only at the external events of Church history, we would have missed the true character of this period. In this chapter we will consider the Church's intellectual life, which in the Middle Ages was a very important element of the Church's self-image.

Just as thinkers and intellectuals helped the *early* Church define itself, so, too, in the Church of the Middle Ages, theologians and philosophers helped to formulate the Church's doctrine. To many Christians of the Middle Ages, intellectual developments within the Church were more important than squabbles between popes and emperors and other external happenings. That is because what people *thought* directly influenced what people *believed*. And what people believe is the core of Christian faith.

CHRISTIAN LEARNING IN CHARLEMAGNE'S EMPIRE

Christian intellectual life in the West was given a boost as far back as the time of Emperor Charlemagne (c. 800). He brought scholars from throughout Europe to his court at Aachen. Charlemagne himself was very interested in Christian learning. Although he never became formally educated in doctrine, he tried mightily to keep pace with his scholars' debates. He even hid writing implements under his bed and practiced every night to learn how to use them. Charlemagne appointed an English monk, Alcuin of York (735-804), to supervise education in the empire.

Alcuin was so successful in restoring interest in education that the rebirth of culture and letters during Charlemagne's reign is sometimes called the *Carolingian Renaissance*. Alcuin and his fellow scholars thought that all learning could be divided into seven essential subjects, which were in turn divided into two groups. These two groups were known as the *Trivium*, comprising grammar, rhetoric and logic, and the *Quadrivium*, comprising arithmetic, music, geometry and astronomy.

The first truly original thinker of the Middle Ages was a monk named John Scotus Erigena (810-877). Before him, scholars had more or less repeated what Augustine had taught. Erigena was highly skilled in Greek and introduced the West to the great accomplishments of Greek thought. He also pioneered the use of syllogisms to arrive at truth. In a syllogism there is a *major premise*, a *minor premise* and a *conclusion*. For example, "All human beings are mortal; John is a human being; therefore John is mortal."

Some in the Church thought that applying logic to theology was sinful. To them, belief was belief and knowledge was knowledge, and the two couldn't mix. Yet, the intellectuals within the Church slowly won out. They showed how knowledge and belief are both essential to Christian life. Augustine himself had thought that faith and reason could be harmonized. "Reason" was the general name given to intellectual pursuits. "Understand," Augustine had said, "so that you may believe, and believe so that you may understand." This became something of a slogan for medieval scholars.

SCHOLASTICISM: SCHOLARSHIP IN THE SERVICE OF FAITH

By the tenth and eleventh centuries a name was being used to describe the method of learning which combined both faith and reason. That name was *Scholasticism*, and the men who engaged in scholastic learning were called "Schoolmen." The Schoolmen were mostly monks or friars who spent a good portion of their days thinking and writing about the truths of the Christian faith.

The father of Scholasticism was Anselm of Canterbury (1033-1109). With him the Church's intellectual life reached a new plateau. Anselm had been abbot of an important monastery, and then Archbishop of Canterbury in England. His writings influenced scholars everywhere.

What sort of issues did the early Schoolmen think and write about? There were many. In particular, they helped to develop the Church's teaching on the sacraments. By about the mid-twelfth century, it was becoming common in the Church to speak of seven sacraments.[1] Confirmation, Matrimony, Extreme Unction (anointing of the sick and dying), Holy Orders and Penance were joined to the two foundational sacraments, Baptism and Eucharist.

The Eucharist received much attention in the Schoolmen's discussions, especially insofar as the idea of the *Real Presence* was concerned. The term "Real Presence" referred to Christ's actual presence in the bread and wine of Communion. The Schoolmen concluded that in the Eucharist there is a "trans-

---

[1] The Schoolman, Peter Lombard (1095-1160), first enumerated the seven sacraments. Thomas Aquinas (1225-1274) accepted this enumeration, and the Council of Florence affirmed it in 1439.

formation of substance," as they put it. Bread becomes the body of Christ; wine becomes his blood.

At the Fourth Lateran Council in 1215 this philosophical concept was formulated into the doctrine of *transubstantiation*. The Council said that "the Body and Blood of Jesus Christ are truly contained in the Sacrament of the Altar under the outward appearances of Bread and Wine, the Bread having been transubstantiated into the Body and the Wine into the Blood."[2] Through such means, medieval scholars helped the Church to define official doctrine.

UNIVERSITIES AND THE RISE OF NONRELIGIOUS LEARNING

Eventually, scholars wanted to do more than just help the Church define doctrine. They wanted to pursue learning for its own sake. In other words, they wanted to learn things that may have had nothing to do with religion. The pursuit of learning separate from theology gained momentum with the rise of the university system, beginning in the twelfth century.

Universities had originally been cathedral schools where men studied theology in order to serve in the Church. That changed, however, with the Crusades. The wisdom of the East began to pour into Western cities. Scholars began separating knowledge into separate subjects, such as law, medicine, science and so on. Previously, it was thought that theology contained all the knowledge there was, and that theology should be studied as the only subject worth knowing.

Scholars began to divide up knowledge largely in response to the rediscovery of writings of the ancient Greek philosopher, Aristotle (384-322 B.C.). Prior to this time, most learning in the West had been based on the philosophical system of Plato (428-347 B.C.). Plato took a more unified, deductive approach to learning, proceeding from the unity of things to the diversity of things. For example, he would first think about beauty, let's say, as an abstract idea. He would then discuss why particular things, a tree, for example, was beautiful.

In contrast, his student, Aristotle, proceeded more like a scientist, using *inductive* reasoning, which moves from many things to a single, unified conclusion about those things. For example, Aristotle would consider all the different trees in the forest, and only then conclude, "Ah, these trees are beautiful!"

As Aristotle's works started to become better known in Europe, he became the rage among university teachers and students. Nearly everyone wanted to base university education on the Aristotelian system of philosophy. This meant that specialized disciplines like law, medicine, and science were set apart from the general theological education which everyone had previously received in universities. Theology proceeded from God to things. Aristotle

---

[2] Fourth Lateran Council, in Jaroslav Pelikan, *The Christian Tradition*, 4 vols. (University of Chicago Press, 1974), vol. 3, pp. 203-204.

proceeded from things to God. Aristotle's philosophy meant that a non-religious way of looking at the world was now possible.

Thus universities became centers of non-religious as well as of religious learning. Scholars then began to question whether learning and education should be used only by the Church and only to bolster the faith. They began to see that learning could have a purely earthly objective. This threw a scare into many Church officials. Some even suspected that any scholar not promoting pure theology was a heretic.

Church officials were particularly afraid of any new doctrine based on Aristotle. They saw his philosophy as contrary to Church doctrine. They didn't want to know about God by first knowing about things in the world. They thought knowing about God was all you needed. *Then* you could ask questions about things in the world. Just as the Inquisition was used to squelch heretics like the Albigensians (see Chapter Seven), so, too, that tribunal was now used to make sure that university professors did not teach ideas contradicting the faith.

FAITH 'VERSUS' REASON, OR FAITH 'IN HARMONY WITH' REASON?

We get an idea of the different approaches taken to Aristotle by considering two of the greatest names in Christian learning, Bonaventure (1221-1274) and Thomas Aquinas (1225-1274). Bonaventure used Aristotle, but preferred Plato. Bonaventure feared that certain aspects of Aristotle's philosophy could not be squared with the gospel.

Bonaventure believed that the human *will* was more important in leading one to truth than the human intellect. Medieval scholars frequently split up the human soul into "faculties," like intellect and will. At any rate, Bonaventure taught that one should give first place to the human heart's desire to believe, rather than to the human mind's desire to *know*. In other words, for Bonaventure, Christians should believe first, and understand second.

Thomas Aquinas, on the other hand, believed that intellect and will are *both* important in helping one to understand the gospel. For Aquinas, belief and understanding are not on a collision course and do not lead to two separate sets of conclusions, one set having to be accepted on faith, and the other set making sense to the mind. When Aquinas's teachings first came under official investigation, they were condemned by the Archbishop of Paris, where Thomas taught. Later, however, it became obvious that Thomas was not contradicting the gospel. In fact he was bringing faith and reason together in a way that made it easier to understand the gospel. Thomas's writings became the most renowned system of thought in Christendom.

It would be impossible here to summarize the many thick volumes of Saint Thomas's thought. As just one example of how he brought Aristotle's philosophy to bear on Christian theology, consider Thomas's *quinque viae*, or "five ways" to know the existence of God from the senses. These are the propositions that (1) for there to be movement, there must be a *prime mover*; (2) from all the caused phenomena in the world, there must be *a prime cause*; (3) the existence of things that might logically not exist leads us to conclude that there is a *necessary being*; (4) to compare the qualities of things implies that there is a *standard of comparison* which is perfect in its possession of these qualities; and (5) the intelligent purposes which unintelligent beings demonstrate show that there is a *purposive intelligence* involved in their creation. While these propositions do not strike us as very original, in Thomas's time it was both daring and risky to proceed from God's creation to God when writing theology. Previously, theology had always started from the nature of God, and reasoned from there to the nature of things.

The Church's intellectual life in the thirteenth century develops as bishops, kings and popes influence the growth of universities and seek their support in various controversies—often with one another. Eventually, *Thomism*, as Thomas's system of thought came to be known, would be used by the Church as its principal method of learning. In the Thomist system, truth is one. It is found both in divine revelation and in earthly creation. With Thomism, the Church had nothing to fear in its search for truth through reason. Not everyone agreed with this principle, however, as events after Thomas's death were to show. Many scholars still believed that reason and faith contradicted each other. Some of these scholars left the Church and practiced "pure science." Others stayed in the Church and continued to be suspicious of non-religious learning.

'REALISM' VERSUS 'NOMINALISM'

The Franciscan scholar, William of Ockham (1285-1349), stayed in the Church, but stirred up a hornet's nest among Church-approved scholars. He studied and taught at Oxford University where he developed a philosophical position known as *nominalism*. This word comes from the Latin word for "name." It means that abstract ideas like truth, beauty, goodness or human nature are simply *names*. For a nominalist, these abstract entities have no objective existence. Nominalism was the opposite of *realism*, which holds that such abstractions do exist. For a realist, truth, beauty and goodness are not just names; they actually exist.

University education now was moving toward Aristotle's philosophy. In that philosophy, priority was given to an investigation of individual things before arriving at unified conclusions. In that setting, nominalism naturally became very popular. Nominalists like Ockham also applied their philosophy to the Church. They argued that the abstract concept of Church does not exist. Only individuals in the Church exist, but not "Church" as a concept. Thus, they concluded, one person in the Church is of no more importance than any other person. "Church" as a whole is no greater than the sum of its parts.

UNIVERSITY SCHOLARS SEEK CHURCH REFORM

Nominalism thus coincided with a growing lay movement calling for clerical reform and for Church authority based on the popular will. The English scholar, John Wycliffe (1330-1384), led a reform movement in England which based itself on the idea that all Christians are priests. All Christians, Wycliffe taught, should base their lives solely on Scripture, rather than on the teachings of an institutional Church.

In Bohemia, a scholar and priest named John Hus (1372-1415), at the University of Prague, echoed many of Wycliffe's teachings. Hus was eventually burned at the stake, and Wycliffe was forced to resign from his teaching position at Oxford. After Wycliffe's death, Church officials in England had Wycliffe's bones dug up and scattered. Yet, this fearful overreaction to what was happening in universities did not stop educated people from examining Church authority in a new light.

Thanks to the work which Scholasticism had begun, educated people now approached religious questions through the eyes of reason. Many intellectuals were now demanding that reason validate every assumption, especially assumptions concerning the Church. Scholars like Anselm and Aquinas had put learning in service of the Church. Now an age was dawning in which scholars would use learning to shake the very foundations on which the Catholic Middle Ages rested.

In about a century, for example, a highly educated Catholic scholar and monk named Martin Luther would seek a major reform of the Catholic Church. Would the hierarchy accept his challenge, and enter into peaceful dialogue? Or would it react in fear and rage as it did in the cases of Wycliffe and Hus? We will answer that question in subsequent chapters.

FOCUS 15

DOCTORS OF THE CHURCH

As its experience with Scholasticism shows, the Catholic Church has consistently encouraged intellectual speculation about the truths of the gospel. From the early Church to theologians like Karl Rahner in our own day, Catholicism has always stood for the proposition that faith and reason can be harmonized. In other words, Catholicism does not require someone to quit thinking in order to be a Christian. That is one of the great contributions of Catholicism to world religion.

In order to show how much the Catholic faith cherishes knowledge and learning, the Church has designated its greatest thinkers as "Doctors" of the Church. The term "doctor" simply means teacher. In order to become a Doctor of the Church a person must have met three requirements: (1) a life of personal holiness; (2) a demonstration of profound wisdom; and (3) designation by either a pope or ecumenical council as a Doctor of the Church.

Who are these Doctors of the Church? The nine "founding doctors" of the faith are—from the Western Church, Ambrose, Augustine, Jerome, and Popes Leo the Great and Gregory the Great; from the Eastern Church, Basil the Great, Gregory of Nazianzus, Athanasius and John Chrysostom. From the period considered in the present chapter, the Church has selected Anselm, Bonaventure and Thomas Aquinas.

Other notable names are Bernard of Clairvaux, Francis de Sales, John of the Cross, Robert Bellarmine, Albert the Great, and Anthony of Padua. At present the list stands at thirty-three names, with twenty-five from the West, eight from the East, two popes, eighteen bishops, nine priests and one deacon. Only three women made the list: Catherine of Siena, Teresa of Avila and Therese of Lisieux.

Perhaps one day the Church will recognize that not all profound wisdom is to be found in books written by ordained men, and that religious women and laypersons, untrained in theology, have made enormous contributions to the Church's intellectual life. When that happens, the list of Church doctors will become more inclusive, and the Church will have acknowledged that the Holy Spirit gives the gift of wisdom as the Spirit wishes.

FOCUS 16

ANSELM'S 'ONTOLOGICAL PROOF' FOR THE EXISTENCE OF GOD

One of the most famous theological "proofs" of the Scholastic period was Anselm's proof for the existence of God from *ontology*, the study of being. Anselm's argument went like this: God can be defined as "that being greater than which nothing can be conceived." This very idea demands that God exists: If God did not exist, then our *imagining* God would be greater than God, which we have already determined by definition to be impossible.

This is an illustration of how the Schoolmen applied *dialectic*, the science of logic, to theological investigation. The point was to make the faith more reasonable and understandable, and for a while they were very successful. Eventually, however, scholars came along who used dialectic to make matters of doctrine seem foolish. They asked nonsensical questions like, "How many angels can dance on the head of a pin?" This example illustrates one difficulty with trying to make the faith logical. Someone can poke holes in any argument. Thus if our faith is based solely on reason and logic, we won't get very far. At some point we have to confess that the great mysteries of the Christian faith—the Virgin birth, the Incarnation, the Trinity, for example—cannot be scientifically explained. In the last analysis, faith is always a conviction about things we do not see (Hebrews 11:1).

CHAPTER NINE

EVERYDAY LIFE IN THE CATHOLIC MIDDLE AGES

WHAT WAS IT LIKE TO BE A CHRISTIAN in the High Middle Ages?[1] The answer depends on where you lived, what sort of work you did, your gender and level of education and whether you were a layperson or in vowed religious life. To some extent those variables are just as important today in describing a Christian trying to live the gospel in the third millenium of Christianity. But there is one important difference to keep in mind when we consider life in the High Middle Ages. That difference involves the concept of secularism.

We take it for granted today that the world in which we live is *secular*, that is, that our modern society is indifferent to or rejects religion and religious values. Thus, in the modern world we compartmentalize our lives between our "job selves," our "family selves" and our "religious selves." It is difficult for us to understand the Middle Ages precisely because the Middle Ages were not a secular age like ours.

To the medieval person life was principally religious. That does not mean that people in the Middle Ages did not have to work for a living or that they were holier than we are or that they gave more attention than we do to the gospel. By and large the Middle Ages were as raucous, lustful and violent a time as our own. Countless deeds of cruelty and evil were performed by people calling themselves Christian—indeed even in the name of Christ.

What do we mean, then, when we say that the High Middle Ages were principally religious? We mean that Christians in this era looked upon the world as the place where the struggle for good and evil was played out according to the script which God had written. To medieval Christians everyday life was the drama of Christianity reflected in every event in their lives.

To the medieval Christian, every deed and event fulfilled some tiny part of God's plan for the universe. People in the Middle Ages would never have

---

[1]As a reminder, we have arbitrarily defined this period as roughly 1150-1350.

asked, as we do today, "What's it all about? What does life mean? Where are we going? Is there a God who takes an interest in humanity?" For the medieval Christian, such questions, had they been asked, were very simple to answer. Life is all about gaining salvation. The meaning of life is found in the gospel. We are going either to heaven or to hell. Yes, God takes an interest in humanity. That is why God has established the Church, which instructs people in the ways of God and tells them how to win salvation and avoid damnation. This was the great medieval life drama. It unfolded day by day in the lives of ordinary Christians everywhere.

LIFE STRUCTURED AS A PYRAMID

Since life in the High Middle Ages was the visible unfolding of God's supernatural plan, life was organized to mirror that plan. Both society and Church, then, were *hierarchically* structured, from supreme power at the top to lesser powers at the bottom. The system by which this was accomplished in society was called *feudalism*. Feudalism was a method of organizing human relationships so that persons with less authority submitted themselves to persons with greater authority. That culminated in the submission of all to the king.

At the top of the political pyramid stood the king, followed by the lesser ranks of nobility. Then came landowning non-nobility, and finally landless peasants and slaves. At the top of the Church's pyramid stood the pope, followed by cardinals, archbishops, bishops and abbots, various grades of priests, various grades of deacons, monks and nuns and, finally, the laity.

Climbing back up the pyramid, people submitted themselves to those in authority over them. The man immediately in authority over someone was called that person's lord. In relationship to one's lord, one was a vassal. Everyone but pope and king had lords, and everyone but the lowest serf had vassals. Thus, to be called lord in the Middle Ages did not necessarily mean that one was wealthy or powerful. Some lords were great nobles, but some were poor landowners barely able to stay alive.

SPIRITUALITY: EXPERIENCING DOCTRINE IN THE HEART

In discussing everyday Christian life in the Middle Ages we reach the concept of spirituality. Whereas theology *thinks* about doctrine, spirituality *experiences* that doctrine in the heart. Thus spirituality has more to do with feelings and belief than with thinking and understanding. Nevertheless, belief and understanding can never be completely separated.

What was the nature of spirituality in the High Middle Ages? The first thing we notice is that medieval spirituality was greatly influenced by monks living in monasteries. The early Middle Ages are sometimes called the "Dark

Ages," when civilized life supposedly disappeared in Europe. It is often said that monks preserved both culture and faith for later generations. This is true to a degree, but should not be overemphasized. There *was* cultural and religious life outside of monasteries. Nevertheless, the monks, walled off from the chaotic world around them, did accomplish a great deal in passing on the traditions of the early Church and Greco-Roman culture to later generations.

Spiritual life for the monks was based entirely on work and prayer. During five or six hours of the day, the monks worked to support themselves. Otherwise, when they weren't sleeping or eating, they prayed, either in choir with the other monks or alone in their cells. Their community prayer consisted mostly of singing the psalms of the Old Testament. Much of their private prayer was made up of reading and reflecting on the Bible. Private prayer had three stages: *reading* a Scripture passage under the guidance of the Holy Spirit, *reflecting* at length on what the passage means, and passing into a type of *wordless communication* with God which today we might call mysticism.[2]

Nearly all monasteries followed the rule of Saint Benedict, but not all monks and nuns were Benedictines. Various monastic groups split off from the Benedictines in order to emphasize a particular aspect of monastic life which they found lacking in the Benedictines. The most important of these offshoot monastic orders was the Cistercians. Their spiritual father was Bernard of Clairvaux (1090-1153), one of the most important figures in all the Middle Ages.

Bernard's wisdom was so valued that he guided not only the lives of monks, but also gave political advice to popes and kings, who readily sought his counsel. Through his preaching, Bernard prodded Catholic Europe into the Second Crusade (1147). When it turned into a disaster, he said that God allowed Christians to be defeated by infidels in order to chastise Christians for their sins. How was it that Bernard, the spiritual guru of the age, a man who preached a life of solitude, peace and holiness, could urge Christians to go forth and slaughter their enemies? For medieval Christians this was no contradiction. For them, all of life was seen as spiritual combat, and only Christians were on God's side. Bernard's legacy, however, lies not in his affiliation with the Crusades, but in his development of a spirituality which influenced both monks and lay people.

BECOMING FEMININE BEFORE GOD

Bernard and the Cistercians believed that everyone is feminine before God. That is, they taught that spirituality depends not on *doing* something, but on surrendering to the movement of God within the human soul. Thus feminine receptivity, rather than masculine activity, was the means to reach God. This type of spirituality eventually reached the laity, who all during the Middle

---

[2] In Latin these three stages were called *lectio, meditatio* and *contemplatio*.

Ages rubbed shoulders with monks and learned spiritual practices from them.

Lay people then began to realize that the life of prayer and devotion was for everyone. People who were not monks began to write spiritual treatises to guide others. The most famous works by laypersons are *The Cloud of Unknowing*, written anonymously in England in the fourteenth century, and two works by women, the *Dialogues* of Catherine of Siena (1347-1380) and *Revelations of Divine Love* by Julian of Norwich (1342-1413).

During this same period, lay spirituality was often organized along community lines, similar to the life lived by vowed religious like the Franciscans. Especially in England, Holland and the Rhineland in Germany, laypersons committed themselves to the *Devotia Moderna* (modern devotion). They lived lives of asceticism and piety based on shared readings from Scripture and common ownership of possessions. The most famous spiritual treatise to come from this environment was *The Imitation of Christ*, by Thomas à Kempis (1380-1471). The heart of lay piety in the modern devotion is exemplified in Thomas's book. There, inner repentance, conversion and apostolic service to the poor are emphasized, as opposed to merely formal participation in the Church's sacramental life.

DAILY LIFE IN PARISH AND DIOCESE

But what about everyday Christian life for those people who weren't monks or educated laypersons involved in movements like the Modern Devotion? What was daily life like in the average parish in the High Middle Ages? Let's look first at the parish itself and the priest who ran it.

Today's visitor to Europe can still visit examples of small, beautifully constructed medieval parish churches and chapels. Usually they are made out of stone and were built by men in the parish. However, most typical parish churches of the age were somewhat inelegant structures. Parish priests, in comparison with monk-priests in the monasteries, were mostly uneducated in theology. Nevertheless, they managed, by hook or by crook to keep their flocks spiritually nourished.

Whereas the local parish church was run on a shoestring budget, most of the medieval Christian's financial and labor resources were poured into the great cathedral churches housing the throne of the local bishop. *Chartres, Notre Dame, Canterbury, Strasbourg*—nearly every episcopal see boasted a masterpiece of Gothic architecture. In the believer's eyes the cathedral was worth every penny and ounce of energy spent to build and maintain it.

The cathedrals served as spiritual headquarters for the growing diocesan bureaucracy. The diocese[3] had been an administrative unit of the old Roman government. It served as a convenient means of organizing the Church along

---

[3] In the West, the word *diocese* was used in its modern sense by the late fourth century, although *parochia* (parish) was interchanged for "diocese" until the ninth century.

geographical lines. Priestly life in the diocese was rigidly structured. Priests who were not monks or friars or otherwise members of a religious order were called *secular priests*. Secular priests affiliated with a cathedral were called *canons*. The canons held meetings called *chapters*, presided over by the bishop. Depending on how much autonomy the bishop allowed the canons, the canons elected *deans*, who served as chief priests of the chapter. Often several deans were selected, who presided over geographical subdivisions within the diocese called *deaneries*.

The bishop also appointed priests to serve as his diocesan assistants, such as the *chancellor*, who handled administrative duties for the bishop. The growing bureaucratic character of the diocesan Church was repeated in Rome. There the popes had large numbers of advisors and clerical workers who made up the papal *curia* (court). Cardinals were in turn appointed to head various offices within the curia. In this way, Cardinals gradually came to be a permanent feature of papal administration.

Back home in the parishes, the ordinary believer led an active spiritual life. Of primary importance was the liturgy celebrated in the parish church. This consisted, first of all, of Sunday Mass (in Latin), and then daily Mass, although not every parish could provide a daily Mass. In some places only the wealthy attended daily Mass. Only they could afford to provide a priest with room and board through the week. Elsewhere, priests often worked in the fields or otherwise fended for themselves to earn a living. It was not uncommon for parish priests to beg for money for their personal upkeep, although most towns and villages could afford to support at least one priest.

Next to the liturgy, the most important element in popular piety was devotion to Mary and the saints. At some point, probably in the twelfth century, recitation of the *rosary* became popular throughout Catholic Europe. The rosary most likely originated with Cistercian monks, who were known for their devotion to the Virgin Mary. The monks then passed the rosary on to laymen working in and around the Cistercian monasteries.

By the thirteenth century, traveling Dominicans carried rosary beads with them and gave them to laypersons who came to hear the Dominicans preach. From then on, the rosary became a favorite lay devotion, largely because anyone, educated or not, could recite it. At the end of the twelfth century the Council of Paris turned a voluntary practice into a rule. The Council decreed that the three major prayers of the rosary—the Creed, the Our Father and the Hail Mary—should be memorized by the faithful.

Sunday Mass, especially in cathedrals and larger parishes, was often regarded as above the mentality of the ordinary believer. In many places the poor were confined in the rear of the churches, where they could barely even see what was going on at the altar, let alone participate in it. One contemporary chronicler records a scene where the congregation shouted, "Higher! Higher!," as the priest elevated the consecrated Host. "Oral communion" decreased and "visual communion" became popular as Eucharistic devotions stressed the purity of the host and the unworthiness of the communicant. Finally, the Fourth Lateran Council (1215) decreed that annual confession and receiving Communion during the Easter season were "duties" binding on all the faithful.

There was a great deal of outright prejudice against the laity on the part of the clergy. Many preachers of the day warned their terrified congregations that most lay people were going to hell. They hinted that the beatific vision was reserved only for holy priests. That prediction proved inaccurate in both respects: The Church never officially taught that any percentage of the laity was damned, and most of the priests were not holy. One famous preacher in the thirteenth century was fond of telling his audiences that only one person in one hundred thousand would be saved. A horrible kind of predestined gloom hung over the Middle Ages.

Because the clergy often ostracized the laity, the laity tended to develop their own spiritual practices. Often such practices were at odds with official Church teaching, or at least, were only on the fringes of orthodoxy. Such a practice was the trade in relics. Body parts or clothing of the martyrs were venerated in the early Church.[4] Saint Augustine endorsed the honoring (though not the worshiping) of relics. With the return of the crusaders from the Holy Land, however, things got out of hand, as shiploads and cartloads of supposedly authentic remains of the apostles, the Virgin Mary and the Lord Jesus himself found their way west.

A frenzy for relics led to the most ludicrous of scandals. Sometimes parishes or towns fought with each other to purchase from relic peddlers such things as a given saint's forearm, or the Virgin Mary's maternity gown. Sometimes ten or twelve skeletons of that same saint were pieced together from collections owned by several towns. It is said that enough vials of the Virgin Mary's breast milk could be collected to have nursed a thousand infants. One monastery proudly displayed its collection of the baby Jesus' first teeth. Another reconstructed the cross of Calvary from bits and pieces of wood gathered over the years.

In its official teaching, the Church tried to suppress the quackery associated with relics. The Church stressed that honoring relics could be useful to a person in meditating on and imitating the holiness of the saint whose relics one possessed. Nevertheless, an exaggerated devotion to relics was never entirely eradicated.

HELL AND PURGATORY

Popular piety influenced another Church doctrine—purgatory. In 1274, the Second Council of Lyons established the Church's official teaching on purgatory, although, as with much else, the medieval doctrine of purgatory was originally developed by Saint Augustine. Purgatory was said to be a place where those who are saved, but who have died without having performed

---

[4] For scriptural parallels, see 2 Kings 2:14, 13:21; Acts 19:12.

penance for their sins, must suffer to satisfy that penance. This already morbid doctrine was often distorted by the faithful and took on exaggerated images of horrific torture.

Although the Church never described what types of suffering the souls in purgatory endured, the popular imagination ran rampant. People applied all the torments of hell, which likewise sprang uncensored from the believer's psyche, to purgatory. Hell was said to have been a place, as Anselm described it, of "sulphurous flames, eddying darkness, swirling with terrible sounds. Worms living in the fire. Devils that burn with us, raging with fire and gnashing your teeth in madness." Such individual imaginings, in the humble believer's mind, were often looked upon as official Church declarations describing what hell and purgatory were actually like.

To this day, conceptions of hell and purgatory are based largely on medieval imagination rather than on anything found in revelation or official Church doctrine. One of the most popular devotions in the Middle Ages was the offering of prayers and Masses for a departed loved one's soul. The purpose was to free that soul from the torment of purgatory. Sometimes, unscrupulous priests would stir the believer's sense of pity with hideous descriptions of the sufferings the departed soul had to endure. Their goal was to exact a higher "stipend" (cash payment) for Masses to release the departed soul from the horrible pit.

AN AGE OF CONTRADICTION

As these contrasting examples of true piety and pseudo-pious humbug illustrate, the High Middle Ages were a time of the greatest contrasts and contradictions. It was a time of great sanctity and a time of much nonsense. It was a time when many Christians made incredible sacrifices on behalf of the gospel, and a time when others grew rich from careers in the Church. It was a time of humility and sincerity, and a time of arrogance and fakery. It was a time for great saints and a time for glaring sinners.

Francis of Assisi called the age in which he lived "times of malice and iniquity." Never before has the gospel been so exalted and so defamed all in one era and culture. Little wonder that as the High Middle Ages came crashing to an end, many people wanted to do away with the Catholic Church altogether, and replace it with something else, as we shall discuss in the next chapter.

But was the Church to blame for all the contradictions to be found in the Middle Ages? A growing number of people answered yes. Criticism came especially from the educated, who had the confidence to think for themselves. Some felt they could live lives of Christian sanctity without the help of priests. Others voiced criticism because of the obvious contradiction between the life-style depicted in the Gospels and the corruption and sham which they observed in both society and Church.

Some people, however, looked upon the Church as more of a victim than victimizer. This latter group thought the Church should be reformed, but not abolished. As we shall see beginning in the next chapter, Church history after the High Middle Ages is in many ways the story of the struggle between those who wanted to reform the medieval Church and those who wanted to abolish it.

FOCUS 17

THE AGE OF THE FEMININE

The Middle Ages differed from all previous historical epochs in that, for the first time, women came to be thought of as essential contributors to life and culture. Ancient civilizations, such as the Greek, Roman and Hebrew, for example, were patriarchal, or male-dominated, societies. The High Middle Ages still gave first place to male values. But for the first time in history some men began to think of women as their equals.

In some ways, women were treated with even more respect than men. In many medieval homes, for example, it was considered un-masculine for boys to read. Thus, it was often the girls who learned reading and writing. The Church took bold and progressive steps for the time to protect women, such as forbidding married men from maintaining mistresses. Such a practice had previously simply been taken for granted in both classical and barbarian societies.

Much of the attention to feminine values stemmed from the popular devotion to the Virgin Mary. She was revered by men and women alike as the paragon of Christian virtue. The devotion to Mary spilled over into popular culture. There, wondering poets known as troubadours extolled feminine virtues. In popular literature, such as the chansons (heroic songs), male characters like Lancelot, Gawain and Percival dedicated their lives to the love and respect of women. The very notion of romantic love was created in the Middle Ages. Prior to that time, marriage had been based entirely on economic and social considerations.

We meet many women in the Middle Ages who were strong individuals in their own right, such as Queen Eleanor of Aquitaine (1122-1204). Her royal court at Toulouse in France rivaled in culture anything the world had ever known. Finally, thanks to the Cistercian contribution to spirituality, feminine values were incorporated into the Christian prayer tradition. Women like Catherine of Siena, Clare of Assisi and Bridget of Sweden were not afraid to tell a pope that some of his decisions should be reversed. By and large, the High Middle Ages did more to promote the worth and integrity of women than any previous age in history, even if much of what was thought of as "feminine" was highly idealized and spiritualized. As the Middle Ages ended, so did much of the culture which honored the feminine.

FOCUS 18

DID THE CATHOLIC CHURCH HIDE THE BIBLE FROM BELIEVERS DURING THE MIDDLE AGES?

In every religious tradition there are legends and stories calculated to show how "our side" has always been in the right, and the "other side" has always been in the wrong. In some sectors of the Protestant tradition one enduring myth is that the medieval Catholic Church hid the Bible from the laity. Such people alleged that if ordinary believers had read the Bible they would have become independent from the clergy. That was the reason, they said, why the clergy wanted to keep the laity ignorant of what Scripture teaches.

One popular Protestant account of bygone years depicted starving peasants stumbling into a cathedral and finding a strange book chained to a pillar. When the humble believers touched the book, angelic music filled the church and a heavenly shaft of light fell onto them. Suddenly, a bestial looking man dressed as a priest charged at the peasants and assaulted them, ordering them never to touch this forbidden book again.

Well, all of us, Catholics and Protestants alike, fall prey at times to silly denominational propaganda like this. Such legends have no relation to the facts. The historical reality is that the Catholic Middle Ages was a biblical age. From time to time there were official decrees against unsupervised lay Bible reading or against translations of the Vulgate into the vernacular. During Pope Innocent III's papacy, such measures were designed to prevent heretics like the Albigensians from spreading their own distorted version of the Bible. One account, for example, depicted Jesus as an angel who didn't really suffer and die on the cross.

On the whole, however, the Catholic Church did all that it could to encourage lay Bible reading. But how was the Church to do this in an age of great illiteracy and no printing presses? It wasn't until the mid-fifteenth century that the printed Bible became available. Before that, the laity read the Bible painted on the walls of churches and public buildings, etched into stained glass windows or sewn into tapestries.

Nearly every story, legend, song or poem learned by the medieval Christian was based on scenes from the Bible. One could not walk a mile in the High Middle Ages without seeing a visual representation of the gospel or hearing some gospel theme repeated in verse, prose or song. Christians in the Middle Ages may not have possessed leather Bibles, but they knew their Scripture, and the Church did nothing to hide God's word from them.

CHAPTER TEN

THE END
OF THE CATHOLIC
MIDDLE AGES

THE CATHOLIC MIDDLE AGES went out with a bang instead of a whimper. One respected historian, Barbara Tuchman, has written a popular book on this subject called, *A Distant Mirror: The Calamitous Fourteenth Century*. That title aptly depicts the chaos and disaster that characterized life during the latter days of the Middle Ages, or the fourteenth and fifteenth centuries. We will now consider that time period in this final chapter of our study of the pre-Reformation Church. Perhaps we could summarize these fateful two centuries by saying that nearly everything that could go wrong, in both Church and society, did go wrong.

At the same time, however, we should not conclude that nothing good came out of this period. Our historical judgment of a given age depends to a large extent upon the perspective from which we are looking at it. To the people who lived in the late Middle Ages, the wars, plagues, intrigues, factionalism and insecurity which they experienced no doubt suggested that things couldn't get any worse. Indeed, we find in the fourteenth and fifteenth centuries a preoccupation with the end of the world. For example, one finds during this period a constant flux of people wandering from town to town proclaiming (as many of today's TV preachers do), "The end is near!"

Yet, it was precisely the fourteenth and fifteenth centuries that brought us the incredible rebirth of culture and learning that we call the Renaissance. Thus, although the late Middle Ages represent a death to one age, at the same time they represent new birth for another age—the modern age which we will consider in later chapters.

As has been true all through our discussion of Church history, it will be somewhat difficult in this chapter to distinguish between what was going on in the Church and what was going on in society at large. That is because so much of late medieval life was involved with developments in the Church and in religious thinking. As we discussed in the previous chapter, people in the Middle Ages were first and foremost religious. Everything they did was affected by their religious outlook on life. As a result, the strife and turmoil in the Church had a tremendous influence on the rest of society. Whereas early Christians found solace and security by looking to the trustworthy leadership coming from Rome in their day, the reverse was true for Christians living in the late Middle Ages.

That is, as people looked at the scandals and divisions within the late medieval Church, they sometimes despaired of finding anything permanent to hold onto. They often wondered whether the gospel had any power to change the world after all. As people's confidence in the institutional Catholic Church began to fade, they looked elsewhere to find meaning in life. They looked, for example, to secular learning, to national politics and the movement toward parliamentary representation. Many were part of the growing dissent from Catholic doctrine that would soon culminate in the Protestant Reformation.

Let's begin our discussion of this chapter then, by looking at the Church's internal condition. We'll see how that condition was part of the general break-up and change that characterized life during the fourteenth and fifteenth centuries.

THE 'BABYLONIAN CAPTIVITY' OF THE PAPACY

The place to start is where we left off in Chapter Seven, when we were discussing the Babylonian Captivity of the papacy. By way of summary, the popes, at the insistence of the French crown, moved their headquarters from Rome to Avignon in southern France, in the year 1309. They stayed there until 1377, remaining completely under the thumb of the French monarchy. Remember that Pope Boniface VIII (1294-1303) had failed to understand how strong a force nationalism was within the countries of Europe. When he tried to exert control over the French king, the French people supported the king rather than the pope. (See pages 66 ff.)

Similar to the days when German emperors ran roughshod over the popes, the institutional Church once again came under the control of strong monarchs, this time French kings instead of German emperors. The seven popes who served as "Bishop of Rome" in Avignon left a disgraceful record behind them. To illustrate how thoroughly Church bureaucracy had succumbed to the French king's control, when Pope Clement V died in 1314, the (largely French) cardinals who assembled to elect his successor were handed a list of four candidates drawn up by King Louis X. The king then ordered them to select the new pope from that list.

The popes in Avignon built a magnificent palace to house themselves and their many friends and relatives—whom they put on the Church's payroll. Altogether, it was one of the lowest points in the history of the Church's leadership. This situation demonstrates all over again the danger to the Church's spiritual authority when Church leadership is identified with power, prestige and possessions.

Yet, to round out the picture, toward the end of the Babylonian Captivity the popes began to admit the harm which moving the papacy to Avignon had inflicted on the Church. Pope Urban V (1362-1370) tried to institute a moral reform of the papal curia, although he was unsuccessful. Pope Gregory XI (1370-1378) finally fled from Avignon, returning the papacy to Rome on January 17, 1377. But too much damage to papal prestige had been done. Christians did not automatically revive their complete and immediate confidence in the institutional Church.

NEW CONCEPTS OF CHURCH GOVERNMENT

By now the writings of scholars like William of Ockham (see page 77) had won many intellectuals to the cause of allowing the laity a share with the clergy in governing the Church. This is what one would expect in an age when, for example, the English nobility were gaining more and more rights against their king through the creation of a strong parliament. Throughout Europe, noblemen and upper-class, university-educated men (no lower-class men and no women) were winning the right to run their own lives along with their kings. This was *not* a movement toward popular democracy as we know it. No one at this stage of political development wanted to do away with kings. Nonetheless, it was a radically new concept of how people's lives should be governed.

Even in the Church, people were calling for a more expanded concept of government. An Italian scholar, for example, Marsilius of Padua, wrote a popular work called *Defender of the Peace* (1324). He called for the Church to be run not by pope and hierarchy, but by "the totality of the faithful who believe in Christ and invoke his name." Thus, by the time Gregory XI returned the papacy from France to Rome, the times were ripe for a new look at how the Church should be governed. When Gregory died, the cardinals who met to elect his successor did something that played right into the hands of those who were calling for Church reform.

THE WESTERN SCHISM: NOT ONE POPE, BUT TWO, THEN THREE

What the cardinals did was to elect not one, but two popes. This happened because a group of cardinals had stayed behind in Avignon when Gregory XI returned to Rome. This French group elected Clement VII as their pope. A faction of cardinals meeting in Rome elected Pope Urban VI (1378-1389). The Catholic Church eventually recognized Urban and his successors ("The Roman Line") as the authentic popes rather than Clement VII and his successor ("The Avignon Line").

During the period when there were two men claiming to be pope (a total of some thirty-seven years), people were naturally in a state of utter confusion. The chair of Peter, the Rock, looked anything but stable to the average

Christian. Some areas of Europe supported one man for pope and some another. One's choice for "universal shepherd" depended on where one happened to be living at the moment. Just as necessity is to the mother of invention, the *papal* (or "western") *schism*, as it is called, was the mother of the *conciliar movement*. Many Christians hoped to reform the Church's leadership by basing it on councils rather than on the direct rule of popes.

THE CONCILIAR MOVEMENT: AN ABORTED ATTEMPT AT REFORM

The first council to meet during this period convened in 1409 at Pisa in Italy. Some five hundred delegates attended. In the early Church, only bishops voted and formulated policy at councils. At the Council of Pisa, however, the majority of the delegates were either priests or lay noblemen. The Council of Pisa met for the purpose of ending the papal schism. However, the most popular topic of discussion at the Council was conciliarism[1] itself. The question was raised whether popes or councils—or both—should govern the Church. The council tried to depose the pope in Rome and the one in Avignon and choose a new pope whom everyone would accept. But they succeeded only in electing yet another pope. Now there were three popes—each with his own set of cardinals! When the council delegates failed to resolve the dispute, they adjourned. But they went back home convinced that a new council should convene to assert its right to at least a share in the leadership of the Church.

It was King Sigismund of Bohemia who convened this new council, in 1414. It met for over three years in southern Germany in the town of Constance. The Council of Constance resolved the papal schism and changed the rules by which the new pope was to be elected. Along with the cardinals, six men (laymen were allowed) from five different nations voted on this new choice for pope. This group of papal electors named as pope Martin V (1417-1431).

Before supervising Martin's election, the council had passed a resolution which declared, "This council holds its power directly from Christ; everyone, no matter his rank or office, even if it be papal, is bound to obey it...."[2] This was a declaration of independence against the way the Western Church had been governed up to this point. To reinforce their belief that they were supreme in matters of Church government, the delegates to the Council of Constance made Martin V promise to convene councils again on a regular basis.

Martin did in fact reluctantly convene the Council of Basel in Switzerland in 1431. Only a small number of delegates attended, and nothing important was accomplished. Martin's successor, Pope Eugene IV (1431-1447), managed to move the council to Florence, where debate over relations with the

---

[1] Conciliarism is the notion that supreme authority in the Church lies with a general council.
[2] "Acts of the Council of Constance," "*Haec Sancta*," in *History of the Church*, Hubert Jedin, ed., 10 vols. (New York: Crossroad, 1982), vol. IV, p. 448 ff.

Byzantine Church dominated the agenda. This permitted Eugene to divert attention from the conciliar movement.

Eventually, European Christians, worn out by plagues, war and social revolts, simply had no energy left to spend on the conciliar movement. By Pope Eugene's death, the papacy was once again firmly in control of Church leadership. Yet, an old issue was left unsettled: Who leads the Church, and who *decides* who leads the Church? This was a question that was asked from New Testament times to the time of Pope Eugene IV (and is still asked today).

Eventually, those who insisted on a model of Church government that was based on something like a representative democracy found that they could no longer support the Catholic Church. When Martin Luther came onto the scene in 1517, such people naturally found themselves attracted to the Protestant cause.

LIVING THE GOSPEL IN A TIME OF CHAOS AND DISRUPTION

Before we reach the Protestant Reformation, however, let's conclude our discussion of the final days of the Catholic Middle Ages by examining what life in those days was like for average Christians struggling to live the gospel. Compare them to today's American Christian family, constantly assaulted by media messages contrary to the teaching of Christ. So, too, the external environment in which later medieval Christians lived presented a strong challenge to the Christian's faith. In the Church's first centuries, it was easy to know what being a Christian meant. It meant choosing to put one's life on the line by disobeying Roman law. In the late Middle Ages, however, as in our own day, Christians were often very confused and disoriented. There was an official, impressively organized institutional Church displaying great wealth and power. Many shrill voices argued for contrary views of what Christianity meant. To make this confusion and disorientation even worse, all of life around the Christian seemed to be in a tailspin toward chaos and disorder.

THE BLACK DEATH

Let's look at just two examples of this external chaos. The first involves the great plague that swept over Europe in the fourteenth century and beyond. The Black Death, as the bubonic plague was called, probably came from the plentiful supply of infested rats. Fleas from the rats bit people, and people caught the disease which the rats carried. This, of course, is what we think now.

The people who contracted the disease and died didn't have our knowledge of the disease. It killed nearly one out of every three Europeans. Often, it was seen as direct punishment by God for society's sins. And since traditional religious piety didn't check the plague, people fell back on their last line of defense against this mysterious cosmic evil—superstition.

In our own day an entire body of "counter-cultural" religion has grown up as a substitute for traditional religion. So, too, in the late Middle Ages, many Christians chose astrology, witchcraft, fortune-telling and trance-induced prophecy as the antidote for disorder, chaos and confusion. Similar to the situation in our own country in 1929, when many wealthy businessmen ruined by the Great Depression committed suicide, many people in the late Middle Ages literally went crazy. They saw their once secure world collapsing all around them. For example, people known as *flagellants* walked from town to town whipping themselves with ropes and lashes, thinking that by hurting themselves they could appease the angry God who was supposedly causing all this turmoil.

SOCIAL UNREST AND REVOLT

The social disorder which arose from the Black Death was mirrored in the second great external challenge to living the gospel in the late Middle Ages— social revolt. Plague and the resulting disruption of economic life affected all ranks of medieval society, from kings to slaves. But it hurt the lower classes the most.

Small landowners, peasants who worked on land but did not own it, urban craftsmen whose businesses were ruined, knights with no lords to pay them an income and many poor priests vented their rage against the established order by rising up everywhere throughout Europe. They madly attacked nobles' homes and bishops' palaces, murdering and looting in a frenzy of pent-up frustration over the suffering inflicted on them from every side.

The nobility's response was brutal and certain. Entire villages of poor people, including those who had not participated in revolt, were savagely murdered by hired thugs masquerading as soldiers. Of course, this had an enormously negative impact on ordinary Christian life. Imagine, by way of analogy, how difficult it would be to keep and maintain the faith in our own age during an all-out world war. To Christians of the late Middle Ages, ravaged society looked every bit as devastated as post-war Germany and Japan looked to us in 1945.

THE HUNDRED YEARS' WAR

And finally, there was the actual, "official" war of the late Middle Ages, the Hundred Years' War between England and France. Every European nation was involved in one way or another. The war lasted from 1337 to 1453. The most telling episode of the war involved a young Frenchwoman named Joan of Arc. At the most hopeless moment for her country, Joan believed she received instructions from the archangel Michael, telling her to present herself to the French king and to lead the French armies in a new offensive against the all-conquering English.

Was Joan's heavenly commission fact or fiction, a miracle from heaven or a simple peasant girl's mad delusions? In the Middle Ages it was often difficult to distinguish one from the other. For Joan herself, however, and for the French people who regarded her as their deliverer, God was directly inspiring Joan to lead the French nation in battle. She did just that, heroically and victoriously.

Then, captured by the English, Joan was accused by Church leaders of being a witch. For many men in the hierarchy, God could not possibly act through simple lay people, and certainly not through a woman. Therefore, the devil and not God had to be influencing Joan. Yet, Joan stood firm, insisting that Saint Michael was guiding her. In an age when violence reigned, English clergymen and soldiers burned the future saint (Joan was canonized in 1920) and patroness of France at the stake, on May 31, 1431.

A SAINT DIES, AN EPOCH DIES

When Joan died in the flames the Middle Ages died with her. Joan combined in her person the nobility and heroism of the warrior fighting to the last breath for a cause. Joan symbolized the richest depth of medieval femininity. She brought to the world the insights of a soul attuned to the inner spirit. Joan, like the Middle Ages themselves, was a great and profound mystery, incapable of being truly defined and contained by rational analysis.

Like Joan of Arc, the Catholic age, too, died in a dream. The dream had been that of unifying all human beings within a single culture and under a single rule in the name of Jesus and his gospel. The simple piety, the respect for feminine virtue, and the humble faith in saints and angels, the childlike belief in the triumph of good over evil, the untroubled trust in a world run by God and his appointed agents on earth—much of this died in the bonfire which killed the Middle Ages' most famous martyr.

From its adolescence in the Middle Ages, the Church would pass to a rude and jarring early adulthood in the Reformation. The Church's life would never be the same again. Simple solutions, black-and-white alternatives, clearly marked paths to heaven or to hell, the transparent gospel lived and proclaimed by countless unnamed saints would never again dominate human consciousness. A great and majestic experiment in the Christian faith had ended. It was time for a new world and a new humanity.

FOCUS 19

'WHATEVER HAPPENED TO THE BYZANTINE CHURCH?'

The year 1453 was one of the most momentous in world history. The Hundred Years' War ended. Johannes Gutenburg perfected his printing press. The citadel of Eastern Christianity, Constantinople, fell to the Seljuk Turks. The Byzantine Empire was no more. But Orthodox Christianity continued to live on—even in the conquered Eastern land where Christianity once ruled supreme.

The "fanatical Muslims" turned out to be much more tolerant of religious differences than Christians were of differences among themselves. The Muslims gave Orthodox Christians some degree of independence in the later Ottoman Empire (today's Turkey), with its capital in Istanbul (Constantinople's new name). Yet, the center of gravity for Orthodox Christianity shifted to a new and unexpected capital—Moscow.

The Church in the Slavic countries was founded when the Bulgar king, Boris, accepted Baptism in the year 865. After several years of waffling between the Western Church's jurisdiction and the Eastern Church's, Boris finally brought his whole tribe into the Byzantine Church. From then on, the Slavic peoples were oriented toward Greek Orthodoxy instead of Roman Catholicism.

Two brothers, Cyril and Methodius (ninth century), proved to be highly successful missionaries to the Slavic tribes. They even invented a written language for the Slavs, based on the Cyrillic alphabet, that is the ancestor of today's Russian alphabet. Beginning in the ninth century, the Duchy of Moscow, a small region in today's Russia, became the center of Slavic culture. The princes of Moscow soon began to call their city "the third Rome." They named their rulers, "Czar"—the Slavic spelling for "Caesar."

After the fall of Constantinople in 1453, the patriarchs of the Russian Orthodox Church argued strongly for Moscow as the new center of Christianity. They regarded Roman Catholicism as an "apostate church." Eventually there was little to tie the Greek Orthodox Church to the Russian Orthodox Church. Today there are three separate branches of the medieval Church remaining—the Roman Catholic, the Greek Orthodox and the Russian Orthodox, along with numerous Churches of different rites united to one or another of these three root Churches.

FOCUS 20

THE CATHOLIC CHURCH'S 'REPORT CARD' ON THE EVE OF THE PROTESTANT REFORMATION

When the Protestant Reformers came along in the sixteenth century, they gave the medieval Catholic Church a "failing grade." Before we reach the Protestant Reformation, let's make up our own report card. Let's grade the Catholic Church on its record at the end of the Middle Ages, using the familiar school grading system of A's, B's, C's, D's and F's.

REPORT CARD FOR CATHOLIC CHURCH GRADUATION DAY, TRANSITION FROM MIDDLE AGES TO MODERN TIMES

Category of Grading...Grade

Intellectual achievement of smartest students
    (Augustine, Anselm, Aquinas, etc.)......................................A

Deportment of "big-name" saints
    (Benedict, Francis, Catherine, Joan, etc.) ....A

Popes' ability to get along with others ....D

Ordinary priest's personal morality ....C-

Bishops' and abbots' practice of gospel poverty ....D

Crusaders' response to the Sermon on the Mount................F

Catholics' and Byzantine Christians' skill in bearing
    with one another patiently and forgiving one another ....F

Clergy's respect for the laity..D

Laity's ability to distinguish between authentic gospel
    and hokum such as relic peddling....................................D

Respect for women ....B

Artistic and architectural skills in
    bringing gospel alive in day-to-day life ....A

Monks' skills in preserving faith and culture
    during "Dark Ages"...A

Church's effort to preach the gospel despite
    hardships and difficulties ....A

Church's effort to adapt evangelization
    to new times and cultures...B

Everybody's love for Mary and the saints.............................A

CHAPTER ELEVEN

ENTERING THE AGE OF REFORMATION

A BRIEF STORY TO SET THE MOOD

To set the mood for the world we are about to enter, let's take an imaginary trip back through time. We'll travel back nearly five hundred years to the year 1520, and to a little town in what is today Poland. We'll eavesdrop on a conversation between a young man, age nineteen, and his little sister, age eleven. Their names are Christoph and Frieda Franck. Christoph has just learned that he must travel for his family on business to a town in Germany named Wittenberg. Actually, in those days, there was no "Germany" as such. Wittenberg was actually in a German-speaking *duchy* named Saxony. But for our purposes, we'll say that Wittenberg is in Germany. Christoph is anxious about going to Wittenberg. He has never traveled more than ten miles away from home. He wonders if the people in Wittenberg will be different from his friends and family in his hometown.

Christoph and his sister sit by the well house behind their father's weaving shop where they have been working all morning. It's time for lunch. Frieda chews intensely at the still warm goose thigh her mother fried earlier this morning, and asks, "Do you believe in God, Christoph?"

Christoph was watching a flock of quail scatter through an elm grove in the pasture. "Of course I do," he answered. "What kind of stupid question is that?"

"I was just wondering," Frieda said. "Papa says there are people in the world today who don't believe in God."

"Oh, he didn't mean that," Christoph said in irritation. "He's just upset by all the arguing going on. Papa thinks that anybody who doesn't walk straight down the middle aisle of church on Sunday morning, like he does, is going to hell. Or at least he *hopes* they go to hell."

What arguments are going on?" Frieda asked.

"The arguments are about all kinds of things," Christoph answered. "You know how Papa says, 'Obey the bishop and keep your mouth shut'? Well, a lot of people are complaining about the priests. They say they're too rich. And they wonder why you need a priest, anyway. Can't you get to heaven without a priest, they ask? Then there's the controversy about indulgences."

Frieda made a funny face at the word. "What's *that*?" she asked.

"It's where the priest lets you say prayers or give money to the Church so you won't have to spend time in purgatory after you die. I think it's pretty stupid, but don't tell Papa I said that, hear?"

"I promise," Frieda said, an earnest look on her face. She scooted closer to Christoph. "You mean you don't believe the *priests*?" she asked excitedly, as if Christoph were letting her in on a secret only kids his age knew about.

"It's not that I don't believe them," Christoph said, "it's just that I question some of the things they teach. Look, promise you won't tell if I show you something?"

Frieda's eyes grew wide and she nodded solemnly. Christoph took out a folded wad of rolled-up paper from his blouse. "I got this from a Franciscan coming from Italy whom I met at the bishop's palace last week. It's got all kinds of ideas in it you never hear about from Papa or the priests. It says councils of free men instead of the pope should run the Church. It says there's no such thing as purgatory, and that indulgences are just a way to get money out of working men like Papa and me."

"Do you believe it's true?" Frieda asked in astonishment.

"I don't know," Christoph answered, "but I'm sure thinking about it."

Christoph wondered if he had told his sister too much. Frieda grew quiet. They finished eating and lay stretched out on the grass looking up at the hazy sky. Frieda noticed that Christoph had clasped his hands behind his head and she adjusted her arms to imitate his posture. They didn't hear their father approaching until he stood directly over them. "Frieda," he said softly, "go to the house and help your mother make our guest comfortable. He has come all the way from Saxony. In the morning he will help Christoph leave for Wittenberg. They will travel part of the way together."

Frieda did as her father asked. When she had gone, the men talked about Christoph's upcoming trip.

"The man I told you about earlier, Christoph—Dietrich is his name—has arrived today from Wittenberg. He has brought money for your trip. He'll go with you to Breslau, and then you will be on your own." Herr Franck looked at Christoph and gently gripped his son's shoulder. "We have confidence in you, Christoph. We will pray the holy angels go with you."

Christoph and his father got up and walked slowly back to the house. That night, the family talked with their guest, Dietrich, about life in Wittenberg. Christoph sat cross-legged on the floor, his back to the hearth. Frieda lay on her back with her head on Christoph's leg, cautiously scrutinizing the strange visitor as he spoke. "Tell me, Dietrich," Christoph asked, "what is this town of Wittenberg like?"

Dietrich seemed puzzled by the question, as if for him all towns were the same. "A good enough city." He shrugged his shoulders and added, "But many strange things happening."

"Tell us!" Frieda exhorted.

"Well," Dietrich said, "there is a priest there who is angry with the pope, and Duke Frederick says the priest is right. No one knows what to think. I don't fool with such matters. Better I stay out of trouble. That's why I go back to Hesse. Better you come to Wittenberg yourself, Herr Christoph."

Frieda turned to her father, who was sitting at the kitchen table chewing on a stubby pipe. "Is the pope a bad man, Papa?" she asked.

"No, of course not, child!" Frieda's mother answered. "And, Christoph, while you are in Wittenberg, you will stay away from troublesome priests who disobey God's leaders. Such men are headed for hell and they are everywhere these days!"

Dietrich cleared his throat and turned nervously in his chair. "Some agree with you, and some don't. Wittenberg, even all Germany, argues over this man Luther. That is why I say, I stay out of trouble."

Christoph stared at Dietrich, trying to imagine what life would be like in Martin Luther's Wittenberg. He saw himself meeting exciting, fascinating people when he got there. "At least people in Wittenberg think for themselves," he said.

"It's fine for them to think for themselves," his father said sternly, "but you keep your nose pointed straight ahead when you get there." He then yawned and stretched, a signal to his family that it was bedtime. His wife fixed Dietrich a pallet near the hearth and then joined her husband in the downstairs bedroom. Christoph and Frieda settled into their beds in the loft.

Frieda whispered across the room toward Christoph's bed, "What do you think about Dietrich?"

"He seems all right, I guess," Christoph replied in a low voice.

"Do you think that priest he talked about, Father Luther, is wicked?"

"I don't know," Christoph answered. "I didn't want to say anything downstairs, but I know about Luther. The bishop is upset about him because there are priests in Liegnitz who like what Luther is doing. Last week, while I was on an errand to his palace, I heard the bishop yelling at somebody. He was screaming like a mad swan, 'I don't want any more of that filth in my diocese!' When I went in to see him, his desk was stacked with pamphlets like the one I showed you today. He was so angry I thought his buttons would pop!"

Frieda sat up in bed and leaned back cross-legged against the dark stained headboard. "But if Father Luther's a priest, why is the bishop mad at him? I thought bishops and priests were friends."

Christoph chuckled, and leaned on his side, his head on his elbow. "Not this priest and this bishop! Luther says the pope has made up all sorts of things that aren't in the Bible and that you should believe the Bible instead of the pope, and so the pope is mad at him. Some people want to burn Luther at the stake because he wants to do away with the pope and the bishops and let people pray to God without going through priests first."

"But who would run the Church?" Frieda asked in a puzzled voice.

"That's the first smart question you've asked," Christoph said. "I guess Luther wants to change the Church around altogether."

Just then a deep thumping sound reverberated up the wall. "Papa can hear us," Christoph said. "Let's go to sleep."

Christoph lay in bed looking through an alcove window at the stars until he was sure Frieda was asleep and then turned onto his stomach and drifted off himself.

FACT OR FICTION?

Let's stop our story for a moment and consider what's happening here. We've sat in on an incident in the life of an ordinary Catholic family living in the time of Martin Luther. As our imagined story illustrates, people in those times were concerned about the religious turmoil that was spreading throughout Europe. As a young man eager for adventure, Christoph is attracted to the exciting news he has heard about a radical priest named Martin Luther. His young sister, Frieda, naturally is influenced by what Christoph thinks. Their parents, on the other hand, are convinced that Luther is the devil's agent. They want their children to adhere steadfastly to their traditional Catholic faith and not listen to talk of religious reform.

Chances are, that as Luther's religious revolt against the Roman Catholic Church spreads in the years after 1520, the Franck family will become polarized. It may be that Christoph will go to Wittenberg and decide to follow Luther's movement. Perhaps his parents will feel sad, even disgraced, about their son's decision. Christoph may have to choose between his conscience and his family. It is a choice that millions of Catholic Christians will have to make during the years that we are about to study. These are dramatic, even tragic years for the Church. They are years fraught with violence and discord. Only rarely will we find people on either side of the religious quarrel acting toward each other in a loving manner as Jesus taught. Instead, we will find that many Christians are frightened, insecure, confused. In such a climate, people often insist that *their* religious beliefs and only theirs are the right ones. Anybody who disagrees with "my belief," many people will say during this age of Reformation, deserves to be put to death.

It would perhaps be more interesting simply to follow the story of the Franck family as it responds to the religious turmoil in the years ahead. That would make our story more personal. To take that approach, however, would mean that we would miss the big picture of what is going on elsewhere and in the lives of other people. As we study Church history during this period, we don't want to ignore major themes and movements. Yet, at the same time, we don't want to get so bogged down in big events that we forget how all this history affected ordinary believers. In the pages ahead, then, we will shift our focus back and forth. We will turn now and then to small, personal events in the lives of ordinary people like the Franck family. Then we will step back and look at the big picture. Let's turn to that big picture now, by taking a quick overview of Catholic Europe on the eve of Luther's religious revolt.

CHANGE IN THE AIR

If we had to pick one word to characterize the age into which Martin Luther was born—the age when the Reformation began—that word would be "change." Those of us who lived in the 1990's, the age of the breaking up of the Communist world in Eastern Europe, can appreciate what Christians were going through in the early sixteenth century. The stable, secure world of the Middle Ages was dying on the vine. We chronicled the life of that world in previous chapters of our study of Church history. For the sake of continuity, let's highlight briefly three of the major factors that will make the Church of the Reformation different from the Church of the Middle Ages.

The dynamic force of nationalism. First of all, in the age of the Reformation, the very conception of the physical world and how it is to be governed is undergoing radical change. In the Middle Ages it was thought that there were "two powers" in charge of people's lives. These two powers were the pope and the emperor. By the early 1500's, neither popes nor emperors possess nearly the power or prestige they had in the Middle Ages. That is because the force of *nationalism* is replacing the idea of a united Christendom.

Take "Germany" itself, for example. This geographical entity of German-speaking principalities that we encounter in the year 1500 is not really a country at all. Instead it is a collection of some three hundred fifty independent territories all vying with each other for power and influence. Yet, one thing unites these territories: their pride in being German in ancestry, language and values. Over the years, the authority of the Holy Roman Emperor in Germany has diminished. In 1519 the leading German princes, called *electors*, choose the man they want to be emperor. His name is Charles V, and he indeed inherits a huge empire to rule. But he is not seen by his subjects as an absolute monarch as were earlier emperors. Christians in Charles' German-speaking territories are very suspicious of Charles. He speaks Spanish (having been raised in Spain) and spends most of his time in Holland (which he prefers to Germany).

To look even more closely at the German situation, let's focus on the duchy of Saxony, where Martin Luther lives. There the powerful elector Duke Fredrick rules. He is jealous of the emperor's power and wants to be independent in governing Saxony. His people support him in this. They prefer to be thought of as citizens of a free and independent Saxony rather than as citizens of a huge, multinational empire. Consequently, when Martin Luther begins to preach against Rome, he can say nearly anything he wants without fear of reprisal. Why? Because he is looked upon in Saxony as a *national* hero. In many Saxons' minds Luther stands for good, holy Germany against wicked, corrupt Rome. This is one illustration of how the force of nationalism will greatly influence the Reformation.

The autonomy of the individual. Along with the growth of nationalism, we find that people in the sixteenth century are looking upon themselves very differently than did people in the Middle Ages. One reason for the change is the effect of the *Renaissance*. The Renaissance was a cultural movement in Europe that stressed the power and creativity of the *individual* as opposed to the collective authority of the Church and the state. People are now beginning to think and do for themselves, rather than simply adhere to group dogmas and traditions. An entirely new class of people is forming: the middle class. Middle-class people are educated and economically self-sufficient. They do not have to rely on the nobility for their upkeep, as did the peasants and serfs of the Middle Ages. In fact, as more and more princes and knights lose their land holdings and feudal income, *they* become economically dependent on the new middle class, who seek to gain more and more political autonomy.

This produces a tremendous "culture shock" in society. The idea is born that hard work and ingenuity, rather than one's noble birth, is the most productive force in people's lives. And when printing is developed and printed books become popular, the influence of the educated individual is made even greater. Educated people communicate with one another through the printed word. Martin Luther and the other Protestant Reformers will succeed precisely because there now exists a class of educated individuals interested in reading the Reformers' writings. This independence of mind extends to independence of soul. People who think for themselves will say they can *believe* for themselves as well. Many will say they no longer need priests, bishops and popes to tell them how to relate to God.

The discoveries in the new world. Another major factor to consider as we enter the age of the Reformation is the effect that the explorations and discoveries taking place in the New World had on the people of the day. Remember that Columbus's voyage to America (1492) took place only nine years after Luther was born (1483). The explorers' discoveries set off a mad scramble among the countries of Europe for colonies, land and gold. It also made people realize that their European society was but a tiny part of a global civilization. As the outer world enlarges in one's perception, one's inner world changes also. No longer are old ideas safe and secure. No longer do old realities work as they did before. Think, for example, of how the astronauts' travels changed our modern understanding of our place in the universe.

EUROPE THE TINDERBOX

The faith of Christians of the time could not possibly have been unaffected by these dramatic changes taking place in society. Old ideas and values were being replaced by new ways of looking at things. What about the Catholic faith? Should it change, too? Or was it an unchangeable absolute? Christians were deeply troubled by such questions. They urgently looked for answers. On one side were those who insisted that the traditional faith must remain untouched. On the other side were those who demanded radical change.

FOCUS 21

MARTIN LUTHER AND POPE LEO X: A STUDY IN CONTRASTS

Martin Luther was raised in a devout but stern German Catholic home. He was very scrupulous as a boy and constantly worried that God had not forgiven his sins. On the day when he was ordained as an Augustinian priest, he was so frightened by his unworthiness before God that he broke out in a feverish sweat and suffered chills and tremors. In the year 1510, his Augustinian superiors sent him to Rome, where he was scandalized by the immorality and lack of faith he saw on the part of the Roman clergy. When he returned to Germany he resolved to lead a holy life, study Scripture and pray for the reform of the Church. It was during one of his prayer periods that he underwent a powerful inner conversion. He believed God had shown him for the first time what Scripture meant when it spoke of salvation by faith. From that time on he began to be more outspoken in his criticism of Rome and its teachings.

Contrast Luther's stark life and rugged faith with the unchristian example set by the man who was pope during the first years of Luther's revolt: Pope Leo X. A member of the powerful and rich Medici family, Leo at age eight had been made abbot of a wealthy monastery, although he never lived there. By the time he was thirteen, Leo had been appointed either bishop or abbot sixteen times over. Yet, he never even visited most of the dioceses and monasteries of which he was supposedly spiritual head. He was made a cardinal at age fourteen, and at age thirty-seven was ordained pope, even though he had not yet been ordained a priest. His inaugural ball cost more than twenty-five million dollars in today's monetary equivalent. He announced to the revelers in attendance, "God gave us the papacy to enjoy, and we intend to do just that!" Leo promptly embarked on a campaign to turn Rome into the art capital of the world, selling curial offices and cardinal's hats to finance his beautification efforts. It is not difficult to imagine what effect Leo's life-style had on pious Martin Luther back in Germany.

FOCUS 22

WAS THE CATHOLIC CHURCH REALLY 'ALL THAT CORRUPT' ON THE EVE OF THE REFORMATION?

One of the stiffest challenges any of us faces is to own up to our own failures and mistakes. That's true likewise for groups of people, especially people who make up religious bodies. We find it much easier to look at the good features of our religious tradition and ignore the bad. We Catholics have been guilty of that when it comes to the Reformation. We accurately point to the harmful effects of the Reformation, such as the splintering of the Church into hundreds of sects and the proliferation of competing doctrines. But we are sometimes not so "historical" when it comes to acknowledging the Catholic sins that contributed to the Reformation. Was the Catholic Church really as corrupt as the early Protestant Reformers said it was? The short answer is, yes it was. Take an eyewitness's word for it, a woman who was a saint. Saint Catherine of Siena, writing a century before Luther, had this to say:

> On whatever side you turn—whether to the secular clergy of priests and bishops, or to the religious orders, or to prelates small or great, old or young...you see nothing but offenses; and all stink in my nostrils with a stench of mortal sin. Narrow, greedy, and avaricious...they have abandoned the care of souls.... Making a god of their belly, eating and drinking in disorderly feast, they then fall thence forthwith into filth, living in lasciviousness, feeding their children with the substance of the poor. (In Will Durant, *The Story of Civilization*, 11 vols. [New York: Simon and Schuster, 1957] Vol. V, pp. 572-573.)

Or if Catherine's words don't convince us, consider what Pope Pius II wrote in 1463:

> People say that we live for pleasure, accumulate wealth, bear ourselves arrogantly, ride on fat mules and handsome palfreys, trail the fringes of our cloaks after us, and show round, plump faces beneath the red hat and the white hood, keep hounds for the chase, spend much on actors and parasites, and nothing in defense of the Faith.... If the truth be confessed, the luxury and pomp at our court is too great. And this is why we are so detested by the people that they will not listen to us, even when we say what is just and reasonable. (Durant, p. 388.)

There were many good clergy and religious on the eve of the Reformation who persevered in the faith and lived according to the gospel. Yet, the historical record is replete with the scandal of corruption throughout the Church. As we begin our study of the Reformation, we Catholics had best start off on the right foot by acknowledging our communal sinfulness. Such an acknowledgment will place us in the right frame of mind to understand the actions of the Protestant Reformers. We may disagree with them on doctrinal grounds, but we can readily appreciate their contempt for Church corruption.

CHAPTER TWELVE

THE REFORMATION: PROTESTANT PHASE ONE

'HERE I STAND'

The date is April 17, 1521. Father Martin Luther of the Augustinian Order has been summoned before a meeting of the Imperial Diet (Council) in the German town of Worms. He is ordered to answer charges of heresy. His inquisitor will be Johann von der Ecken, the chief lawyer for the archbishop of Trier. The tribunal is scheduled to convene at seven o'clock in the evening in the audience hall of the local bishop's palace. The palace is the most ornately decorated building in town. Three stories high, its facade bears many traces of Italian design. Large green shutters protect the windows, and an iron gate, four meters high, guards the entrance way. Only people directly connected to the proceedings before the emperor or those wealthy enough to purchase a seat are permitted into the hall.

By six o'clock, everyone except the emperor and the seven electors of Germany is in place. Luther sits at a table to the left of the emperor's throne, silently reading through some notes and every now and then turning to read a passage from his Bible. At a table to the right, von der Ecken and another inquisitor are whispering with one another. At a quarter to seven a trumpeter announces the arrival of the electors. By order of seniority, they enter the room. Duke Frederick of Saxony, Luther's prince and protector, is fourth in line behind the archbishops of Mainz, Trier and Cologne. Behind Duke Frederick march the three younger princes who make up the contingent of men who elect the emperor. Frederick wears a long purple cape and carries an ostrich-plumed white hat in his left arm. A silver, gleaming sword hangs from his belt.

Finally, Emperor Charles enters the room, at first to the fanfare of trumpets and then utter silence. Everyone stands respectfully. People are struck at how young the twenty-one-year-old looks and how shy he seems. He is led to the throne by his guard and the archbishop of Mainz. Dressed in a white satin blouse with his gold imperial pendant hanging around his neck, Charles stands for a moment, his plush velvet hat on his head—the only man in the hall still permitted to have his head covered. Around his shoulders is a green silk cape bound together at the neck by a gold chain. His leggings are of the Spanish style—something which is not lost on his German spectators—multicolored stripes of blue, red and orange with each stripe bordered in gold thread. Instead of boots, he wears delicate purple sandals. Charles seems almost afraid to address the audience, most of whom are much older than he and far more experienced at wielding power.

"Be seated," he says at last, and then he sits down himself. An attendant removes his cape, and he hands the man his hat. "My lord archbishops," he announces, "my lord princes, you may begin."

Von der Ecken stands to open the case against Luther. Pointing to a stack of some twenty of Luther's books, the red-cheeked prosecutor looks directly at Luther and asks, "Martin, are these your books, and are you prepared to repudiate what you have written in them?"

Luther stands and answers in a tense voice, "How could I repudiate *all*, sir, since by common agreement those portions of my writings which deal with the corruption of popes, bishops and priests are accurate and fair."

The emperor suddenly stamps the butt of his sword on the floor and shouts, "No! They are not 'accurate and fair'!" A hush falls over the crowd. Charles regains his composure, looking around as if he is embarrassed for having made such an outburst.

Von der Ecken waits for the emperor's nod before continuing. "Do you repudiate your writings, Martin, in full or in part?"

"I will gladly repudiate any parts, sir, which you can show me are contradicted by Scripture."

"Ah yes," von der Ecken replies wearily. "'If I can show how they contradict Scripture.' Martin, you make the same response heretics throughout the centuries have made: 'Show me where I deviate from Scripture.' Don't you see, Martin, that your words lead to anarchy? Were every man given the right to judge Scripture for himself, every man would become pope. There would be no order, no unity within the Church. How dare you substitute your reading of Scripture for that of the successors of the apostles? Yes, Martin, you have retreated into the same lair in which all heretics hide, but I will not follow you there. Let us not argue fine points of Scripture so as to deter this diet from the investigation at hand. I ask you again, do you or do you not renounce what you have written in your books?"

"Very well, my Lord," Luther replies, in a voice that now shows no trace of hesitation, "if you want a simple answer, I will give it to you. Since I do not accept the authority of either popes or Church councils, because the two have on numerous occasions contradicted each other, I *will* not and *can* not retract anything I have written unless I am shown in Holy Scripture why I should do so. To do otherwise would be to betray my conscience. That is my answer. Here I stand."

The audience murmurs excitedly until the emperor's guard reestablishes order. Von der Ecken begins to interrogate Luther on the issue of Church councils, but after a brief exchange the emperor interrupts. "Enough! We have heard his answer. He denies the authority of Church councils and he says that every man may interpret Scripture free of guidance from the Church. What more need we hear?" Charles stands up, prompting the entire assembly to do likewise. "I have given my pledge that this man will not be harmed," he shouts, his young voice cracking at one point. "I will keep my pledge, but I have more to say on this matter. The accused will remain in Worms until I have declared my intentions more fully." The emperor turns and storms out of the hall. The audience bursts into excited chatter.

THE ROAD TO WORMS

How did Martin Luther reach this point? How is it that a pious and devout priest could break with the Church and lead millions of other Christians to do likewise? Let's retrace Luther's steps to the tribunal at Worms.

First we must ask the question, was Luther simply upset with the corruption he saw in the Church? Or would he have disagreed with traditional Catholic doctrine even had the Church not been corrupt? If it were just the former, we could perhaps conclude that Luther's revolt amounted to "sour grapes." Perhaps, we could say, he was just an angry priest who should have been more patient and forgiving with human sinfulness. By this line of reasoning, we could say that the entire Reformation might have been avoided if the Church had rooted out the sin and immorality among its leaders.

This response would be too simplistic. Yes, Luther was an angry, volatile man. Yes, he often threw temper tantrums and spoke and acted emotionally when it came to criticizing the pope and the clergy. But that is not all that motivated him. Although he hated the corruption in the Church, his principal reason for breaking with Rome was *doctrinal* and not *emotional*. Although we can never know for sure, history leads us to speculate that even if the Church had been untainted by corruption, Martin Luther would still have broken with Rome. Yet, would his doctrinal disagreements have been as passionate had it not been for the corruption in the Church? Likely not. To understand Martin Luther we must understand *both* his anger at corruption *and* his theological attack on traditional Catholic doctrine. Let's start with his response to corruption and then turn to an analysis of his theology.

ST. PETER'S BASILICA
AND THE CONTROVERSY OVER INDULGENCES

For Luther, the straw that broke the camel's back involved, of all things, a building project. Pope Leo X's predecessor, Pope Julius II, had begun work on the greatest church ever built—St. Peter's Basilica. Leo wanted the basilica substantially finished during his pontificate so that his family, the Medicis, would get most of the credit for the project. The problem was that Leo didn't know how to handle money. To be more precise, he wasted money, spending vast amounts on all sorts of trivial things. Consequently, as his papacy progressed, he found himself on the verge of bankruptcy. Each day, he looked with despair at the huge basilica looming up from the earth before his Vatican apartments. The basilica project had become something like one of those "cost-overrun" government boondoggles of our own day. The more money Leo spent on the basilica, the more money it required.

Leo devised a scheme. He turned north to wealthy Germany. The prince-elector of Mainz, an archbishop, Albert of Brandenburg, was himself a poor steward of money. He was in arrears on his financial obligations to Rome. Leo proposed a deal. He would authorize a campaign in Albert's diocese to grant plenary indulgences. For purchasing indulgences, Catholics would be promised in a papal document that all their sins would be forgiven and all time in purgatory for those sins remitted. Albert could keep half of the money he collected, and the pope would get the other half. Albert's back taxes would be wiped out, and Leo would raise money to continue building St. Peter's.

By today's standards, Leo's plan was grossly unscrupulous. Catholics in that era, however, were accustomed to paying for spiritual benefits like indulgences. Nowadays, the Church makes it clear that neither sacraments nor indulgences nor any other means of grace can be bought. Even so, there are still those who think they can buy their way to heaven—despite what the Church teaches.

Such people were numerous in Leo's time. His sin was to exploit their superstitious tendencies in order to raise money. Archbishop Albert made matters worse by using priests to preach on indulgences who were interested only in their "cut" from how much money they raised. Some of these priests told their audiences that a plenary indulgence guaranteed the buyer that all *future* sins would be forgiven as well as past sins. In other words, these men said in effect, "Buy one of our indulgence documents and sin all you want without fear of going to hell or purgatory."

The most notorious of these indulgence peddlers was a Dominican named Johann Tetzel, who sold indulgences near the borders of Luther's Saxony. He went beyond telling his audiences that they could they keep their own souls out of purgatory. He told them they could free the souls of their loved ones already in purgatory as well. His co-workers sang a little ditty to persuade the crowds: "As soon as the coin in the coffer rings, the soul from purgatory to heaven springs." When Catholics from Luther's Wittenberg went to hear Tetzel and succumbed to his sales pitch, Luther grew furious. He wrote his now famous *Ninety-five Theses*. There he attacked not only indulgences but the conception of papal and Church authority that supported indulgences. The

Theses were an overnight "best-seller."[1] Spurred on by this favorable reaction, Luther began to compose pamphlets (in German) in which he elaborated on his doctrinal disagreement with Rome.

LUTHER'S THEOLOGY

We must distinguish between "Luther's" theology and "Lutheran" theology. In his early days, some of what Luther taught was not radically different from ideas being advanced by other Catholic theologians. Later, however, as the controversy raged out of control, Luther's followers shaped his thoughts into a more formal body of doctrine. That body of doctrine—Lutheran theology proper—gradually took shape as being irrevocably opposed to traditional Catholic teaching.

What is the Church? Luther's principal grievance in the indulgence controversy was his opposition to the idea of the Church that the indulgence peddlers advanced. They taught that the Church contains a "treasury of merit" from which grace can be dispensed. This "treasury" contained all the "merits" earned by Christ on the cross. This idea turned salvation into an accounting system, where sinners must earn *grace* to blot out their sins and accumulate *merit* to reduce their time of punishment for committing those sins.

By this view, only ordained ministers in the Church can dispense grace. The clergy hold the "keys" to the Church. They can unlock the treasury of merit and allow the laity to gain access to the grace of salvation. Luther vehemently disagreed. Christians, he taught, can gain access to Christ's grace of salvation without going through the treasury of merit. They can go directly to Christ, bypassing the clergy and their indulgences. The institutional Church, Luther believed, is Christ's body on earth and is helpful to salvation. But if the Church is corrupt and does not truly represent Christ, Christians can receive Christ's love and grace without the assistance of the institutional Church. Further, Luther rejected the idea of purgatory altogether.

Few in the Catholic Church today believe in the mechanical, legalistic view of grace that the indulgence peddlers taught. Many Catholics today find Luther's views on grace and indulgences compatible with their own. At Vatican II, the bishops stressed the importance of the "priesthood of all believers," as did Luther. By this, Luther meant that each Christian ministers to other members of the Church. All Christians are priests to each other. Ordained priests do not have God's grace all locked up in some imagined "treasury of merit." Everyone, ordained or unordained, has direct access to Christ's love and grace.

Yet, Luther did not want to do away with the distinction between ordained and lay believers. He stressed the need for a community of believers governed

---

[1] Although they were written in a scholarly Latin that few could understand, several vitriolic translations circulated almost at once.

by full-time shepherds. He did not teach a "Jesus-and-me" doctrine; he did not profess that individuals can get to heaven without the Church. Only later would other reformers argue against the need for any institutional structure at all. Luther believed in the need for an organized Church, but he wanted individual Christians to be more aware of their autonomy and freedom before Christ than the Catholic clergy of his day would allow. Each Christian, Luther taught, freely receives Christ's grace without paying for it or otherwise adhering to mechanical rules or legalistic requirements.

What are the sacraments? Nor did Luther want to do away with the concept of *sacrament*. True, he wanted to limit the number of sacraments. He thought that only Baptism and Eucharist were sacraments because he believed these were the only two begun in the New Testament. He said the other five traditional sacraments were beneficial to Christian life but were not true sacraments. He believed Baptism truly empowers a person to become a member of the Church. It was not just a sign of one's faith, as later reformers would teach. Luther thus accepted infant baptism.

Nor did Luther feel that the Eucharist was just a *memorial* of the Last Supper as later reformers would teach. It is true that he did reject the Catholic doctrine of transubstantiation. That is, he did not believe that the bread of the altar becomes Christ's body and the wine Christ's blood. But he did believe that Christ was somehow really present in the bread and wine. It was just that he did not believe that the bread and wine actually changed into the Body and Blood. Rather, for him, they remained bread and wine, but were somehow mysteriously filled with Christ's presence at the same time.[2]

As for the Mass itself, Luther did not accept that it was a sacrifice, or that one could gain spiritual "merits" from the Mass. The liturgy for Luther was a devotional act. It was an act of worship in which Christ was present in the preached word and the bread and wine of the altar. But for him, the liturgy did not continue the work of Calvary, as Catholics believed.

The Bible as God's word. For Luther, Christ is most present to the believer in the gospel. That is why Luther placed so much emphasis on Scripture as the word of God. Yet, Luther was no literalist who opposed the written Bible to Church authority or Church tradition, as would later reformers. For Luther, final authority in the Church is in the gospel that Jesus preached and lived. If the Church teaches and lives that gospel, Luther believed, well and good. But if the Church does not, then the Bible is a better source for the gospel than the Church. He was not opposing the Bible to the Church. He was subordinating both Bible and Church to the *gospel.*

Faith versus works. The final point we should make about Luther's theology involves the difference between faith and works. He thought that indulgences, penance for the forgiveness of sin, the Mass and other means of receiving

---

[2] His position was called consubstantiation.

116

grace were "works." He relied on Paul's words in Galatians to the effect that "a person is justified not by the works of the law but through faith in Jesus Christ" (Galatians 2:16). In other words, Luther did not believe that anything one *does* makes one holy. He condemned Catholic doctrine for teaching that people can gain grace by "doing things" such as going to Mass, performing penance, or buying indulgences.

However, he did not condemn good works such as serving the poor or fasting and almsgiving. He merely taught that such good actions did not make one holy. As he put it, "Good works do not make a man good, but a good man does good works." In other words, first comes faith in Jesus Christ as savior, which makes one holy before God. Then come works. Luther thought that Rome had this backwards. Through its many spiritual practices, dispensations and indulgences, the Catholic Church taught that people could become holy. Luther said this was wrong. He advocated participating in spiritual practices as *acts of devotion*, not as means to grace.

In actuality the Catholic Church had always taught the primacy of faith as the essential prerequisite to salvation. And the Church had always taught that faith is a free gift, given to people irrespective of what they do. Yet, because of the corruption of the time, it *looked* as though the Church was professing one thing and doing another. It preached faith, but sold indulgences. It taught that the grace of salvation is a free gift, but encouraged people to buy their way out of purgatory. For Luther, this was an abomination which he could not tolerate. For him, "works" put the emphasis on human effort, on "working one's way" to heaven, whether by going to Mass, saying novenas or buying indulgences. He wanted to make it clear that only God can get one to heaven. And the only way that one comes to God is through faith in Jesus Christ, not through religious practices.

LUTHER: CHAMPION OF FREEDOM

The capstone of Luther's theology was this: that Christians must be free in their relation to God. What makes someone free? Purely and simply the salvation won by Jesus Christ. And how does one receive that salvation? Through faith in Jesus Christ. Nothing one *does* makes one free. No ordained minister, no Church practice, no outward observance of rules and regulations can make one free. For Luther, the Church of his day imprisoned people in man-made religion rather than setting them free. He believed God had called him to preach the gospel of freedom. He dedicated his life to that calling. Luther's teaching was marked by inconsistencies—as was the life-style of the Church he condemned. But for the moment, let's simply note Luther's initial impulse, his burning desire to preach as Saint Paul did, "Christians, you were called for freedom!" (Cf. Galatians 5:13)

FOCUS 23

LUTHER THE MAN: A LIFE MARKED BY INCONSISTENCY

Luther is such an interesting historical figure precisely because he was so human. He wore his heart on his sleeve and never feared speaking his mind. This was an attractive feature of his personality. It also meant that he was often overcome by his emotions. It was perhaps his susceptibility to emotional swings that led to many inconsistencies in his teaching. For example, he taught that all people can find salvation through faith in Christ, but insisted at the same time on predestination. He taught that God knows ahead of time who will believe in Jesus as savior and who won't. God, Luther taught, withholds the grace of salvation from the latter and gives it only to the former. It is a very limited kind of "freedom in Christ" that sees a large part of the human race damned by God before they are even born.

Then there was Luther's intolerance of those who disagreed with him. He could proclaim in one breath, "Faith is a free work to which no one can be compelled," while in the other breath he could say, "He who does not receive my doctrine cannot be saved." The peasants and the poor attempted to use Luther's teachings on personal freedom to throw off the rule of princes by starting a social revolution in 1524. Yet, Luther reacted angrily to the peasants' revolt, urging the princes to "smite, slay and stab" the peasants. Luther said that the peasants should be reduced to slavery so that the princes could ensure the peasants' adherence to his doctrine. He called the rebels "mad dogs" who must be killed. And his words for the Catholic clergy were even harsher. The pope was "the devil's sow," and bishops were "ignorant apes." His views on women were not much better. According to Luther, "they are good for nothing.... They are made for bearing children." Luther preached freedom in Christ, but frequently tripped over his own narrow beliefs and prejudices. By these, he would have kept some people enslaved to tradition—the very thing he accused the Catholic Church of doing.

FOCUS 24

'PROTESTANTS' VERSUS CATHOLICS

As Luther's movement gained momentum, a growing number of German princes broke with Rome and embraced Luther's doctrine. They did this largely for political rather than for religious reasons. Luther's chief lieutenant, Philip Melanchthon, wrote: "Under cover of the gospel the princes were only intent on the plunder of the churches." The princes' desertion of Catholicism greatly alarmed Emperor Charles. To quell the political revolt, he convened a diet at the town of Speyer in 1529. A committee he appointed made certain recommendations about religious freedom. Among these were a recommendation that Lutheran doctrine be tolerated throughout Germany and that the Catholic Mass be celebrated everywhere. Some of the Lutheran princes formally "protested" to the emperor, insisting on governing religious matters for themselves in their own principalities. This "protest" led to these princes being called "Protestants." That name was eventually attached to all those who disagreed with Rome and accepted the new doctrines. Hence our term *Protestant.*

Eventually, the Protestant princes' revolt against the Catholic emperor led to open warfare. The Protestant princes forced Charles to give them the right to control religion in their own territory. Charles was so broken by this defeat that he resigned his office and entered a monastery in Spain. His brother Ferdinand succeeded him and presided over a conference at Augsburg in 1555. There the following agreement was reached. In Latin it was phrased, *"cuius regio, eius religio."* This means literally, "whose region, his religion." In other words, Protestant princes could demand that their subjects be Protestant, and Catholic princes that their subjects be Catholic. People who didn't like this arrangement were given freedom to migrate to a principality that supported their choice of faith. From that time onward, some areas of Germany became Protestant and some Catholic, and largely have remained so to this day.

CHAPTER THIRTEEN

THE REFORMATION: PROTESTANT PHASE TWO

LUTHER SET OFF A STORM that had long been gathering. He was by no means the first reformer within the Church who taught the doctrines discussed in the last chapter. Luther succeeded where others failed because of a unique blend of factors: among others, the strength of his personality, the sharpness of his intellect and the quickness of his pen, the protection he was offered by the powerful Duke Frederick of Saxony, the passion of German Christians to end their subservience to Italian churchmen.

Success breeds success. When other reformers saw that Luther was succeeding, their courage was fortified and they, too, challenged Rome's authority. In addition, princes in other places saw their colleagues in Germany gaining politically from Luther's movement. Promoting a movement that promised independence from pope and emperor looked to these princes to be a good way of furthering their own ambitions.

RADICAL REFORM EFFORTS: THE 'LEFT WING'

But "Luther's movement" did not remain *his* movement. As soon as his ideas became better known, other reformers thought they could improve upon Luther's teaching. One wing of the reform movement saw Luther as too timid. Radical preachers from this "left wing" of the Reformation wanted a full-scale return to the days of the early Church, where all things were owned in common. These radicals preached overthrow of the established order and the downfall of princes.

Needless to say, the princes didn't go for *this* kind of religious revolution. The princes accepted Luther, because he stood for the independence of princes against the tyranny of pope and emperor. But the radical reformers wanted to do away with government by Church and state altogether. This the princes could not abide. The princes moved angrily to suppress radical, communitarian Christianity root and branch. In one year they put to death over a hundred thousand peasants and urban workers who were aligned with one kind of radical movement or another.

A group known as the Anabaptists grew out of the radical movement. The Anabaptists are not to be confused with the later Baptists,[1] of whom we shall say more later. The Anabaptists were radical and communitarian, but most were pacifists. They did not want to achieve their goals through violence, as did some radical reformers.

Their principal doctrine was the rejection of infant baptism. They taught that people are first "saved" through a conversion experience in which they put their faith in Christ as savior. Then they are baptized, but only as a sign that they have already been saved. This sign, they believed can only be made by adults. In other words, for the Anabaptists, Baptism was not a sacrament, but merely a ritual. It did not bring one the grace of salvation. It was merely a public acknowledgment that one had been saved.

For the times, this was an extremely radical doctrine. Luther was horrified at the Anabaptists' teaching and urged the princes to condemn them. Both Catholic and Lutheran princes responded eagerly. Anabaptists were expelled from nearly every city where they were found. In many places they were drowned simply for believing as they did. The Reformation had now turned into a persecution. The Anabaptists were the first group of Protestant believers to suffer for their faith.

RELIGION OR POWER?

The Anabaptist experience shows that the Reformation was not concerned simply with religion. More importantly perhaps, it was concerned with *power*—ecclesiastical and political power. The Catholic Church wanted to keep its power against the Lutheran princes. The Lutheran princes on the other hand wanted to expand their power against the pope and emperor. Both Catholics and Lutherans wanted to eliminate radicals like the Anabaptists. We will see how important the addiction to power was as we proceed with the unfolding story of the Reformation. We will look at three major examples: John Calvin's movement in Geneva, Henry VIII's revolt in England and the struggle of Catholics against Protestants for supremacy in France. By necessity, we will have to compress many details into a generalized picture.

CALVIN'S THEOCRACY

John Calvin (1509-1564) was actually more significant to the future development of Protestantism than Martin Luther. He was twenty-six years younger than Luther and had the time and energy to take up where Luther left off. He

---

[1] Perhaps the best example today of Anabaptist descendants are the Mennonites.

was a Frenchman, highly educated (in both theology and law) and intelligent. Persecuted in Catholic France for espousing his theology, he traveled to Geneva, Switzerland, in 1536. There, Protestant reform was already firmly entrenched. A council of sixty men had been elected by the populace to run the city according to "Reformed" principles established in Zurich by a reformer named Ulrich Zwingli (1484-1531).

Reformed and Calvinist theology. Let's say something about the word *Reformed*. It means something more than simply a church that is part of the reforming movement. *Reformed* came to take on denominational significance. In other words, just as some Christians were saying they were Lutherans or Anabaptists, other people were now saying they belonged to the Reformed Church. Calvin moved into Geneva when the city was accepting and experimenting with Reformed theology. He added his own thoughts to Reformed doctrine. The result was a new presentation of Reformed doctrine known as Calvinism. In the future, more Protestants would belong to the Reformed churches than to the Lutheran Church. This especially would be true in America, where Puritans, Congregationalists, Baptists, Dutch Reformed and Presbyterians all based their faith on certain tenets of Calvinism.

Calvin's theology. What was Calvin's theology? We find it principally in his major work, *The Institutes of the Christian Religion* (1536). It was, and is, a tremendously influential treatise. Calvin went much farther than Luther in establishing the Bible as the sole source of Church authority. For Calvin, it was impossible to know anything at all about God that is not in the Bible. Thus, Church tradition and the teaching of Church councils were for Calvin attempts to usurp the authority of the Bible. Unlike Luther, who emphasized the primacy of the *gospel*, Calvin stressed the primacy of a written document—the Bible itself. This was the origin of Protestant literalism, and was perhaps aided by the fact that Calvin had studied law.

Calvin emphasized the majesty of God and the depravity and smallness of humanity. Thus he read the Bible as revealing an angry, wrathful God whom Christians had to serve in fear and trembling. The source of humanity's "frightful deformity," as Calvin called it, is original sin.[2] Original sin has so weakened and debased human nature that human beings can do nothing on their own that is pleasing to God. In fact, Calvin believed, the vast majority of human beings will never be saved from the devastating effects of original sin. Thus, most people are going to hell.

Calvin's doctrine of *predestination* was even sterner than Luther's. Luther based his version of predestination on God's *foreknowledge* of those who will accept Christ and those who won't. Calvin, however, saw God as *creating* some people for hell and some for heaven. It's not, as it was for Luther, that God knows in advance who will accept Christ and who won't. Rather, for Calvin,

---

[2] Calvin relied heavily on Saint Augustine for the concept of original sin in his doctrine.

God *chooses* some to go to hell and some to go to heaven. For Calvin, this was not a frightening or pessimistic doctrine. Rather, for him it emphasized God's power and majesty. Only God could have the power and autonomy to send some to hell and some to heaven. The fact that we humans can't understand this mystery, Calvin believed, shows how small we are and how glorious God is.[3]

Another difference between Calvin and Luther concerns their respective views of the Eucharist. Both Catholics and Luther, although in differing ways (Catholics believing in transubstantiation, Luther in consubstantiation), believed Christ is present in the bread and wine of the altar. Calvin disagreed. For him, Christ remains in heaven during the liturgy. By receiving Communion, the believer is united with Christ in heaven by the work of the Holy Spirit. This was a position that stood halfway between Luther on the one hand and the followers of Zwingli on the other. The latter taught that the Eucharist is simply a memorial service. It *commemorates* the Last Supper, but that is all. Calvin was not willing to go that far. He believed that the Eucharist was something like a traditional sacrament. Yet, he was unwilling to locate Christ in the bread and wine themselves.

Life in Geneva. Calvin wanted his theology to be applied on the political level. In 1541 he became head of the council of elders that governed Geneva. This governing body came to be known as the *Presbytery*. Calvin and the Presbytery established a *theocracy* in Geneva. This means that they united religious law and civil law. They believed that God—through them—was in direct charge of Geneva. The most recent example of this type of government is the ayatollahs' Iran, where people who sin against the Islamic law are likewise guilty of breaking the Iranian civil law. So, too, in Geneva, Calvin ordered corporal punishment of fornicators and adulterers. He regulated people's dress, especially that of women, by forbidding jewelry and certain hairstyles. He forbade theater and other cultural works, and censored books and literature. He used torture to impose his doctrine.[4]

In Calvin's movement, then, a concern with religion spilled over into a concern for power. Until Calvin's death in 1564, it was power rather than religion that governed Christian life in Geneva. Traveling now to England, let's turn to another example of how the quest for power outstripped religious reform.

HENRY VIII AND ANGLICANISM

Since it's such a familiar story, we won't recount in detail King Henry VIII's motivations in breaking with Rome. The reader is referred instead to movies

---

[3] From a modern psychological viewpoint, one wonders if Calvin was not "projecting" his own grandiose need for power onto God.

[4] The Catholic inquisitions likewise used torture. Both the inquisitors and Calvinists hideously distorted the gospel in their zeal to force their views on others.

like *Anne of a Thousand Days* or *A Man for All Seasons*. They are accurate, fascinating reproductions of Henry's conflict with Rome over his desire to divorce his wife and his subsequent angry break with the Catholic Church.

Henry, head of the English Church. Ironically, Henry started out by *condemning* Luther and the Reformation. Pope Leo X was so pleased with Henry for doing this that he named the king, "Defender of the Faith." Henry proudly bore this title, thinking himself the most loyal Catholic monarch in Europe. Yet, when his wife failed to produce a male heir to the throne, and the pope failed to approve Henry's request for an annulment, he turned colors and became the most determined opponent of Rome that one could find. In 1531, he ordered English priests and religious to acknowledge him "the protector and only supreme head of the Church and Clergy of England." From that point on, Henry governed the English Church as authoritatively as any pope.

In 1534, Parliament, now completely subservient to Henry, passed the Act of Succession. This Act required all Englishmen to swear an oath to Henry as head of the Anglican Church. It also required them to support Henry's daughter, Elizabeth, as his heir, rather than Mary. Mary was Henry's daughter by Catherine of Aragon (his partner in the marriage he had tried to have annulled). Many Catholics refused the oath. The most famous of these was Sir Thomas More. More had been Lord Chancellor of England. When he refused to take Parliament's oath, he was imprisoned in the Tower of London and eventually beheaded for his faith. (See Focus 25.)

Cranmer and new theology. How did Henry's new establishment of the Anglican Church affect theology? The name to note here is Thomas Cranmer, Archbishop of Canterbury. When Henry was King, Cranmer had to tread lightly. Henry was still a Catholic in religious sentiment. He refused to allow Lutheran or Calvinist doctrines into his Anglican Church. Henry, for example, kept the Catholic Mass and accepted the Catholic theology of the Mass. After Henry's death, however, Cranmer began openly to promote Lutheran and Calvinist theology. He repudiated Catholic teachings on the Mass such as transubstantiation and the idea of the Mass as a sacrifice. Cranmer was put to death during a brief Catholic resurgence under Queen Mary Tudor ("Bloody Mary"). But when Mary died and was succeeded by her half-sister Elizabeth I, Cranmer's theology returned to style.

Queen Elizabeth molds the new Anglican Church. It was really Queen Elizabeth rather than her father Henry VIII who established for the Church in England its distinctly Anglican character. Elizabeth first moved to persecute Catholics. Persecution was nothing new in England. Elizabeth's Catholic half-sister, Bloody Mary, had put Protestants to death. Henry VIII had executed Catholics, Anabaptists, Calvinists and anybody else who would not accept his direct political control of the English Church.

Elizabeth consolidated her theological grasp on the Anglican Church by having her advisors publish *The Book of Common Prayer* and the *Thirty-nine Articles*. The former was meant to be the standard for Anglican belief. It attempted to steer a middle path between traditional Catholicism and Protestant doctrines that rejected the sacraments altogether. For example, on the Eucharist, the prayer to be recited at the Anglican liturgy joined together a little bit of traditional belief in the Real Presence, and a little bit of the idea that the Eucharist was only a memorial of the Last Supper. The prayer read: "The body of our Lord Jesus Christ, which was given for thee, preserve thy body and soul unto everlasting life. Take and eat this in remembrance that Christ died for thee, and feed on him in thy heart by faith, with thanksgiving."

The *Thirty-nine Articles* was likewise something of a compromise document. It upheld the validity of "traditions and ceremonies of the Church which be not repugnant to the Word of God." At the same time, it rejected purgatory, confession of sins to priests and indulgences. Elizabeth realized that many of her subjects were still very much Catholic. She thus tried to give them some leeway to accept Anglican doctrine. But when push came to shove, she angrily persecuted anyone who accepted the authority of Rome. As in Germany, the Reformation in England was more about power than about faith. Elizabeth wanted to shape the Church in England according to her views mostly for *political* reasons rather than for *religious* reasons. Let's look across the Channel to France and see how this theme was repeated there.

'PARIS IS WORTH A MASS'

The Reformation never gained a foothold in France as it did in Germany, Switzerland, England and elsewhere. There are several reasons for this. Perhaps the two most important are these: (1) Although reforming intellectuals like Calvin were prominent in France, most intellectuals stayed with Catholicism. (2) In addition, the French Catholic Church was already semi-independent before Luther's revolt. French Catholics had long been French first and Catholic second. They weren't about to tolerate Italian churchmen telling them what to do. King Francis I, only a year before Luther published his *Ninety-five Theses*, had gained from Pope Leo X the right to appoint French bishops and abbots in France.

Yet, Luther's and Calvin's respective doctrines did gain popularity in France. And when King Francis persecuted and murdered large numbers of Protestants in southern France, the outrage produced more converts for the Protestant cause. The French converts called themselves *Huguenots*. Huguenot power spread throughout southwestern France. French princes, like their German counterparts, thought they, too, could use religion to further their political ambitions. They wanted to be independent from the French Crown and rule their own duchies independently. They hoped the Protestant movement would help them do this.

By 1559, the resulting religious turmoil had reached fever pitch. Perhaps half of the French nobility had deserted Catholicism for one Protestant sect or another. Even more important, the large, educated, skilled middle class in France was moving swiftly toward conversion to Protestantism. In 1562, religious warfare broke out. Cruelty and persecution were practiced by both sides.

The worst incident occurred in 1572. The French queen, Catherine d' Medici, persuaded a powerful duke to assassinate the Huguenot leader. The attempt failed. Panic-stricken, the queen persuaded her son, King Charles IX, to slaughter Huguenots in their homes before they could retaliate. Some ten thousand were murdered in this "St. Bartholomew's Day Massacre," as it came to be known. When Pope Gregory XIII in Rome heard the news, he attributed the action to God's divine intervention on behalf of the Catholic cause and called for a celebration. The pope, too, thus showed that he was more interested in power than he was in the gospel.

When the Catholic king, Charles, died, the crown eventually descended to a Protestant prince, Henry of Navarre. However, French Catholics refused to accept Henry. Henry wanted desperately to conquer Paris, the Catholic stronghold. War waged back and forth. When Henry at last stood before the walls of Paris, he felt unconfident about proceeding further. He realized that the vast majority of the lower classes were Catholic. And since the lower classes in France comprised most of the population, Henry admitted to himself that a Protestant king could never rule the hearts of his subjects.

He thus took a step motivated purely by expediency. "Paris is worth a Mass," he said, as he converted to Catholicism. Henry restored order to France and ended the religious strife. He even granted the Protestants a good deal of freedom in worshiping as they chose.

But Henry's opportunistic conversion proved to everyone that the Reformation was not so much concerned with religion as it was with power. What had started out with Luther as a religious revolt, ended up a half-century after Luther as competition for political control of the Church and the accompanying control of people's lives by the state.

FOCUS 25

THOMAS MORE: SAINT, REBEL OR PATRIOT?

Four hundred years after he was put to death for refusing to accept King Henry VIII as head of the English Church, Thomas More was made a saint of the Catholic Church. But why did More refuse the oath he was told to take? Let's look at the details. Had More accepted Parliament's Act of Succession, he would have agreed that Henry was sovereign of the English Church. He also would have accepted Elizabeth as Henry's heir. To More's way of thinking, Elizabeth was an illegitimate child. She had been born to the King's former mistress Anne Boleyn. More felt that Henry's first wife, Queen Catherine of Aragon, was Henry's lawful wife. Thus, for More, Catherine's daughter, Mary, was lawful heir to the throne. In refusing the oath, More, a highly skilled lawyer, acted as any English lawyer might have done. That is, he refused to condone the king's attempt to subvert the laws of royal descent.

But a close reading of the events leading to More's death reveals something else at work in More's heart. He primarily refused Henry's oath because he realized that if Henry were to succeed, the Church in England would be splintered into dozens of competing bodies. In this he was proven to be right. More hated the corruption in the Catholic Church and frequently condemned it. Yet, he preferred Rome and all its folly to a Church that was torn by doctrinal strife and contradictory teachings. He realized that if Henry became head of the Church in England, there would soon be not one pope competing for Christians' loyalty, but dozens. For More, the Church, sinful as it was, had to remain unified. He could not participate in its being divided. For that conviction he was willing to pay with his life. Thomas More died as a man who loved his country and his Church equally. He was an English patriot who died for his faith and for his king.

FOCUS 26

HEALING THE BREACH: A FIRST STEP TOWARD RESOLVING THE THEOLOGICAL QUESTION THAT UNDERLIES THE PROTESTANT-CATHOLIC SPLIT

As we leave the Protestant phase of the Reformation era, let's notice that recently there's been some good news on the theological front. Recall that Luther's bedrock doctrine was "justification by faith apart from works of the law" (cf. Galatians 3:11). For Luther, as well as for all later Protestant reformers, this doctrine was virtually a theme song by which they rallied their troops to combat Catholicism, with its supposed insistence on "works" as the means to salvation. On June 25, 1998, the Pontifical Council for Promoting Christian Unity, as approved by Pope John Paul II, published its Lutheran-Catholic *Joint Declaration on the Doctrine of Justification*, which in turn had been approved in Geneva by the Lutheran World Federation (an organization which represents fifty-seven million of the world's sixty-one million Lutherans). In the *Joint Declaration*, Catholics and Lutherans now profess together:

> By grace alone, in faith in Christ's saving work and not because of any merit on our part, we are accepted by God and receive the Holy Spirit, who renews our hearts while equipping and calling us to good works....We confess together that good works—a Christian life lived in faith, hope and love—follow justification and are its fruits.... When Catholics [as at the Council of Trent] say that persons "cooperate" in preparing for and accepting justification by consenting to God's justifying action, they see such personal consent as itself an effect of grace, not as an action arising from innate human abilities. (*Joint Declaration on the Doctrine of Justification*, in *Origins* [Catholic News Service: Washington, D.C.] Vol. 28: No. 8, July 16, 1998, pp. 120-124.)

Catholics do not believe that they are saved by their own efforts, any more than Lutherans do (cf. Focus 8). Yet, although Catholics share this faith, sometimes we have acted as though we believe otherwise—with our scores of devotions, novenas, indulgences, miraculous medals and so on.

All of these practices do nothing to "earn grace," as often seemed to be the understanding in the pre-Vatican II Church. If they fit in anywhere in the Christian life, they fit in as responses to God's goodness for having already earned all the grace for us that was ever available—when Jesus died on the cross. In the *Joint Declaration*, it is stated, "Catholics can share the concern of the Reformers to ground faith in the objective reality of Christ's promise, to look away from one's own experience and to trust

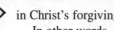

in Christ's forgiving word alone" (page 120).

In other words, we Catholics, in our spirituality have sometimes acted as if our salvation is a question of accumulating spiritual bonus points, when in reality it depends on what God has done in Jesus Christ, rather than on anything we do. With the *Joint Declaration*, we move at least a little closer to reconciling the long and painful separation between Christians that began in the sixteenth century.

CHAPTER FOURTEEN

THE REFORMATION: THE CATHOLIC PHASE

CATHOLIC REFORM BEFORE LUTHER

It would be inaccurate to think that there was no reformation within the Church before Martin Luther initiated the Reformation. Well before Luther, Catholics had sought to reform the Church. In actuality, the Church is always in need of reformation and the Church has repeatedly responded to this need. Think, for example, of the Cluniac reformation that we studied earlier. Think also of the debate in the fourteenth century over the Church's wealth and over ownership of private property by the clergy. Many Franciscan preachers condemned such ownership, allowing themselves only to "use" property, not own it. These radical Franciscans were not very successful. Clerical ownership of property and clerical competition for money and power were commonly accepted in the late Middle Ages.

Yet the reforming impulse within the Church continued. One of the most notable examples of this was the foundation of religious orders whose very purpose was to reform the Church. The Theatine Fathers, for example, were founded shortly after Luther's revolt by Gaetano di Tiene, Paolo Consiglieri, Bonifacio da Colle and Cardinal Gian Pietro Carafa. Cardinal Carafa would later become the stern, reform-minded Pope Paul IV (see below). The Theatines dedicated themselves to improving both the educational level of the clergy and the clergy's spirituality. More than two hundred Theatine priests were appointed bishops. They carried Theatine reforming zeal into their dioceses.

Ironically, the very age in which Church corruption had sunk to the depths was also the age in which Catholic reform preaching reached a high point. John Capistrano, Bernardino of Siena, Vincent Ferrer and Archbishop Antoninus of Florence all flourished in the fifteenth century. They were all masters of reforming oratory. They preached reform to clergy and laity alike, calling many within the Church to return to the gospel. It was said that Bernardino of Siena, by his preaching alone, converted entire towns. Along with preaching there were reform writings, such as Cardinal Gasparo Contarini's book, *On the Duty of the Bishop*. In this influential book, Cardinal

Contarini strongly criticized the life-styles of bishops and urged them to reform.

CATHOLICISM RESPONDS TO THE PROTESTANT REFORMATION

Yet, to be historically accurate, we must say that the Catholic Church didn't take reform seriously until Luther's revolt started succeeding. To be blunt, the Catholic Church didn't reform until it had to. A clear sign that the Catholic Church was going to take internal reform seriously was given during the papal election following the death of Pope Leo X. Prior to Pope Leo's death, Italian politics, including bribery and intimidation, assured that candidates only from wealthy Italian families could be elected pope. In 1522, however, the cardinals who met in the electoral conclave turned to a reform-minded Dutchman. The new pope kept his own name, Adrian, and was known as Pope Adrian VI.[1]

The reforming Dutch pope. Adrian Dedel (1459-1523) was one of the most interesting figures of his day. He had taught the famous Erasmus of Rotterdam. Erasmus was the most respected scholar in Europe and a leading Catholic advocate of reform. So scathing were Erasmus's reform writings that it would later be said, "Erasmus laid the egg that Luther hatched." In addition, Pope Adrian had tutored Emperor Charles. Then, he had been appointed archbishop of Tortosa in Spain. It was in Spain that he learned of his election by the cardinals to the papacy. Before leaving for Rome to accept the papal office, he wrote a stern letter to the Sacred College. In it, he told the cardinals that he was coming not to celebrate with them, but to chastise and correct them.

Similarly, he wrote letters to Catholic princes throughout the Empire, criticizing them for creating a climate in which clerical corruption could flourish. For example, consider the letter Pope Adrian wrote to a Diet of German princes and bishops.

> All of us, prelates and clergy, have turned aside from the road of righteousness and for a long time now there has been not even one who did good.... You must therefore promise in our name that we intend to exert ourselves so that, first of all, the Roman Curia, from which perhaps all this evil took its start, may be improved. Then, just as from here the sickness spread, so also from here recovery and renewal may begin.[2]

Had Adrian lived to enforce his reforming policies, it is highly possible that the Protestant Reformation would have been nipped in the bud. The fact is, however, that Adrian served as pope for only a year, dying in 1523. It was

---

[1] In some lists of the popes he is called Hadrian, after the Roman emperor of the same name.
[2] Pope Adrian VI, "Instruction to the Diet of Nuremburg" (1522), in Hubert Jedin, ed., *History of the Church*, 10 vols. (New York: Seabury Press, 1980), vol. V, p. 108.

well known that he had incurred enemies within the ranks of the cardinals for proposing reconciliation with Luther. It was rumored that the pope wanted to make the following concessions to Luther and his followers: acceptance of a married clergy, acceptance of communion to be received by the faithful as both bread and wine, and acceptance of Mass in the vernacular. Indeed, twice conferences between Lutherans and delegates from Rome met to discuss these proposals. With Adrian's death, the conferences came to nothing.

Set-back under Clement. Instead, the cardinals meeting to elect Adrian's successor, returned to their policy of choosing wealthy Italians from powerful families. Adrian's successor, Pope Clement VII (1523-1534), was a Medici. Clement profoundly underestimated the gravity of Luther's movement. Clement should have turned all of his attention to the still-healable breach between Luther and Rome. Instead, Clement spent his papacy involved in political intrigues and schemes calculated to improve his political fortunes. He even plotted against the one man who could have helped him prevent the spread of Luther's movement—the Catholic emperor Charles. Clement encouraged Charles's enemies, and Charles grew so angry that he sent his German troops to sack Rome. During one week in 1527, both Catholic and Lutheran soldiers under Charles's authority laid waste to Rome. In order to avoid arrest by Charles's soldiers, Clement had to sneak out of Rome in disguise.

Clement's reign was a debacle. With Adrian, the Catholic Church had considered the possibility of reconciling with Luther. With Clement, all hope of reconciliation was lost. It was Clement who mishandled Henry VIII's demand for a divorce. The pope stood fast in disallowing Henry's request. He did so largely for political reasons and without using tact in dealing with Henry. Clement sided with Spain in the controversy. Spain wanted to uphold the honor of their Spanish queen, Catherine of Aragon, when she resisted the divorce. Henry's rage against Rome was directed as much at Clement's favoritism toward Spain as it was at the pope's canonical reasons for denying Henry an annulment. Had Clement been more compassionate and tactful, Henry might never have broken with Rome. By Clement's death in 1534, not only England, but many other areas of Europe had become firmly Protestant. This was due largely to Clement's ineptitude in confronting the religious crisis that had engulfed Europe.

THE COUNCIL OF TRENT

Clement's blunders led to his successor's call for a reforming Church council. Pope Paul III (1534-1549) announced the council in 1535. Yet, for six years, bishops and princes stalled and argued with each other about where they should meet. Finally, in 1541, Emperor Charles intervened. He suggested that the council meet in the German town of Trent, which lay just over the Italian border. Even with the emperor's urging, however, it took four more years for the bishops to quit fighting with one another and agree to meet in council at Trent.

The Council of Trent (1545-1563) was concerned with two agendas: ending corruption in the Church and solidifying Catholic dogma against the new Protestant doctrines. The Council was not as successful in achieving an end to corruption as it was in clarifying doctrine. The struggle to end corruption would be taken over by reform-minded popes like Paul IV. He would be aided by new religious orders that insisted on adherence to gospel life-styles for its members. The most notable of these reforming orders was the Jesuits, of whom we shall say more shortly.

Trent on dogma. As for its doctrinal thrust, the Council of Trent made many lasting accomplishments. We can only highlight some of these. In response to Luther's teaching on the Bible, the Council had this to say:

> The Church receives and venerates with a feeling of piety and reverence
> all the books both of the Old and New Testaments, since one God is the
> author of both; also, the traditions, whether they relate to faith or to
> morals, as having been dictated either orally by Christ or by the Holy
> Ghost, and preserved in the Catholic Church in unbroken succession.[3]

In other words, the Council made it clear that God's revelation is to be found *both* in Scripture and in Church tradition. This position was at odds with the teaching of Protestant theologians. They taught that "Scripture alone" is the source of God's revelation—not Scripture *plus* Church tradition.

On the key issue which led Luther to break with Rome, justification by faith, the Council stated that God alone, through Jesus Christ, justifies human beings. Further, the Council stated, the gift of justification is just that—a gift. It cannot be earned by human effort. Even in the sacraments, the Council stressed, it is *God's* initiative, and not human initiative, that makes the sacraments efficacious. So far, Luther would have been in agreement with the Council on this point.

Where they differed was in speaking of the role of human will. It is erroneous, the Council taught, to say, as Luther and Calvin taught, that God saves people apart from any apparent good works they may perform. For Luther and Calvin, the human will was powerless to do any good at all until God had justified a person. The Council, on the other hand, said that sinners can "convert themselves to their own justification by freely assenting to and cooperating with God's grace."[4] Thus, in this sense, the Council taught that both faith and good works lead to salvation.

Yet, the Council stressed that one can gain spiritual merits from good works only after one has been justified by God's grace of salvation as received in Baptism. For the Council fathers, salvation is both a "grace and a

---

[3] In Justo Gonzalez, *A History of Christian Thought*, 3 vols. (Nashville: Abingdon Press, 1983), vol. III, p. 54.
[4] This was essentially Saint Augustine's position on grace and free will, as summarized by the Synod of Orange (529); see p. 32.

reward." It is a grace "promised to the sons of God through Jesus Christ." It is "a reward promised by God himself, to be faithfully given" because of the believer's good works and spiritual merits.

The means by which faith and works come together in the believer's life is the sacraments. The Council said the sacraments are necessary for salvation. It upheld the traditional seven sacraments (those tabulated by Peter Lombard during the Middle Ages), and upheld the doctrine of transubstantiation. It also said that the sacraments confer grace in and of themselves. That is, the sacraments do not give grace merely because of the believer's faith, as some Protestants taught.

Rather, the Council taught, the grace of the sacraments is always present. This is so regardless of one's state of holiness. The sacraments are efficacious by themselves. They are not "stirred into action" as it were, by the faith or holiness of the believer. Likewise, the lack of sanctity in a priest cannot nullify the effectiveness of the sacraments.

For Protestants, the Council's declaration on the sacraments meant that Rome still upheld "works" as a means to salvation. That is, Protestants believed that through its teaching on the sacraments the Catholic Church still held out to people the possibility of "earning their way" to heaven. The Council insisted, however, that it is Christ working in the sacraments that makes them efficacious. Christ's presence in the sacraments, the Council said, means that God always takes the initiative in giving grace through the sacraments. Thus for the Council of Trent, the grace of the sacraments is not "earned," as the Protestants said. Rather, in the sacraments, the believer responds in faith to God's initiative.

THE JESUITS:
PUTTING TRENT'S DECREES INTO ACTION

Historically, the hierarchy had shown itself to be inadequate at implementing its own reform. Thus, all that was needed for the decrees of the Council of Trent to be implemented was someone to implement them. The Catholic Church found this "someone" in the Society of Jesus—the Jesuits. This religious society was founded by a Basque knight named Ignatius Loyola (1495-1556). Like Luther in many respects, Loyola was scrupulous and stern in his faith. Unlike Luther, he had been converted from a life of pleasure. He became the most ardent advocate of Catholicism in the entire age of Reformation. In opposition to the Protestant doctrines, Loyola and the Jesuits preached "the Tridentine faith." (The word *Tridentine* referred to the dogma clarified at Trent.)

Showing his military perspective on things, Loyola made his followers take a vow "to serve the Roman pontiff as God's vicar on earth and to execute immediately and without hesitation or excuse all that the reigning pope or his successors may enjoin upon them." Loyola wrote that the Jesuits "ought always to be ready to believe that what seems to us white is black if the hierarchical Church so defines it." Within twenty-five years of their founding in 1540, the Jesuits had attracted over a thousand of the most educated, zealous, reform-minded men in Europe.

They fanned out from Rome on missions into every corner of the globe. They became the leading Catholic educators and missionaries, both in Europe and in the new world. After the Jesuits' founding, Loyola himself served as "general" or administrator of the Society. His associates, Francis Xavier, Peter Faber, Peter Canisius, Francis Borgia, James Laynez and other first-generation Jesuits, spread the Tridentine faith throughout the world. The Jesuits stemmed the Protestant tide. After they began preaching, no further principalities or countries in Europe would go over to Protestantism.

HEALTHY REFORM—
AND REFORM TO AN EXCESS—
UNDER POPE PAUL IV

Healthy reform. What happened to the Catholic Church because of the Council of Trent? The most obvious answer is that the Catholic Church now took reform seriously. The Jesuits took the lead by setting a no-compromise example of poverty, chastity and obedience. These vows had always been professed by the clergy, but now the clergy started to live them. The entire climate changed within the Church. Popes and bishops quit winking at corruption. They insisted that the lower clergy lead moral lives. Bishops were appointed to their sees and told to live there. They could not be absentee administrators as before. Further, they could no longer serve as bishop or abbot of more than one benefice (place) at a time. The Catholic Church also moved against simony by prohibiting the sale of Church offices.[5]

It likewise banned nepotism by prohibiting the appointment of one's relatives to Church offices, a practice that had been common during the Renaissance.

Reform to an excess. The man who first imposed many of these tough restrictions was Pope Paul IV (1555-1559). Paul was known for his iron will and no-nonsense attitude toward Church reform. In a sense, he became a Catholic Calvin. Paul instructed the magistrate who administered the city of Rome to punish immoral conduct as a violation of the civil law. The pope also proclaimed that no book could be published unless it first cleared the Church's censors. The book must then bear the word *Imprimatur*, which means, "Let it be printed." In 1559, Paul published an *Index of Forbidden*

---

[5] This was principally a reaffirmation of earlier Councils' (Chalcedon [451] and Third Lateran [1179]) condemnations of simony.

Books and ordered mass burning of suspect books. All Protestant works plus any Catholic works critical of Rome were consigned to the flames. Paul then restored the dreaded Inquisition.[6]

The pope turned the Inquisition into a means of persecution every bit as intolerant as the methods used in Calvin's Geneva. Tolerance and acceptance of religious differences were not to be permitted within the Catholic Church. As Paul himself wrote, "No man must debase himself by showing toleration toward heretics of any kind, above all toward Calvinists." The Inquisition eventually became a means of Church-sponsored terrorism. One contemporary cardinal observed, "From no other judgement seat on earth were more horrible and fearful sentences to be expected." Pope Paul even had people burned at the stake "by proxy." When the Inquisition acquitted a cardinal whom Paul had accused of heresy, the pope burned the accused's brother at the stake instead.

TOWARD THE AGE OF RELIGIOUS INTOLERANCE

Was Paul's papacy an aberration? The Jesuit Peter Canisius said of Paul, "Even the best Catholics disapprove of such rigor." Paul's successor, Pius IV (1559-1565), sought to distance himself from Paul's tactics by telling the papal inquisitors to "proceed with gentlemanly courtesy rather than with monkish harshness." Yet, the damage had been done. Paul's actions encouraged overzealous Protestant reformers, in effect, to go the Catholics one better. Protestants thus developed their own cruel and violent means to squelch Catholicism.

In the next chapter we shall see how the Reformation degenerated into a battle to prove one's own faith "right" and the other side's faith "wrong." At first a *debate over doctrine*, the Reformation would now be a *war among Christians* seeking to outdo each other by their intolerance. The age of "us versus them" in the Church had arrived.

---

[6] This was the "Congregation of the Inquisition," which was the final court of appeal from the lower inquisitions. It had been established by Pope Paul III in 1542.

FOCUS 27

MOVING FROM THE COUNCIL OF TRENT TO VATICAN II

Until about 1965, Catholics and Protestants alike thought that Catholicism came only in one "package." Then Vatican II came along and showed that the way in which Catholics practice the traditional faith can change. While this encouraged many Protestants, it frightened many Catholics. Most Catholics of that era had grown up as Tridentine Catholics, but without realizing this. The Catholic Church had been very self-assured and strict in its preaching of Tridentine Catholicism. Thus, most Catholics didn't realize that this model of the Church went back only to the sixteenth century, and that it was not incapable of being updated. For example, priests wearing Italian *birettas* (liturgical hats), nuns dressed in seventeenth-century French costumes, believers "going to confession" in a dark box, celebrating Mass in Latin and in the manner defined at Trent, were all mistakenly thought of by many Catholics as the way things had always been done in the Church.

In fact, Trent introduced many innovations into the practice of Catholicism. The sixteenth-century model of the Church was no more valid than that of the tenth century, or the eighth or the fourth. Yet, until Vatican II, the Catholic Church often made it seem as though only Trent's version of Catholicism was valid.

A famous Catholic theologian, Bernard Lonergan, S.J., once said of Tridentine doctrine on the eve of Vatican II that "It was so fixed and inflexible that it did not require a mind to think it." Vatican II changed that. Vatican II showed Catholics that the faith of the apostles could be professed in a twentieth-century model. No longer was it necessary for Catholics to live in the sixteenth century. Yet, Trent's lesson is valuable. Vatican II is not carved in stone either. Once the Catholic Church implements the teachings of Vatican II, it must then move onward toward the new and the unknown. Christianity is ever looking forward. To present the gospel in only one "package" is to restrict the work of the Spirit, who continually makes all things new.

FOCUS 28

TERESA OF AVILA:
A WOMAN CONTRIBUTES TO CHURCH REFORM

Not many would think of the mystic Saint Teresa of Avila (1515-1582) as a Church reformer. Yet, her entire life was in one sense dedicated to reforming the Church. To begin with, when she was prioress of her Carmelite convent in Avila, Spain, Teresa was widely sought out by male Church leaders for spiritual direction. The life of contemplative holiness that Teresa passed on to her spiritual disciples radiated throughout the Church. Teresa could be blunt in her correctives. Like Saint Catherine of Siena before her, Teresa did not shrink from telling powerful bishops and cardinals to reform their lives and turn to the gospel.

Teresa's most lasting contributions to the age of the Reformation were her writings: *Vida*, *The Way of Perfection* and *The Interior Castle*. In them she encouraged Christians to devote themselves to contemplative prayer. She defines this prayer as "friendly intercourse and frequent solitary converse with Him Who we know loves us." Teresa was a great mystic, blessed with amazing insights into the ways of God. In one of her visions she was granted a special insight of the Trinity, the greatest of mysteries. Yet, Teresa constantly stressed that the way of contemplative holiness was for everyone, and not just for monks and nuns shut away in monasteries.

She also stressed that the purpose of contemplative prayer is to lead Christians toward service of the Church. Teresa practiced what she preached. She would often interrupt her solitary prayer life to attend to the most mundane duties of her convent, or to counsel someone whose faith needed strengthening. She was truly a contemplative in action. Her faith and her teachings spread throughout the Catholic world. She motivated Catholics to achieve the only true "Church reform" that is possible—the reform of the human heart from within by the power of the Spirit.

CHAPTER FIFTEEN

THE REFORMATION: ITS BLEAK AFTERMATH

NOT SUCH STRANGE BEDFELLOWS

In this chapter we will discuss the political situation in Europe during the seventeenth century. In doing this, however, we will not be departing from Church history. The reason is simple. In the seventeenth century religion meant politics and politics meant religion. In the minds of seventeenth-century Christians, religion and politics didn't make strange bedfellows at all. No one in that age believed in separation of Church and state. In fact, everyone believed in the *coalescence* of Church and state. The problem started when the state advanced a religion in which some people did not believe. Then the tragedy for the Christian Church became evident.

Protestants and Catholics were constantly at each others' throats. Further, various types of Protestants violently fought with each other. This religious hatred and intolerance would eventually lead to a devastating war—more devastating in its effect on Europe than even World War II. The war and devastation in turn would lead to a climate of religious indifference and cynicism.

The seventeenth century started off with Christians fighting with each other to establish their respective beliefs as superior to all others. The century ended with many people "burnt-out" over Christians' profoundly unchristian behavior. By the start of the eighteenth century—the "Age of Enlightenment"—many educated Europeans didn't want anything to do with Christianity in *any* form.

A HATRED-FILLED CONTINENT

A quick tour around seventeenth-century Europe does not present a pleasant picture for advocates of the gospel. The gospel got lost in sectarian hatred and intolerance. To give a highly generalized picture, we could summarize the situation as follows.

The great competing powers are no longer the German Empire and France. England has come to the fore as Europe's principal contestant with France for prestige and power. Catholic Spain, defeated on all fronts by Protestant England, is slowly slipping from the stage of history, except for her American colonies. The Scandinavian countries, largely Lutheran, get drawn into the conflicts and shifting religious alliances among the larger countries. The new player on the board is the Netherlands, highly important despite its size, because of its educated citizenry and advanced commercialism. Religious hatred will divide these "Low Countries" into Protestant Holland and Catholic Flanders, with Catholic Belgium gradually asserting its own separate identity.

The warfare and rivalry among the European powers extend to their colonies in the new world. We will take up the story of the non-European Church in the next chapter.

Finally, the bishop of Rome loses more and more influence among the states of Europe. Lost in its own conflicts and uncertainty, the Catholic Church seeks in vain to regain its lost political authority. Princes, and not prelates, will henceforth guide the destiny of the European states and their colonies.

Let's turn now to some important details of this generalized picture.

ENGLAND: PURITANS VERSUS ANGLICANS VERSUS CATHOLICS

The Puritans. The Anglican faith did not appeal to all Protestants. Many felt that Anglicanism was still too Catholic. If judged by external rituals and observances, such critics were right. Yet, a chasm still separated English Catholics and Anglicans. That chasm was authority. Anglicans may have kept some Catholic externals, but they utterly rejected papal authority. They also greatly feared ever coming again under the control of a Catholic monarch. The Puritans, for their part, were much more Calvinist than the Anglicans. They felt that the Anglican Reformation had gone only halfway. They wanted to rid the Church of any vestige of "popish superstition," as they characterized the Catholic tendencies within Anglicanism. Their intention was to "purify" the Church of England—hence their name *Puritans*.

Stuarts versus Puritans. The great anxiety in England involved who would rule the country. The Stuart family had replaced the Tudors (Henry VIII's family) as monarchs. The Stuarts were Scottish rather than English. The Scottish crown had long been associated by marriage with Catholic France. Thus, the English suspected that the Stuart monarchs were at heart Catholics, even though formally Anglican. The second Stuart king, Charles I, was married to the sister of the French king. The Puritans feared that Charles was a Catholic at heart. He instructed the Anglican archbishop of Canterbury to make the Anglican faith even more Catholic in appearance than it already was.

By 1640, the Puritans had gained control of Parliament. They accused

King Charles of plotting a Catholic takeover of England. Their leader, Oliver Cromwell, eventually came to power and had Charles beheaded. Cromwell tried to make England into another Calvin's Geneva. For five dreary years Cromwell and the Puritans turned merry England into a drab, cultural backwater. Most of the English hated it. Anglicans returned to power and drove Cromwell out. The new king, Charles II, longed to be a Catholic, but was persuaded by his advisors to remain at least an ostensible Anglican. On his deathbed, he converted to Catholicism.

Parliament intervenes. Parliament feared a Catholic resurgence under Charles's brother, James, who became King James II in 1685. The Anglican Parliament controlled the country. Persecution of Catholics reached an all-time high. It was a capital offense to be a Catholic priest in England. Lacking good sense, King James made Catholicism fashionable again at his court. He elevated four Catholic bishops to a position of equality with the Anglican bishops. This was the last straw. Parliament expelled James from the throne and made James's Protestant daughter, Mary, queen.

Then Parliament brought in a Protestant prince, William, from Holland to marry the queen. Beginning in 1689, the couple ruled jointly as William and Mary—Protestant monarchs first, last and always. In installing the royal couple, Parliament declared, "It hath been found by experience that it is inconsistent with the safety and welfare of this Protestant kingdom to be governed by a popish prince." Catholics went underground; Puritans went to America. England would remain steadfastly Anglican in its orientation until the Wesleyan (Methodist) movement of the eighteenth century.

FRANCE: 'ONE KING, ONE LAW, ONE FAITH'

During the seventeenth century, it would have been inaccurate to speak of the "Roman Catholic Church in France." A more accurate label would have been, "The National French Catholic Church." France remained Catholic, but Catholic in belief only. When it came to authority, France was staunchly independent.

Dealing with Rome. Actually, there were two schools of thought on the issue of France's ties to Rome. One school of thought was called *Ultramontanism*. This word came from two Latin words that literally meant, "beyond the mountains." In other words, this camp believed that France should align itself with centralized papal authority beyond the Alps in Rome. The other school of thought was called *Gallicanism*. This word comes from the Latin for "Gaul," or France. Members of this camp insisted on a completely independent Catholic Church in France.

Richelieu and the national Church. During the seventeenth century, the Gallican party was much more powerful and influential than the Ultramontanist party.

This was so largely because of the two strong personalities who governed France during the century. The first was Cardinal Richelieu (1585-1642). Formally, he was chief advisor to King Louis XIII (1610-1643). In actuality, he was the power behind the throne and ran the country. Richelieu turned the Catholic Church in France into a nationalized Church—just as the English rulers had turned their Anglican Church into a nationalized Church.

One example of how this nationalized French Church operated under Richelieu involves his treatment of the Huguenots (the French Protestants). Richelieu led a war against them in order to limit their political power. But as soon as the Huguenots were defeated, he opened French society to them, thereby using their skills and education for the good of the country. This annoyed Rome to no end. The Vatican wanted the Huguenots to remain second-class citizens. Richelieu, however, was more interested in *French* power than in Catholic power. To prove this, he spent a good deal of his energy making alliances with Protestant princes to fight the Austrian Catholic emperor.[1]

Louis XIV. The second great personality of the seventeenth century was King Louis XIV (1643-1715). Louis believed in and successfully practiced absolute monarchy. His motto was "I am the state." Louis's power and influence in Europe made the seventeenth century the French century. French language and culture swept over Europe, much like American TV shows today are watched around the globe. As for religion, Louis's policy was summarized in the slogan, "One king, One law, One faith." In other words, for Louis, law and religion were inseparable. The king embodied the nation and he also embodied the French Church. In addition to saying "I am the state," he could just as well have said, "I am the French Church."

In 1682 Louis promulgated "the Four Articles." The Articles invalidated the pope's authority over temporal matters, proclaimed Church councils superior to popes, reaffirmed the king's right to name French bishops, and denied that the pope was infallible unless his teaching agreed with that of a Church council. Louis's action made the French Catholic Church every bit as independent from Rome as any German prince's state-run Protestant Church, or as independent as the Anglican Church in England. The only tie that the French Church had to Rome was its loyalty to Catholic dogma and Catholic devotional practice. Rome sat by, helpless to deter Louis from his course of nationalizing the French Church. Eventually, Louis modified his policies. Yet, he still retained the right to name French bishops.

Persecution of Protestants. Beginning about 1661, Louis reversed Richelieu's policy of tolerating the Huguenots. Instead, he began to persecute them, depriving them of both religious and civil liberties. He even housed French troops in Huguenot homes. This policy was known as "the drag-

---

[1] The former Holy Roman Emperors of Germany were now members of the Austrian Hapsburg family, whose capital was Vienna.

onnades." It infuriated and frightened the Huguenots to such an extent that they began fleeing the country. On one side of the Channel—France—Protestants were being persecuted. On the other side—England—Catholics suffered the same fate. Underlying both policies was the quest for power on the part of strong rulers who didn't want religious dissenters to sidetrack their political plans.

Even though there was no "Protestant problem" in France, the country was wracked by religious turmoil nonetheless. The principle issues were belief versus unbelief, and the *Jansenist* problem. Years of religious warfare, hatred and intolerance, and religious cynicism on the part of its rulers, had made France a very jaded country. Educated Catholics, principally in cities, scoffed at the Catholic faith—or at *any* faith. The country's most respected spiritual leader, Vincent de Paul (1580-1660), who founded the Sisters of Charity, observed that Mass attendance was shrinking drastically in France. Another contemporary observer wrote that in Paris, "Piety is turned to ridicule...and the disorder of religion has gone beyond anything ever seen in the Christian world."[2]

Jansenism. Then there was a problem to the other extreme: religious fanaticism as expressed in the heresy of Jansenism. This distortion of Catholic belief was named after a Dutch bishop, Cornelis Jansen (1585-1638). Jansen believed like Calvin, although he tried to say he didn't. In fact, he preached a doctrine of predestination that was pure Calvinism. French followers of Jansen were called Jansenists. Like Calvin's followers in Geneva, the Jansenists believed in an angry God who was very difficult to please. They thus walled themselves off from the wicked world and practiced self-mortification and asceticism.

A heated controversy began in 1642 when Pope Urban VI condemned Jansenism as a heresy. Meanwhile, Jansenists had started criticizing the Jesuits. They took exception to the Jesuits' practice of *casuistry*. Casuistry was a method of dispensing spiritual advice to penitents. Using casuistry, Jesuits tried to look at the totality of circumstances that led a person to sin, in order to determine if the sinner had lacked the will to do wrong. This seemed to the Jansenists to be too lenient on sinners. A group of Jansenist zealots at a French convent in Port-Royal[3] undertook a campaign against the Jesuits. The Jansenists' most famous supporter was the philosopher Blaise Pascal (1623-1662). Pascal called for French Catholics to return to the austerity and asceticism of the early Church.

France became polarized over Jansenism. Many Catholics regarded its rigorism and sternness as a way to return to authentic Catholicism. King Louis XIV, however, saw it as Protestantism in disguise. He thus moved to suppress

---

[2] Polls in France to this day regularly show that while a majority of the French regard themselves as Catholics, only about ten percent regularly attend the liturgy.

[3] Eighteen miles southwest of Paris.

it. The king's struggle to exterminate Jansenism made it all the stronger. Catholic France was roughly divided into two camps—those who didn't believe much of anything, and those who tried to outdo monks in their rigorism and purity. Among the latter group, Jansenism became very strong. By the eighteenth century, one contemporary journalist opined, Catholic France had become "Jansenist from top to bottom."

Jansenism's legacy. Much of Catholicism in France had become distorted. It emphasized suffering rather than joy, angelic purity rather than the goodness of creation, the wrath of God rather than God's mercy, pessimism rather than hope. This gloomy vision was passed on to future generations of Catholics as the authentic presentation of the Catholic faith.

GERMANY IN SHAMBLES

Germany, the home of the Reformation, continued to disintegrate into a welter of religious factions. By 1600, the greatest hatred was not among Catholics and Lutherans, but among Lutherans and Calvinists. Religious bigotry flourished. Lutheran writers called Calvinists "baptized Jews and Mohammedans."

Just as the Reformation owed its existence to the printing press, so now religious bigotry fed the presses of Germany. One historian had counted eighteen hundred religious tracts printed in Germany in 1618 dedicated to the condemnation of one version of Christianity or another. For the times, this was a huge number. It might have been similar to the entire output of all American publishing houses for one year.

With all the verbal warfare, actual warfare could not be far behind. It had been brewing for years, and finally began in 1618. The war lasted until 1648, and hence is called The Thirty Years' War. Like everything else connected to religion during this period, politics and the lust for power overshadowed the religious motives for the war.

The Thirty Years' War was one of the most savage in all history. Religious hatred raised the fighting man's capacity for cruelty and barbarism to a new level. Had Europe had the same population during the Thirty Years' War that it had during World War II, the casualties of the former would have been twice those of the latter. As it was, Germany and Austria alone suffered a combined population decline of some eight million people because of the war—a percentage unprecedented in the history of warfare.

It is unnecessary to our study of Church history to examine the war in detail. All that is germane to our task is to speak of the effect of the war on the life of Christians. Through its clever manipulation of alliances and exploitation of religious intolerance, France came out the winner. Germany was the big loser. It was devastated by the war in every sense—physically, emotionally, morally. German victims of the war were reduced to eating dead animals, grass, tree bark and, in some cases, human flesh to survive.

Transportation and commerce were destroyed, keeping Germany far behind other nations until the nineteenth century.

The Peace of Westphalia (1648) granted Protestantism equal status with Catholicism in Germany. It made Calvinism legal. By now German Christians didn't care *what* religion people practiced, so long as there was no more bloodshed.

The real loser of the war was Christianity. The question that was in everyone's mind was this. How could followers of the "Prince of Peace" possibly justify the carnage and inhumanity of a war to the death for control of his Church? The answer many educated people arrived at was simple: There is no justification for warfare among Christians. Thus, it was argued, the people who were fighting with each other were not Christians. There are no Christians, such cynics said. The Christian gospel is a fraud. Educated Europeans thus looked to another source than the gospel for religious truth. They found it in the world view of the *philosophes* of the Enlightenment. (See Focus 30.)

THE SECULAR AGE IS BORN

Into the vacuum created by religious hatred among Christians stepped the French *philosophes*. These were intellectuals who proclaimed the death of the Christian God. The universe, they proclaimed, runs according to mechanical law that can be ascertained by scientific study. Science, not religion, leads humanity to the truth. Formerly Christian Europe eagerly heeded the new gospel of this Age of Enlightenment.

FOCUS 29

HAVE AMERICAN CATHOLICS SOMETIMES BEEN MORE JANSENIST THAN CHRISTIAN?

What was behind Jansenist spirituality? Ultimately it was an attempt to control the human passions through self-denial, mortification and asceticism. Why was control so essential to Jansenism? Because Jansenists feared that if they could not publicly demonstrate control of their passions, they had perhaps not really been chosen by God for salvation after all. A person predestined to salvation, it was thought, will act in a certain way. Calvinists who professed the "Puritan ethic" said that a person can judge whether one has been saved by looking at how hard one works and how much wealth one achieves. Jansenists said that a person can judge whether one has been saved by seeing how "pure"—usually meaning asexual—one's life is.

Have American Catholics sometimes been Jansenist? Look at our history. Many of our churches and schools were founded and staffed by Irish priests and sisters. These were trained in seminaries and con-vents that were steeped in French theology and spiritual method. If one reads this French theology and spirituality closely, one will find in it an undeniable strain of Jansenism: "Deny your body, mortify your flesh, suffer, keep your nose to the grindstone, accept misery and shame as punishment for your sins."

Anyone raised in pre-Vatican II Catholic America will have to admit that Jansenism was a strong undercurrent of one's Catholic upbringing. Only rarely did one hear preached the theology contained in Jesus' words, "I came that they might have life and have it to the full" (John 10:10). Instead of focusing on the grandeur, victory and joy of Easter, Catholic spirituality in America focused on the pain and sorrow of Good Friday. Catholics were taught to be a *suffering* people, estimating how many days their aches and pains would get them out of purgatory. They were seldom taught to be a joyful people proclaiming the gospel of a savior who loves and saves us in spite of our sins.

FOCUS 30

A LOOK AT THE *PHILOSOPHES'* GOSPEL: ENTER THE MODERN AGE

The Enlightenment was a philosophical and scientific renaissance of the seventeenth and eighteenth centuries. How did the Age of Enlightenment's "gospel" differ from the Christian gospel? The Enlightenment stressed the perfectibility of the human person apart from God. Unaided by religion, Enlightenment thinkers said, humanity can find truth and live a life of happiness and progress. The French thinkers of the Enlightenment, called *philosophes*, became the enemies of organized religion, and especially of the Catholic Church. Their leader was Voltaire (1694-1778), whose motto was, "*Ecrasez L'Infame*," or "Crush the infamous [Catholic Church]." Voltaire explicitly traced the Enlightenment's doctrine back to the Reformation. He spoke of the Protestant Reformers as "our fathers." He said to the *philosophes*, "We must have the courage to go a few steps further."

The *philosophes* taught that only sensory knowledge can be trusted. Faith is an illusion and a superstition. One philosopher put it this way: "The nerves of the body are all there is to man." In their most famous work, the multi-volume *Encyclopédie*, the *philosophes* spelled out their gospel in more detail. Overall, it was an attempt to substitute science and reason for religion and faith. It saw the world purely in secular terms. And since the world we live in today is a secular world, we can say that the *philosophes* were the founding fathers of the modern age of liberalism. In this age science, the state, intellectual achievement and the cult of the body overshadow religion and the life of the spirit.

Indeed, the *philosophes* prophesied how the modern age would arrive and what it would look like. One of them wrote of "a great revolution coming in both religion and government." It will be an age, he said, that will "get rid of all revelation and mystery." Another wrote that the human soul was "an empty word." Still another wrote, "I would sacrifice my life if I could annihilate forever the notion of God." Another said, "Live for yourself.... The friend of mankind cannot be a friend of God, who at all times has been a real scourge to the earth."

Is the Enlightenment gospel or the Christian gospel more popular in the world today?

CHAPTER SIXTEEN

THE CHURCH
IN THE NEW WORLD

CATHOLIC OR EUROPEAN?

At this point in our study, the Church was no longer limited to a European environment. By chance or divine providence—take your pick—the age of Reformation and the age of European colonization coincided in time. The new world colonies received from their mother countries European culture and the European way of understanding Christianity. They likewise received all the problems, prejudices and religious conflicts that their mother countries were experiencing in the age of Reformation. Thus European colonization also meant the exportation of European religious turmoil.

Missionaries in that age—who were often in a combative state of mind to start with—were not likely to change when they encountered new peoples and new cultures. Often, as Catholic and Protestant evangelists traveled to non-European regions of the world, they took with them the "us-versus-them" mentality that they had grown up with in Europe. Often, missionaries looked upon native peoples as potential "points" to be scored in a contest with an opposition Christian body. The native peoples were "souls to be won" for one's side in the contest. The letters, diaries and journals of famous Catholic missionaries, for example, are full of stories of "winning the savages" to the "one, true faith"—and "for the glory of our most Catholic monarch." By this approach to missionary work, Christian evangelists brought their European perspective on the gospel to native peoples. They did not consider that the native peoples may have wanted to look at the gospel from their own perspective. Missionaries felt that once native persons were baptized, they should act not only in a Christian way but in a *European* way.[1]

This attitude caused tremendous hardships for the native peoples. In many instances native people couldn't swallow the European baggage associated with the missionaries' evangelization efforts. In some places, native people who didn't accept baptism were punished or even put to death by soldiers

---

[1] This was another version of the same tendency the Church had shown when it first moved out of its Mediterranean base into the barbarian kingdoms. See Chapter Three.

accompanying the missionaries. In South America, for example, whole tribes of native peoples were wiped out by Spanish soldiers for resisting colonization and the accompanying evangelization effort of Spanish missionaries.

Catholic Spain and Catholic France were initially much more successful at colonizing than was Protestant England. Thus, since most European missionaries were Catholic, the Catholic Church in particular was responsible for exporting European culture along with the gospel. Yet, many Catholic missionaries gradually realized the problems associated with preaching the gospel in a completely different culture than the one they had known in Europe.

Early on, Jesuit and Franciscan missionaries were confronted with the problem of what to do about native customs among their converts. This was nothing new. The Apostles themselves had this problem. Consider, for example, the account in Acts about the dilemma caused by the admission of Gentiles into a largely Jewish Christian Church (see, for example, Acts 15).

The Jesuit experiment. The Jesuits were great innovators in the area of evangelizing native peoples. They went to China and Japan and learned Asian languages and culture. When they went to evangelize at the courts of Asian leaders, they would dress as orientals, and relate the Christian gospel to Asian religion. The Jesuit Matteo Ricci (1552-1610), for example, wrote a book in Chinese for the educated Chinese, as well as a Chinese Catechism for catechumens and the many converts he made.

The Apostle Paul had done the same thing. In his mission to Athens, for example, he had addressed his audience not in the rabbinical style he used elsewhere, but in the Greek style, using arguments from Greek philosophy (see Acts 17:22-34). Paul became "all things to all, to save at least some" (1 Corinthians 9:22).

Yet, Rome was displeased with some of the Jesuit experiments. Rome ordered Jesuit missionaries not to stretch Christian dogma too far in adapting it to the non-Christian religions. This raised the question whether Rome was interested in the *evangelization* of the native peoples or in the *Europeanization* of these peoples. Consider, for example, the tragic story of the Jesuit missionary, Roberto dé Nobili (d. 1656). Son of a prominent Italian family, dé Nobili went to India to spread the gospel. So long as he dressed and taught like a European, he got nowhere.

Then he changed his method. He dressed in the robes of Brahmin priests, practiced meditation as they did, and taught the gospel from a perspective which the Brahmins would understand. As the Brahmins (who were the highest caste) converted to the gospel, they brought thousands of lower-caste Hindus into the Church. By some estimates, after dé Nobili had changed his tactics, he supervised the conversion to Christianity of over one hundred thousand Indians. Yet, Rome ordered him to quit using the innovative strategy he had devised for preaching the gospel.

A change of attitude. Nowadays, the Catholic Church honors and respects native and local customs, and attempts wherever possible to integrate these customs into its preaching and liturgy. Consider, for example, Pope John Paul's trip to the American southwest, where he celebrated a liturgy fashioned after a traditional Native American ceremony.

Then, too, we must acknowledge that the first Christian missionaries to the new world were often confronted with native ways that were clearly opposed not only to the gospel but to human dignity. For example, the Mayas in Mexico practiced human sacrifice in their religion. Christian missionaries— European or not—could hardly have incorporated beliefs and practices of this sort into their gospel message.

ROME AND THE AGE OF REVOLUTION

Beginning in the late eighteenth century, another problem complicated the spread of Christianity to the new world. Enlightenment ideas[2] as discussed in the last chapter, were breeding political revolutions all over Europe. Revolutionary sentiment spread to America, where Enlightenment thinkers like Benjamin Franklin and Thomas Jefferson became prominent leaders in the movement for American independence. In Europe, the center for revolution and revolutionary ideas was France.

Revolutionary France and the Catholic Church. The French revolution of 1789 was based on the idealistic slogan, "liberty, equality, fraternity." When the revolutionaries came to power, they revealed another side to their agenda. They were virulently anti-clerical and anti-Church. And in France, of course "anti-Church" meant anti-Catholic. For the French revolutionaries, the Church stood for wealth, privilege, superstition and all the customs and traditions which enslaved people rather than set them free. When the alliance of throne and altar was toppled (as in the French Revolution), Catholics paid a heavy price.

Under the dictator Maximilien Robespierre (1758-1794), for example, the French government forced priests to take an oath in support of revolutionary ideas as contained in the revolutionary manifesto, *Declaration of the Rights of Man and the Citizen.* Pope Pius VI condemned this document and forbade French Catholics from adhering to its doctrine. When French priests refused to take the oath, Robespierre put hundreds of them to death, closed churches and confiscated Church property all over France.

Later, when Napoleon came to power, things improved for the Church. Napoleon was practical rather than ideological. He realized he needed the Catholic lower classes to fight his wars of conquest. He thus entered into a *Concordat* (1801) with Rome. The *Concordat* restored to the Catholic Church

---

[2] In this context, the Enlightenment meant a distrust of authority and tradition, both religious and political, and the belief that through reason alone humanity could bring about justice, morality and material prosperity.

many of its lost privileges. One by-product of the *Concordat* was that it steered French Catholicism away from *Gallicanism* to *Ultramontanism*, or, as we discussed in the last chapter, the desire to have Church authority centralized in Rome.

Napoleon dealt directly with the pope, bypassing the French bishops. The bishops were thus no longer as important to the national French Church as they had been under Louis XIV. Further, French Catholics now began to look to Rome for protection from their government's arbitrary religious policies. Submission to Italian prelates didn't look as bad as it did in the days of Louis XIV. Now, many French Catholics looked upon Rome as the preserver of order, and stability and tradition. When Napoleon was defeated a second time, the European Congress of Vienna (1815) brought monarchy back with its trusted ally, the Church.

Rome's attitude toward the new ideas. Rome was horrified by the revolutionary ideas spreading throughout the world. It placed all such ideas under the heading of "liberalism," and condemned liberalism as anti-Christian. To the popes of the day, revolutionary ideas were nothing less than Protestant reform doctrines dressed up in different garb. Rome most detested the concepts of popular democracy and separation of Church and State. Rome wanted society to be run the old way, with aristocrats protecting the Church's interests and the lower classes humbly submitting to the authority of prince and prelate. Europe became divided between *reactionaries* who opposed the spread of democracy, and *liberals* who favored it. The vast majority of Catholics, encouraged by Rome, were reactionaries.

As just one example of Rome's hostility to the new democratic ideas, consider the encyclical *Mirari Vos*, written by Pope Gregory XVI in 1832. In it, the pope defined liberalism as "this false and absurd maxim, or better this madness, that everyone should have and practice freedom of conscience."[3]

As for freedom of the press, the pope called it, "this loathsome freedom which one cannot despise too strongly." Little wonder, then, that the new democratic governments looked upon Rome as the bastion of reaction, royalism and conservatism. Little wonder also that citizens in the new democracies feared allowing Catholics to enter fully into the democratic process. People in the new democracies asked themselves, "Can democracy and the Catholic Church coexist in the same country?" and, "Can Catholics truly be citizens of a democratic nation?"

Let's now look at the significance of such questions for the life of the Catholic Church in the most prominent of the new democracies, the United States of America.

---

[3] "Acts of Gregory XVI," pp. 169-174, in Hubert Jedin, ed., *History of the Church* (New York: Crossroad, 1982), vol. VII, p. 287.

CATHOLICISM IN AMERICA: A STRUGGLE FOR RESPECTABILITY

Until the 1960's, Catholics in America were constantly involved in a struggle for respectability. In other words, they constantly had to prove that they could be both loyal Americans and faithful Catholics at the same time. This was a *twofold* struggle. Catholics had to earn respectability *at home*, from non-Catholic citizens. Catholics also had to earn respectability *away from home*, in Rome.

At home, non-Catholics feared that Catholics could not be loyal citizens of a democratic republic. Non-Catholics feared that Catholics' first allegiance would be to Rome. Ironically, Rome had the opposite fear. Rome feared that Catholics in America would become too "American-minded" in their thinking. That is, Rome feared that American Catholics would be converted to democratic ideals and quit supporting a hierarchical Church in which democracy was regarded as evil.

American Catholics were thus stuck in a very difficult position. They had to convince their fellow citizens that they were loyal Americans. At the same time, they had to convince the Church in Rome that they were faithful Catholics. In the present chapter, let's look at the first problem American Catholics had to face—the struggle for respectability at home. In the next chapter, we will consider how American Catholics had to win respectability in Rome.

ANTI-CATHOLIC SENTIMENT IN AMERICA

Right from the start, Protestant colonists (the vast majority) in what would be the original thirteen states, demonstrated their strong anti-Catholic bias. Every colony placed restrictions on Catholics' liberties.[4] No colony would permit them to serve in a leadership capacity in colonial government. Some colonies placed even harsher restrictions on Catholics, such as refusing to allow them to settle permanently. In the early days, Catholics were sometimes exiled from a given colony, depending on the attitude of a particular colonial governor.

The Maryland experiment. One colony that tried to tolerate people of all faiths was Maryland. Maryland became home to more Catholics than any other colony. It had been founded by Cecil Calvert, Lord Baltimore. He had lost his post as England's Secretary of State because he had converted to Catholicism. He came to America intent on founding a colony in which Protestants and Catholics could live together in peace. On March 25, 1634, this first colony in America dedicated to religious freedom was founded. In

---

[4] Since the original thirteen colonies were tied to England, and since England itself barely tolerated Catholics (Catholics were excluded from Parliament until 1829, for example), it was natural to expect the English colonists to bring anti-Catholic fears and attitudes with them to America.

1649, the colonial legislature passed the historic Toleration Act, which made Lord Baltimore's policies of religious freedom the law of the colony. At that time the colony was independent of the English Crown. It was still Lord Baltimore's private "patent."

In 1652, Puritans seized power in Maryland. Catholics were driven from public office. Some were put to death by Puritan leaders. The Toleration Act was repealed. In 1691, Maryland became a Crown colony. The Anglican Church became the official Church of the colony. Catholics were taxed against their wills for the Anglican Church's support. Catholic religious services were forbidden. Catholics could not hold public office and could not vote. As bad as things were in Maryland, they often were even worse in other Crown colonies.

Yet, in the midst of this persecution, Catholics proved their loyalty to America. Let's stay with Maryland as an example. As the revolutionary period approached, the prominent Carroll family became leaders of the independence movement in Maryland. Charles Carroll (1737-1832) was invited to sign the Declaration of Independence on behalf of the colony, and he did so with a flourish. He added "of Carrollton" after his signature, explaining, "Now King George will know with which Carroll he is dealing!"

Charles's cousin, Daniel Carroll, greatly influenced the drafting of the Constitution. His leadership was largely responsible for the drafters' rejection of a proposal to have the president elected by Congress, rather than directly by the people. He likewise persuaded the Constitutional Convention to add the tenth amendment[5] to the Bill of Rights. After his service to the Constitution, Daniel Carroll was chosen by the Continental Congress along with two other men to select the site of the national capitol. He alone chose the present site for the White House.

Finally, Daniel's younger brother, John Carroll, was named first bishop of Baltimore in 1789—the first Catholic bishop in the United States. Although appointed by the pope, Carroll had been nominated by the American priests after Rome sought the priests' views on who would be the best candidate. This was a privilege that would be denied to the American priests after Carroll's appointment. Following Carroll's appointment, Rome would once again directly and without consultation from Americans appoint American bishops.

ANTI-CATHOLICISM AFTER INDEPENDENCE

With the adoption of the First Amendment[6] in 1789 and its guarantee of religious freedom to all citizens, Catholics should have experienced a reversal of their misfortunes. This was not necessarily the case. At this early stage of

---

[5] "The powers not delegated to the United States by the Constitution, nor prohibited by it to the states, are reserved to the states respectively, or to the people."

[6] The opening clause of this Amendment provides, "Congress shall make no law respecting an establishment of religion, or prohibiting the free exercise thereof...."

American history, the Supreme Court had not yet extended the liberties of the Bill of Rights to citizens of the various states. Thus, although the *federal* government was prohibited from discriminating against Catholics, *state* governments were not. For example, New Hampshire, North Carolina, New York, New Jersey, Delaware, Pennsylvania and Georgia explicitly restricted public office to "citizens other than Papists."

Anti-Catholic sentiment began to mount in the 1830's when President Jackson appointed the Catholic jurist, Roger Taney, Chief Justice. Then, President Franklin Pierce named William Campbell the first Catholic cabinet member. Anti-Catholic newspapers reviled the selections of "Romanists in government." The so-called Native American party, founded in 1837, mounted a campaign to limit immigration from abroad to persons from Protestant countries in Europe. In 1852, the Know-Nothing Party was founded. Its members claimed to "know nothing" about what its policies were. Yet, it was obvious that the principal agenda of the party was to persecute Catholics and restrict their civil rights in America.

The Know-Nothings were responsible for stirring up anti-Catholic riots. In some cases, they murdered Catholics in their homes. The Know-Nothings gained control of several state legislatures. They secured passage of "nunnery inspection" laws, which made it legal to invade convents at any hour of the day or night. The Know-Nothings also saw to it that Catholics in some cities were kept from polling places on election day.

Public opinion and Supreme Court decisions eventually reduced the Know Nothings' power. Abraham Lincoln was a strong opponent of the party. He wrote that, because of parties like the Know-Nothings, the Declaration of Independence had virtually been changed to read, "All men are created equal, except Negroes and foreigners and Catholics. When it comes to this," Lincoln said, "I shall prefer emigrating to some country like Russia where they make no pretense of loving liberty."

The Civil War proved that Catholics could be loyal citizens—whether of the Confederacy or of the Union. Yet, after the Civil War, the Ku Klux Klan was founded. Its main purpose was to oppress blacks, but it also had a strong anti-Catholic (and anti-Jewish) agenda. After World War I, the Klan's membership rose to perhaps ten million men. It was largely responsible for the campaign against the first Catholic presidential candidate, Al Smith, who lost the election of 1928.

TOWARD RESPECTABILITY ON THE HOME FRONT

Yet, the vast majority of Americans no longer believed the anti-Catholic propaganda of groups like the Know-Nothings and the Klan. American Catholics had sacrificed too much blood and energy on behalf of their country for anti-Catholicism to remain credible. Then, too, by the turn of the twentieth century, vast waves of immigration from Catholic countries had greatly increased Catholic population, resulting in increased Catholic political clout. By 1960, when John F. Kennedy was elected the first Catholic president, American Catholics were no longer regarded as second-class citizens. They had won their struggle for respectability on the home front. Would they be as successful in their effort to gain respectability from Rome?

FOCUS 31

THE SPANISH IN AMERICA: REVISING THE WAY WE UNDERSTAND AMERICAN HISTORY

History is written from the perspective of "winners," rather than of "losers." Nowhere has this been more true than in the writing of American history. Every American school child learns of the English contribution to the settling of America. The colonies of the Atlantic seaboard are the starting place for the usual history textbook's discussion of American history. This focus on the English experience gives the impression that "America" initially meant only the English colonies. And since English values are upheld as superior to all others, English Protestantism is upheld as the norm of American religion.

In actuality, early America meant more than the English, Protestant experience in America. Leaving aside the reality that "American" can in truth be applied only to the native peoples who were already here, who were the first European American settlers? Clearly, the Spanish. They were exploring and settling Florida and the American southwest well before the English settled Jamestown in 1607. True, the English colonies were more significant to the future development of the new republic. But all during the early period of American history, the nation continued to expand in the Spanish southwest and in Spanish California. In fact, judging by today's results, we could say that the Spanish contributed as much to the founding of America as did the English. California is now the most populous state. It is inconceivable to imagine California history without the Spanish contribution. Its four most populous cities, Los Angeles, San Diego, San Jose and San Francisco, derive their names and their tradition from the Spanish.

In short, early America was not just an English, Protestant country. It was Spanish and Catholic as well.

FOCUS 32

AN AMERICAN CATHOLIC HALL OF FAME— THE 'TOP TWENTY-FIVE'

Attempts at selecting notable people in any field are risky. The same holds true for selecting a list of those American Catholics who made significant contributions as Catholics to their country. At the risk of giving offense for leaving out many others who deserve to be here, let's make an arbitrary list, roughly in chronological order, of notable American Catholics.

1. *Francisco Vasquez de Coronado* Spanish explorer who opened up the southwestern United States to Spanish settlement.
2. *Pedro Menendez de Aviles* Founder of America's first city, St. Augustine, Florida.
3. *Francisco Eusebio Kino* Jesuit missionary to Arizona, founder of numerous churches and towns.
4. *Junipero Serra* Franciscan missionary to California, founder of nine missions that became cities.
5. *Isaac Jogues* Jesuit missionary to the Iroquois, martyred for the faith.
6. *Kateri Tekakwitha* Mohawk Christian, martyr and evangelist.
7. *Jacques Marquette* Jesuit Missionary to the upper Mississippi, explorer and geographer.
8. *Cecil Calvert, Lord Baltimore* Founder of Maryland
9. *Charles Carroll* Patriot, signer of the Declaration of Independence.
10. *Daniel Carroll* Patriot, shaper of the Constitution.
11. *John Carroll* First American bishop.
12. *John Barry* Founder of the American navy.
13. *Elizabeth Ann Seton* Founder of Sisters of Charity of Emmitsburg, Maryland, and of first parochial school.
14. *Catherine Spalding* First superior, Sisters of Charity of Nazareth.
15. *Roger Brook Taney* Chief justice of the United States.
16. *Kit Carson* Scout, explorer, mountain man.
17. *John-Baptiste Lamy* First archbishop of Santa Fe.
18. *Edward Sorin* Founder, University of Notre Dame.
19. *John Lancaster Spalding* Bishop of Peoria, "founding father of Catholic Education."
20. *Isaac Hecker* Founder of the Paulists, ecumenist.
21. *James Gibbons* Cardinal, author of *Faith of Our Fathers,* Archbishop of Baltimore.
22. *Theodore Hesburgh* President, University of Notre Dame.
23. *Dorothy Day* Social activist, founder, *Catholic Worker* movement.
24. *Thomas Merton* Monk, author, ecumenist.
25. *John F. Kennedy* First Catholic president.

CHAPTER SEVENTEEN

THE CHURCH REACTS TO THE MODERN WORLD

PIUS IX—'PIO NO-NO'—AS POPE

Years after the French Revolution in Europe and the establishment of a republic in the United States, Rome had refused to budge from its reactionary stance toward democracy. In the eyes of many in the Church hierarchy, modern times in their entirety were the work of the devil. This attitude became firmly entrenched with the election of Pope Pius IX in 1846. Seen as a liberal at first, Pius IX became reactionary after his expulsion from Rome by Italian nationalists in 1848. His Italian name, Pio Nono, is thought by some to be appropriate, since the Pope's policy was to say "no-no" to everything new.

The fortress mentality. The Congress of Vienna (1815) redrew the map of Europe and restored the monarchy in France. Alliance of throne and altar began anew, entering Europe into an age characterized by "the fortress mentality." According to this school of thought, the Catholic Church was the bastion of the truth, while the modern world was thoroughly wicked and the source of all lies. And, indeed, as the history of the twentieth century would affirm, there was much in the modern world that was wicked and false. The question became whether to engage the world or to wall oneself off from it. Rome seemed to think that the best that Catholics could do was to retreat to the "fortress" of Holy Mother Church and save themselves from the world's venomous attacks.[1]

During the era of the Reformation, "us versus them" had meant "we good Catholics versus those bad Protestants." Now, during the era of Pio Nono, "us versus them" meant "we Catholics, the preservers of Western Christian tradition" versus "those liberals who have perverted all that is decent and good in Western civilization."

---

[1] Another issue was understanding just what was an "attack." Certainly the writings of Karl Marx, for example, were incompatible in most respects with Christianity, but were his methods open to use by Christians?

"Liberalism" then and now. We should point out that "liberalism" in Pio Nono's day was not the same thing as it is today. Rather, liberalism in that era essentially meant opposition to a society governed by aristocracy. Influenced by the Enlightenment, liberalism also was characterized by belief in such innovations as freedom of speech and of the press, separation of Church and state, and by the belief that individuals through their own efforts can achieve their full potential as human beings.

True, some liberals were outright socialists, wanting the state to control society. Yet, many nineteenth-century "liberals" would, by today's standards, be very conservative. Most liberals of that age were not socialist. They would have opposed, for example, the large-scale involvement in the private sector by the government that characterized the presidency of Franklin D. Roosevelt. Thus, we should not imagine in the pages ahead that we are opposing one political philosophy in vogue today against another. It would be wrong, for example, to think that the Catholic hierarchy were conservative Republicans and all others were liberal Democrats.

What was it that made Pio Nono and the hierarchy so afraid of modern times? First, we should look at the reasons behind their fears. Liberalism as summarized in the teachings of the *philosophes* (see Chapter Fifteen) was in many ways contrary to the gospel. To the extent that Rome warned against a philosophy that ignored God and deified the human intellect, Rome was acting responsibly. Liberalism in this sense was anti-gospel, and Christians could not accept it.

But there was another side to liberalism. Not all liberal thinkers wanted to do away with God or turn human beings into deities unto themselves. Many liberal thinkers considered themselves loyal Catholics. They simply wanted human progress to be thought of in a more positive way. These liberals said that Jesus himself had set the example of how human beings should live. According to this school of liberalism, every human being has dignity and worth in the eyes of God. This is so regardless of the social or economic position into which a person is born. To the extent that the Church sides with the state in denying to individuals their God-given right to freedom and self-determination, the Church frustrates the will of God. In the eyes of Catholic liberal thinkers, not only was the gospel not opposed to democracy and individual freedom, it encouraged democracy and individual freedom.

To Rome, such ideas were frightening. The Church, Rome believed, knows what is best for "her children." Catholics flirt with disaster when they think they can decide for themselves what is the best way to live their lives. Things work best, Rome believed, in a world in which divinely appointed monarchs rule the state and divinely appointed prelates rule the Church. To many Catholics, Rome's ideas were hopelessly behind the times.

Yet, Pio Nono was firmly in control of Church thinking for thirty-two years (1846-1878). Rome was not about to look favorably upon the modern world. As odd as it may sound today, Vatican officials during Pius IX's papacy condemned use of the lightning rod, the steam engine and the telephone. Pio Nono's nickname became "the prisoner of the Vatican," because he so rarely ventured out into the world.

***The* Syllabus of Errors.** The Catholic Church's reactionary thinking especially manifested itself in the pope's broadside volley against liberalism—his notorious *Syllabus of Errors* (1864). The *Syllabus* was a list of eighty propositions condemned as erroneous. Among them were the following: The pope said that it was wrong for there to be public education of children in "any Christian State."[2] By this he meant that only Catholic schools should educate children in Catholic countries. (To the Pope's way of thinking, only Catholic countries were "Christian States.")

Pius IX proclaimed it erroneous to propose that "it is possible to please God in [the Protestant Church] as well as in the true Catholic Church."[3] He also stated it was erroneous to propose that the Church could not use force to impose its beliefs, or that it does not have temporal power. Likewise, the pope condemned the idea of separation between Church and state. By this he meant that the Catholic Church and Catholic aristocrats should jointly rule in Catholic countries. He likewise condemned the idea that Catholic countries should grant freedom of worship to other religions. It was error, the pope proclaimed, to propose "that each person is free to adopt and follow that religion which seems best to the light of reason."[4]

In a catch-all proposition, Pius stated it was erroneous to proclaim that the Pope "can and ought to recognize and harmonize himself with progress, with liberalism, and with modern civilization." By the pope's own words, the Catholic Church had made itself the enemy of modern times. Of course, it is important to remember that "modern civilization" and "progress" in Pius IX's Italy meant instances where Church property was seized, religious were expelled from their houses and belonging to a religious community was illegal. Given this context, some of his reactionary statements are more understandable.

Toward papal infallibility. Reading the *Syllabus of Errors* might prompt one to ask, "By whose authority was the pope making all these dire proclamations of error?" Had he consulted other bishops? Had he convened a council? Had he solicited the opinions of responsible Catholics? In fact, Pius IX had done none of these things. He believed that he was authorized in and of himself, as pope, to make such proclamations. Just as Louis XIV had said, "I am the state," Pius IX believed, "I am the Church." In fact, during one of his many temper tantrums, he screamed at a Cardinal who asked him to submit to Church tradition, "Tradition! *I* am tradition!"

---

[2] "Quanta Cura," #45, in Justo Gonzalez, *A History of Christian Thought*, vol. III (Nashville, Tenn.: Abingdon Press, 1983), p. 367.
[3] Gonzalez, p. 367.
[4] Gonzalez, p. 367.

The Immaculate Conception. In 1854, after polling bishops around the world, Pius IX declared as dogma the doctrine of the Immaculate Conception. In his papal bull, *Ineffabilis Deus*, he proclaimed that the Virgin Mary, "From the first moment of her conception...was, by the singular grace and privilege of Almighty God, and in view of the merits of Jesus Christ...kept free from all stain of original sin."

The First Vatican Council. In 1869, Pius IX convened the First Vatican Council. The principal achievement of Vatican I was its proclamation of the constitution, *Pastor Aeternus*, in which the doctrine of papal infallibility was formally declared.

The Council declared that when the pope speaks *ex cathedra*,

> that is, when in discharge of his office of pastor and doctor of all Christians...he defines...a doctrine of faith or morals...[he] is endowed with that infallibility with which our divine redeemer willed that the Church should be furnished in defining doctrine of faith or morals.[5]

Further, the constitution continued, "such definitions of the Roman pontiff are irreformable of themselves and not in virtue of the consent of the Church." In other words, the document stated, the pope's teaching on faith and morals is final and authoritative because he is the pope—despite what anyone else in the Church might think.

The decree on papal infallibility was clearly an innovation in Church doctrine. That is not to say that many in the Church had not long believed that the pope is infallible in matters of faith and morals. What was new about the decree was this: It rejected any consultation between the pope and other bishops on the promulgation of dogma. Few Catholic thinkers, even in the Middle Ages, would have gone this far in establishing the pope's authority to proclaim dogma.

Further, the decree was made canonically binding on Catholics. In other words, one could not legitimately consider oneself a Catholic unless one accepted the decree on papal infallibility. Again, few theologians would have gone this far in the Middle Ages. The concept of papal infallibility had been debated by theologians. Yet, it never had been thought that papal infallibility was as important a doctrine as, say, belief in the Trinity or the divinity of Christ. Now, eighteen centuries after the Church was founded, Catholics awoke to find that they must believe the pope infallible if they were to consider themselves orthodox believers.

Pius IX was at least consistent. He preached a world ruled by divinely appointed monarchs, and he acted in accordance with his preaching. Yet, in a democratic age, was it necessary or even helpful to proclaim a doctrine based on divine-right concepts of authority that now had been laid to rest? The

---

[5] *Pastor Aeternus*, in Gonzales, vol. III, p. 367.

decree on papal infallibility, more than anything else, was an attempt on the part of the Pope to bring back the good old days. In Pius's view, the good old days meant that kings and popes governed society, and everybody else obeyed. Unfortunately for Pius and the Church, the good old days were over. Yet, for a century more, Pius's vision of how the world should operate remained in effect in the Catholic Church.

THE FORTRESS MENTALITY
AND THE AMERICAN CHURCH

It should go without saying that Pius IX's ideas "didn't play well in Peoria." The pope's medieval views struck American ears as a throwback to concepts that they had fought to eradicate in the Revolutionary War and in the drafting of their Constitution. The decree on papal infallibility in particular confirmed the suspicions of many Americans that Catholicism and democracy were irreconcilable. Rome's out-of-date ideas fueled the fires of American anti-Catholicism. Transcribed records of the debate over papal infallibility at Vatican I were printed and circulated by anti-Catholic groups in America. Such publications were offered as evidence of Rome's hostility to the American way of life.

What about American Catholics? Where did they stand in regard to Rome's claim of absolute authority to define what it meant to be a Catholic? Most American Catholics were steadfastly faithful to Rome's decrees. As if to assure Rome of the American Church's loyalty, the American hierarchy generally professed its dedicated support for all proclamations coming from the Vatican. (Some United States bishops left the Council to avoid voting against the definition of papal infallibility.) Many observers thought that the American hierarchy was the most submissive in the world. As we will soon see, they had good reason to appear submissive.

The "Americanism" controversy. After Pius IX's death, Rome openly expressed its suspicions of the American Church's loyalty. This took place during the so-called *"Americanism"* controversy. Rome's fear of "Americanism" was related to its fear of *"Modernism."* "Modernism" was a label Rome had given to a movement among Catholic theologians to update Catholic scholarship. In particular, Catholic biblical scholars were applying certain new methods—developed by Protestant scholars—to the study of the Bible. These scholars wanted to know the historical context in which the Bible was written so that they could better understand the Bible on its own terms.

At about the same time, an American priest named Isaac Hecker (1819-1888) founded the Paulist Fathers (see Focus 33). Hecker was a convert to Catholicism. He took a dim view of the way Rome arbitrarily imposed its authority on the American Church. Hecker thought many of Rome's decrees were an attempt to impose European ways on Americans rather than an attempt to safeguard Catholic doctrine.

In the introduction to Walter Elliot's biography of Hecker, Archbishop John Ireland of St. Paul, Minnesota, praised Hecker as "the priest of the future." Elliot's book made its way to France. There, a French editor spoke of Hecker's attitude toward Rome as the "American way." French bishops read this as signaling a break with Rome on the part of the American clergy. Fears and suspicions escalated, and the Americanism controversy was launched.

By the time word of Americanism had made its way to Rome, Americanism was said to stand for the following propositions: (1) that Catholics are not to heed the clergy; (2) that Catholics are not to submit to divine revelation, but are to arrive at truth only by natural means; (3) that monks and nuns should leave their cloisters and do something practical with their lives; (4) that religious vows should be abolished; and (5) that Catholics should live in a conciliatory fashion with non-Catholics. No one was able to point to any actual document in which these so-called Americanist views had been professed.

Nonetheless, Rome became convinced by alarmists that the American Church was on the verge of anarchy. Pope Leo XIII (1878-1903), Pius IX's successor, wrote a stern letter to the American cardinal-archbishop of Baltimore, James Gibbons. The pope instructed Gibbons to repudiate Americanism.

Gibbons wrote back in rebuttal, stating that no Catholic in America believed the supposed doctrines underlying Americanism. "I do not believe," Gibbons wrote, "that there is a bishop, priest, or even a layman in this country who knows his religion and utters such enormities. No, this is not, has never been, and will never be our 'Americanism.'"

Despite Gibbons's reassurances, the Paulists withdrew Hecker's biography from publication. Eventually, the Americanist controversy ended. It had proven to the American Catholic public that American Catholicism was still suspect in Rome's eyes.

It soon became obvious to both proponents and critics of the fortress mentality that a people who fearfully hides behind walls cannot bring the gospel to the world. By hiding in the fortress of past ideas, the Catholic Church of Pius IX's day was, in effect, admitting defeat. It was saying, "The world's ideas are so frightening and shocking, that all we can do is hide our heads in the sand and hope the world goes away."

Many critics within the Church said that the Church should have used all that was good in the modern world to spread the gospel. Such critics saw the Church's fear of the modern world as a sign that the Church still needed reform. Yet, after Pius IX, the Catholic Church, by and large, would languish in its medieval torpor for almost another century, until Pope John XXIII would issue the call for another Vatican council—Vatican II. Before we reach the story of Vatican II, however, let's turn in the next chapter to a discussion of our interrupted account of the growth of the Protestant side of the Church.

FOCUS 33

ISAAC HECKER: A CATHOLIC AHEAD OF HIS TIMES

Isaac Hecker (1819-1888) was born a Methodist in New York City. He became a restless, searching intellectual. His studies convinced him to become a Catholic. Having spent his early years among intellectual non-believers, Hecker felt called to preach the gospel to such people. As he put it, "Providence calls me to convert a certain class of persons amongst whom I found myself before my conversion." He became a priest of the Redemptorist order in 1851. Yet, his life with the Redemptorists was unfulfilling. He felt called to establish a new religious congregation in which he could devote his full attention to explaining the teachings of Catholicism to educated non-believers. After a painful struggle, he finally persuaded Pope Pius IX in 1858 to allow him to form the Paulist Fathers. It was the first American religious community for priests founded in America.

The goal of the Paulists, Hecker wrote, was to "meet the needs of the Church as they arise." Gradually, Hecker found himself becoming a Catholic spokesman to Protestants. He lectured and wrote widely on relationships between Protestants and Catholics. He was the American Church's first ecumenist, even though in his day few would have known what "ecumenism" meant. Hecker communicated with Protestants not with fear and mistrust, but with openness and acceptance. He admitted what was good about Protestantism. And he forthrightly told Protestants why he thought Catholicism could provide what Protestantism lacked.

In his day, Hecker's conciliatory style was quite radical. Yet, he became one of the most respected American Catholics of his day. The American bishops chose him to lecture them on his ideas at the Second Baltimore Council of 1866. His writings and talks bridged many gaps between Catholic and Protestant intellectuals, not only in America, but in Europe as well. He was a man ahead of his times. His spirit and energy unquestionably affected Vatican II, a council that began three-quarters of a century after his death.

FOCUS 34

THE SISTERS IN AMERICA: HOW COULD THERE HAVE BEEN A CHURCH WITHOUT THEM?

The story of Catholicism in America could not be told without accounting for all that religious women contributed to the Church. Yet, women in the Church frequently had to endure suffering and deprivation that their male counterparts did not know. In addition, their contribution to the Church was largely unheralded. We could not possibly do justice to all of the American women's religious congregations here. Let us note just two examples that are typical of the faith and courage of American women religious.

We start with Elizabeth Ann Seton. A widowed mother with five children, she converted to Catholicism in 1805 and shortly thereafter founded the Sisters of Charity in Emmitsburg, Maryland. Under her direction, the first Catholic parochial school was started. Although originally devoted to teaching, the Sisters of Charity branched out into hospital work as well. They established foundations in Baltimore, Philadelphia and New York. Elizabeth Ann Seton, now canonized a saint, laid the seeds for one of America's largest congregations of women religious.

Another important congregation was the Sisters of Charity of Nazareth, founded in Bardstown, Kentucky, in 1824. This congregation's first mother superior was Catherine Spalding. At age nineteen, she took over the leadership of a "congregation" of two other sisters. Their first convent was a log cabin with two rooms on the ground floor and sleeping quarters in the loft. The sisters were so poor that they were known for carrying their shoes with them wherever they went. When they arrived at church, they would put them on—but only for the time they spent there. The sisters founded an academy in Bardstown in 1815 and had thirty-four girls as boarders. Mother Catherine Spalding died in 1858. During the Civil War, the sisters interrupted their teaching duties to attend to the injured and dying on both sides of the conflict. President Lincoln was so impressed by the sisters' service that he ordered Union soldiers to protect their property from damage and destruction.

These examples of "sisters of charity" are but two illustrations among many we could cite of Catholic women who built the Church in America.

CHAPTER EIGHTEEN

THE PATH OF PROTESTANTISM

IN THIS CHAPTER WE WILL CONTINUE our account of the growth of Protestantism. We will look at the growth of Protestantism on two fronts. First, we will scan the development of Protestantism in Europe after the deaths of the first-generation Reformers, Luther and Calvin. Next, we will see how Protestantism came to be shaped in America. Just as Catholicism in America took twists and turns peculiar to its environment, so, too, did American Protestantism. But before examining the American Protestant scene, let's turn to Europe.

AFTER LUTHER AND CALVIN

Scripture and tradition. One of the major themes in both Luther's and Calvin's writings was the rejection of Church tradition as a source of God's revelation. What did they mean by *tradition*? Essentially, they meant the elaboration by Church teachers of doctrines that could not be traced to particular passages in the Bible. Neither Luther nor Calvin rejected Church *customs*, such as hymns, church architecture or liturgical dress. What they rejected was the formulation of *doctrine* unrelated to Scripture. As an example, they rejected the seven sacraments because some of the seven could not be found in Scripture as having been instituted by Christ.

Even so, however, Luther and Calvin waffled a bit. Both of them for example, accepted the great creeds of the faith that had been formulated in the early Church. They did this even though some formulations in the creeds could not be traced explicitly to the Bible. Then, too, Luther and Calvin were great students of Augustine. They based much of their writings on Augustine's thought as well as on the Bible. Thus, right from the start, Protestant theology was not as strictly biblical as it seemed to be.

First- versus second-generation Reformers. If we call Luther and Calvin "first-generation" Reformers, then those who came immediately after them may be considered "second-generation" Reformers. The latter were intensely concerned with the debate over Church tradition. They asked, "Should we allow Luther's and Calvin's teachings to be turned into a formal body of doctrine? Or should we prevent this?" What some feared was the formation of a Protestant tradition that would be every bit as "man-made" as Catholic tradition.[1]

Sola Scriptura. All Protestants believed in Luther's principle of *"sola Scriptura."* This was Latin, for "Scripture alone." Yet, Protestant theologians of one school of thought gave *sola Scriptura* a somewhat liberal interpretation. This school of thought was largely academic and intellectual in its orientation. Everyone, the academic Protestants said, brings a certain emphasis to interpreting Scripture. There is nothing wrong, they said, in developing one's own emphasis in distinction to someone else's emphasis.

This, of course, was precisely what the early Fathers of the Church had said. The early Fathers, too, had based their theology on Scripture. Out of these differing perspectives, Catholic tradition had taken shape. In a sense, then, the academic Protestants were starting all over again on the path followed centuries ago by Catholic theologians. Without really saying so, the academic Protestants were forming a Protestant *tradition*.

This Protestant tradition presumably was based on "the Bible alone." In other words, the second-generation Reformers all professed to be following Scripture to the letter in formulating their differing, often contradictory doctrines. But the question then became, which part of the Protestant tradition more faithfully adhered to the Bible? As that question was pursued, Protestants accused each other of ignoring the Bible, of mocking it or destroying it. As the attacks intensified, the number of Protestant sects proliferated.

Lutheranism. In the Lutheran Church, angry debate took place over who best adhered to Luther's own views on *sola Scriptura.* Some Lutherans developed a doctrine known as "full and verbal inspiration" of Scripture. By this they meant, first, that God has not revealed to humanity anything other than what is found in Scripture. Second, the writers of Scripture were simply passive instruments that God used in dictating what God wanted in Scripture. The authors of Scripture did not use their own intellects in writing Scripture.

Another wing of Lutheranism became prominent in the new Lutheran universities established by Lutheran princes. These Lutherans took a less restrictive approach to Scripture. They even used *philosophy* in elaborating upon Scripture—something Luther himself would have abhorred. As this wing of Lutheranism developed, it virtually became "Protestant Scholasticism." That is, it developed theology according to a form of scholarship that had previously been used in Catholic universities.

Lutheran theology thus became every bit as much an academic discipline

---

[1] Actually, the Catholic Church regards as authentic only those traditions which in the estimation of the magisterium, were inspired by the Holy Spirit, who likewise inspired the "man-made" Bible.

as Catholic theology had been for Catholic theologians. Later, Lutheranism developed along the lines of a compromise that had been reached in 1577 with adoption of the *Formula of Concord*. In the *Formula* certain hard edges of Luther's teaching had been smoothed away. For example, the *Formula* kept Luther's teaching that good works are not needed for salvation. Yet, it stated that good works "are not detrimental" to salvation. It also allowed more freedom to Lutherans in accepting non-scriptural "externals" in their churches. Some of these externals made the Lutheran Church in some places (Sweden, for example) look very Catholic on the surface. For example, Lutheran ministers leading liturgical services in some places dressed just as Catholic priests did who celebrated Mass.

Calvinism. Calvin's doctrine likewise underwent further development. Second-generation Calvinists were particularly preoccupied with Calvin's doctrine of predestination. They made it more pessimistic than Calvin's own version. In developing this doctrine, the Dutch Reformed Church led the way. At the Calvinist Synod of Dort in Holland in 1618, Dutch Calvinists expressed Calvin's doctrine in a way that would greatly influence future Calvinist theology, particularly in America.

They stressed five points of doctrine:[2] (1) Humanity's *total depravity*. Human beings are so inherently depraved that they can make no response at all to God's grace. (2) The saved are *unconditionally predestined*. God chooses who is to be damned and who is to be saved, and gives the latter the *will* to accept the grace of salvation. (3) *Limited atonement.* Christ did not die for all, but only for those whom God had predestined to salvation. (4) Thus God's grace is *irresistible*. The human will is not free. It is either enslaved to sin or forced to be saved by God's grace. (5) Those whom God saves will inevitably *persevere to heaven*. This was the doctrine of "once saved, always saved." That is, a person predestined to heaven cannot fall from grace and fail to make it to heaven.

It could be argued that later Calvinism virtually repudiated the most important doctrine on which Luther originally had based his teaching. That doctrine was the supremacy of faith. In later Calvinism, faith was useless. A human soul is irrevocably damned or saved depending on God's predetermined choice for that soul. The human will is powerless to place its faith in God. There are only two choices: (1) one's will is conquered by God's irresistible grace and one goes to heaven; or, (2) one's will remains locked in original sin and one goes to hell. Of what benefit is faith in such a belief system?

It is not difficult to see how Calvinist doctrine could lead to a religion of elitism, and that is in fact what happened. Those who believe themselves predestined seek to find evidence in their lives in which God's choosing them for heaven is somehow manifested. According to the "Puritan ethic," wealth and

---

[2] The five points are more easily remembered by the acronym T-U-L-I-P, the first letter of each doctrine, respectively.

material prosperity, for example, might show that God had selected someone for heaven. An elitist attitude was often strong in colonial America, especially in Puritan colonies like Massachusetts.

Protestant reactions. There were a number of Protestant reactions to both the intellectualism of Lutheranism and the rigid elitism of Calvinism. These reactions sought to base Protestantism on the heart rather than on the head. That is, Protestants opposed to the intellectual path which Protestant tradition was taking, emphasized the *personal* and *emotional* dimension to religious experience. They did not think doctrine and theology were as important as the experience of *inner conversion*.

JOHN WESLEY AND METHODISM

By far the most significant of this new breed of Protestant thinkers was John Wesley (1703-1791), who founded the Methodist movement. An Anglican priest, Wesley eventually broke away from the Church of England. In 1738, Wesley had a conversion experience in which, as he wrote, "I felt my heart strangely warmed.... [A]n assurance was given me that [Christ] had taken away *my* sins, even *mine*, and saved *me* from the law of sin and death."

In his theology, Wesley shunned the strictness and sternness of Lutheranism and Calvinism. He also rejected what he saw as the dry rationalism of Anglicanism. To his way of thinking, Anglicanism had become a religion of sterile intellectualism reserved for the upper classes.

Instead of the dread doctrines of Calvinism, Wesley preached a merciful God who continually offers the grace of conversion to *all* humanity. Unlike Lutheranism or Anglicanism, Wesley's gospel was phrased in words that the working person could understand. He was spectacularly successful, winning thousands of lower-class English to his doctrine.

In some ways, Wesley was very Catholic in his orientation. He believed in the gradual perfecting of the human soul and in the importance of continual spiritual effort toward salvation. He did not believe in "once saved, always saved," or in an elitist doctrine in which only some are predestined to salvation. And he regarded both Baptism and the Eucharist as sacraments.

Methodism in America. Whereas Calvinism was elitist, Methodism was popular. Yet, both impulses in American Protestantism—the elitist and the popular—coexisted in early America. Generally speaking, the elitist version predominated in the northeast and among the highly educated. The popular version was more prevalent in the middle Atlantic and southern states and among the rural and urban working classes.

It was the need for Methodist ministers in America that led Wesley reluctantly to break with the Anglican Church. Because the Anglican Church would not ordain any of Wesley's disciples for work in America, he ordained them himself. His new Church was thus started. Methodism was very popular in America. Many English-American Protestants rejected their ties to the "old Church" back home and became Methodists.

Through the preaching of Wesley's disciple[3] in America, Francis Asbury, Methodism thrived in colonial settlements in the frontier regions. Eventually, the American Methodist Church split off from Wesley's Church in England. American Methodists called their Church the Methodist Episcopal Church. Whereas the English Methodists, following Wesley, didn't ordain bishops, the American Methodist Church did.

PROTESTANTISM IN AMERICA

The American Methodists' spirit of innovation was not new in colonial America. Before Methodism's success, Protestant Americans of every denomination had developed their own versions of Protestantism. Whereas American Catholicism feared venturing from Rome's supervision, American Protestantism was independent and free to innovate. Let's take a quick bird's-eye view of early American Protestantism by looking at the various colonies in which Protestantism flourished.

New England. In New England Puritanism originally predominated, but several new denominations, all of which adhered to Calvinism, but each of which showed a different flair for faith and practice, became popular. *Congregationalists*, for example, believed in Church government by participatory democracy on the part of all members. *Presbyterians*, on the other hand believed that a *presbytery*, or body of elders, should govern the Church. *Baptists* believed that Christians should have a conversion experience before professing one's faith through the "ordinance" of Baptism.

The Puritan experience in New England was not always in accord with the gospel. Many Puritans had fled England because they had been persecuted for their faith. Yet, as soon as they reached the new world, they, too, became persecutors. They excluded Catholics, in some places denying Catholics the right to own property. They also tried to set up theocracies in some parts of New England, similar to Calvin's theocracy in Geneva. They tried people as criminals for breaching Puritan doctrine. About 1692, the Puritans of Salem, Massachusetts, conducted trials to expose "witchcraft," ultimately executing fourteen women and six men. By 1712, the hysteria had died down, and the Puritans began losing power in New England.

The Southern colonies. Virginia had been the first English colony. The Puritans had at first been strong in Virginia. However, after the Puritans lost power in England, the Anglican Church returned to supremacy in Virginia, as in the other American colonies. Most of the wealthy, land-owning aristocracy

---

[3] Wesley's brother, Charles (1707-1788), gave the Church numerous beloved hymns, such as "Hark, the Herald Angels Sing!"

(e.g., George Washington) in Virginia were Anglicans. The lower classes turned to other denominations. This situation held true for most of the southern colonies—the Carolinas and Georgia for example. In the southern colonies the lower classes usually were attracted to Methodism or the growing Baptist denomination.

Roger Williams and Protestant toleration. Not all colonial Protestants were intolerant. Roger Williams (1604-1683), for example, was a Baptist pastor who opposed the Puritan Church's domination of the civil authorities. He was a radical for his time in that he favored separation of Church and state. Eventually, the Puritans expelled Williams from Massachusetts. He went back to England and in 1644 got permission to found the colony of Rhode Island. There he established a colony in which religious freedom was guaranteed to all. The oldest synagogue in the United States was built in 1763 in Newport, Rhode Island. Baptists, Quakers and Catholics all settled in the state and worshiped in relative peace.

The Middle Atlantic colonies. In the middle Atlantic colonies the picture was more complex. Pennsylvania was founded by the Quaker, William Penn (1644-1718). Quakers[4] believed in non-violence and pacifism. They also believed that the individual believer's conscience was directly guided by the "Inner Light" of the Holy Spirit. They practiced silence and contemplation in order to stay in touch with the Inner Light.

William Penn believed strongly in religious freedom. Like Lord Baltimore's Maryland and Roger Williams's Rhode Island, "Penn's-sylvania" (Penn's forest), and his new "city of brotherly love," Philadelphia, offered toleration for all beliefs. Penn was even more innovative than most in that he sought to include the Native American tribes among those whose beliefs and practices were tolerated.

New York and New Jersey were likewise home to Christians of many faiths, although in those colonies tolerance was not widely practiced. The Dutch Reformed Church was at first strong in New York. The Dutch by and large were more tolerant of religious differences than were the English. Catholics could usually worship openly in Dutch New York. As the English moved in increasing numbers into New York, however, the Anglican Church gradually rose to a position of prominence in this colony. Whenever Anglicanism became the official religion, religious toleration suffered.

THE GREAT AWAKENING

We could not understand Protestantism in America unless we understand a uniquely American phenomenon. This is religious revivalism. From time to time in the history of the American Protestant Church, great stirrings of fervor

---

[4] Their formal name is *The Society of Friends.*

have moved large numbers of Protestants to renew their faith. The earliest of these revival movements began about 1734 under the leadership of the famous Calvinist preacher, Jonathan Edwards (1703-58). For a reason unknown even to Edwards, people suddenly began to experience outbursts of intense spiritual emotion during his sermons.

Another famous preacher, George Whitefield (1714-70), had the same experience during sermons he gave. All over New England, during religious meetings in this period, otherwise unemotional Protestants burst into tears, shouted, danced or fainted from a sudden rush of enthusiasm. The emotional outbursts were matched by public acclamations of repentance and promises to return to a devout life.

Collectively, the burst of religious enthusiasm during this period was called "the Great Awakening."[5] People who had been touched by this fervor often found it difficult to return to the more placid Congregationalist and Presbyterian Churches from which they had come. And since the Baptists and Methodists were open to religious enthusiasm, their ranks swelled during this period.

This was especially true in the frontier regions of the colonies. As frontier regions like Tennessee and Kentucky, which were not colonies, grew through immigration, they became largely Baptist and Methodist. The growth of these denominations in the frontier regions led to further "Awakenings."

The second Great Awakening began in 1801 in the little settlement of Cane Ridge, Kentucky. It was significant to the future of American religion for the following reason. The fervor it stimulated led to the wholesale exodus of Protestants from European-founded Churches and into newly forming, independent Baptist and Methodist denominations. These independent groups were self-governing and not tied to any formal governing body. This was a peculiarly American approach to religion. It was the origin of the "non-denominational" sects which are still popular today.

Further, as Protestants left the Churches of their homelands, ethnic identity ceased to have religious meaning in America. Irish-Catholics and Scottish Presbyterians became Baptists. German-Lutherans and Anglicans became Methodists. America was truly becoming a religious melting pot.

Protestantism before the American Revolution, marked by the independence and autonomy of its proliferating sects, created a religious climate that naturally supported the movement for political independence from Great Britain. The political revolution in turn encouraged independence of religious thinking. Unlike any country on earth, America had truly become the land of religious variety and unique expression. No state Church could have existed in America—even if the Constitution had not forbade it.

---

[5] It was at its height during the 1740's.

FOCUS 35

AMERICAN CHRISTIANS AND SLAVERY

Slavery was an issue that divided many American Protestant denominations. Originally, the Methodists and Baptists, along with the Quakers, had condemned slavery. The Anglican Church in America (called the Episcopalian Church after the Revolution) tolerated slavery. This was because many Episcopalians in southern states were slaveholders. After the Revolution, the various denominations wavered on the issue. Methodists and Baptists in the south assured slave holders that there was a place for them in their denominations. By one reckoning, in 1843, over a thousand Methodist ministers owned slaves. The Presbyterian Church opposed slavery, but at the same time punished ministers who worked for abolition. By the start of the Civil War, only the Quakers were firmly on record as opposed to slavery.

Disagreement within the Protestant denominations on the slavery issue led to the formation of splinter denominations. For example, today's largest American Protestant denomination, the Southern Baptist Convention, was established in 1845. It came into existence after a dispute over the credentials of a Georgia Baptist preacher who owned slaves. Likewise, the Methodists split over this issue, forming the Methodist Episcopal Church, South. Southern Presbyterians, too, formed their own denomination. Because of the ambiguity of stance by the white denominations, blacks formed their own denominations. The two most significant of these were the African Methodist Episcopal Church and the African Methodist Episcopal Zion Church. The leadership and community spirit that was formed in these black churches eventually gave birth to the civil rights movement of the 1960's.

And what of Catholics? In 1839, Pope Gregory XVI had condemned the international slave trade, but did not specifically address the situation in the United States. In an age in which Catholics were allowed virtually no freedom of conscience on any issue affecting their faith, slavery was the one exception. It was un-Catholic to question whether the pope is infallible. Yet it was not un-Catholic to question whether one human being could own another human being as property. Because of Rome's "hands-off" attitude toward the slavery issue, there were as many opinions on slavery among Catholics as there were Catholics.

FOCUS 36

NEW CHURCHES AND NEW RELIGIONS IN AMERICA

Aside from molding Churches founded in Europe to their liking, American Protestants also formed distinctly new bodies. Chief among these was the "Christian Church," also known as "The Disciples of Christ." It was founded by Thomas and Alexander Campbell in an attempt to end the ever-increasing spread of Protestant sects. The Campbells hoped to unite all Protestant denominations into one. This attempt failed, and the Disciples became a new denomination of their own (founded 1811).

Another major movement was the foundation of the "holiness churches." They grew out of an impulse among Methodists to return to the original piety and enthusiasm that had characterized John Wesley's preaching. The leading denomination among holiness churches was the Church of the Nazarene, founded in 1908. Other holiness churches believed in the manifestation of the gifts of the Holy Spirit. They spoke in tongues, uttered prophecies and worked healings as part of their services. A group of such sects gathered together about 1914 to form the Assemblies of God, still of the leading "Pentecostal" denominations in America.

The turn of the twentieth century also saw the growth of Fundamentalism. Fundamentalism was a reaction to the increasing growth of liberal Protestant theology as developed in universities. Fundamentalists insisted on five "fundamentals": the literal inerrancy of Scripture (the Bible contains no errors, even in history or grammar); the divinity of Jesus; the Virgin birth; the substitutionary atonement (Jesus died on the cross in our place as an offering for sin); Jesus' bodily Resurrection into heaven and his imminent return to earth. Fundamentalism gained adherents especially in the south.

In addition to the new Christian groups that were born in America, there were a number of new religions that significantly departed from traditional Christian teaching. The Mormons were founded by Joseph Smith. His *Book of Mormon* was published in 1830. In it, Smith spoke of his new religion as superseding Christianity, just as Christianity had superseded Judaism. The official name of the new religion was Church of Jesus Christ of Latter-Day Saints. Under the leadership of Brigham Young, Mormons settled principally in Utah in the 1850's. At one point they engaged in active warfare with the United States over the issue of polygamy, as Mormons then (not now) allowed men to have multiple wives.

Christian Science was founded by Mary Baker Eddy in 1879. She taught that illness was only an illusion, based on incorrect thinking. The Church of Christ, Scientist, as it is officially known, interprets the Bible much like the Gnostics of old. They give purely metaphysical interpretations to words like "Christ," "salvation" and "truth."

The Jehovah's Witnesses were founded by Charles T. Russell and reorganized and named by Joseph F. Rutherford in 1931. The Witnesses reject the doctrine of the Trinity and the divinity of Jesus. They believe in the swift return of Christ and end of the world, although they have picked several dates for the end that have not proven accurate.

CHAPTER NINETEEN

THE AGE OF VATICAN II

CATHOLICS AND PROTESTANTS fighting with each other, religious persecution on all sides, a backwards-looking Catholic hierarchy, the splintering of Protestant sects proclaiming scores of competing doctrines. All in all, Christianity has not always put its best foot forward. Based on the example we Christians have set, we shouldn't wonder why so many people today reject Christianity altogether.

Is there anything hopeful to report? The answer depends on one's definition of *hopeful*. For one person, the Church may be going in a hopeful direction if it retreats into the Middle Ages, as Pius IX tried to do. For another, hopeful may mean fundamentalism. For such a person, TV preachers predicting the end of the world are a good sign.

A 'THAW' BEGINS

Up until the age we are entering, it was as if the Church were the emperor parading around with no clothes on. As in Andersen's fairy tale, the Church was professing to be "all dressed up" in the gospel, when in fact it was "naked" with power and fear. It took a few courageous Christians to come along and say, "Why, the emperor has no clothes on!" before the Church could change.

In this chapter, we'll name a few of those courageous Christians—Catholic and Protestant—who called the Church back to its better self. What we'll see is that something like a "thaw" begins. Here and there, gradually and with increasing vigor, the Church begins to retreat from fear and insecurity. It leaves the frozen wastelands of yesteryear and heads for the warm climate of hope and reconciliation.

POPES WHO LOOKED AHEAD

Popes after Pius IX would continue to be conservative. But they had learned from Pio Nono's negative example. They realized that the solution to the

Church's conflict with the modern world did not lie in going backwards.

Leo XIII. For example, Pius IX's successor, Pope Leo XIII (1878-1903), was hardly a progressive liberal. But he realized that the Church had to take an active, leading role in the modern world. Consider Leo's encyclical *Rerum Novarum*, written in 1891. It shocked conservatives within the Church.

In it, Leo supported the right of workers to form associations and to enter into collective bargaining with their employers for just wages and decent working conditions. Some conservatives asked, "Isn't this just what the socialists advocate?" But Leo didn't support socialism. In fact, he condemned it. He was not calling for the overthrow of conservative governments. He was simply calling on those governments to help workers live a humane life in an industrialized society.

Rerum Novarum was a daring innovation on the part of the old-fashioned Church. It showed that Catholicism could proclaim gospel values in modern language. At the same time, *Rerum Novarum* was conservative. It looked upon industrial workers largely as children to be protected by a paternalistic Church and a well-meaning state. It saw the workers as the victims of liberalism and argued that it was the task of conservative governments to protect the workers from liberalism.

Still, the encyclical was a start. In 1931, Pope Pius XI (1922-1939) followed up on *Rerum Novarum* with *Quadragesimo Anno* ("On the fortieth year" after *Rerum Novarum*). He amplified Leo's ideas, proclaiming the right of workers to take control of their lives in the workplace.

Pius XII bridges the gap. A highly educated, intelligent man, Pope Pius XII (1939-1958) laid important foundations for Vatican II. In 1947, he issued the encyclical *Mediator Dei*, in which he spoke of the laity as true participants in the Mass. In *Humani Generis* (1950), he encouraged Catholic theologians to use some of the benefits of modern scholarship in their research. Pius was very much a conservative Italian churchman. Yet, he had keen insights into the way the modern world worked and he wanted the Church to speak effectively in that world.

Pius XII had signaled a truce in the Church's war with "Modernism" when he issued *Divino Afflante Spiritu* in 1943. Prior to that encyclical, the popes had been on record as opposing modern biblical criticism. Catholic scholars had to proceed as if the Bible had no textual errors in it. And they were not to probe beneath the surface of the text. They were not to concern themselves too greatly with the form or the historical context in which biblical passages were written.

In his encyclical, Pius changed this situation. He encouraged the application of modern methods of criticism to study of the Bible. It was not until later that Catholics were permitted to read other versions of the Bible than the *Vulgate* or its translations. But Pius XII paved the way for updated Catholic versions of the Bible.

A man called John. Finally, Catholicism's war against modern times came thundering to an end with the election of Pius's successor, Pope John XXIII (1958-1963). John opened his pontificate by urging the Church, in his words, to "gain new strength and energies, and look to the future without fear." He criticized those in the Church for whom "the modern world is nothing but betrayal and ruination." He stated, "We feel bound to disagree with these prophets of doom who are forever forecasting calamity."[1]

John's great achievement was the convocation of Vatican II. He declared as the Council's purpose the study and proclamation of Catholic doctrine "in the light of the research methods and the language of modern thought. For the *substance* of the ancient deposit of faith is one thing," he continued, "and the *way in which it is presented* is another."[2]

Before proceeding to a discussion of John's brainchild, Vatican II, let's look at the Protestant contribution to the Church's process of updating itself.

PROTESTANT INNOVATORS

Let's first note that Protestantism had in many ways become as stagnant as Catholicism. Luther's early fervor had largely been replaced in Protestantism by a dry, sterile legalism based on an intellectualist approach to the faith. Even after Wesley's revival, Protestantism, especially in Europe, was largely uninspiring. It appealed mostly to middle-class urban dwellers who looked upon membership in the Church as if it were membership in the local Chamber of Commerce. In other words, Protestantism had become socially respectable, but it had little life or energy to it.

Two Protestant thinkers who helped Protestantism thaw out were Friedrich Schleiermacher (1768-1834) and Søren Kierkegaard (1813-1855). Schleiermacher, who wrote in the early nineteenth century, is regarded as the father of modern Protestantism. He disdained the intellectualist approach to the faith that characterized the Protestant Church of his day. While he did not deprecate *understanding*, he was more interested in *feeling*. For him, Christianity should be "a universal pulsing of joy."[3]

Kierkegaard attacked the dry, middle-class Lutheranism of his era. He called the clergy "shopkeepers' souls in velvet."[4] He urged Christians to move beyond the identification of Christianity with civic virtue. Christianity, he wrote, is not the same thing as good citizenship.

A later Protestant thinker, Rudolf Otto (d. 1937), did much to continue Schleiermacher's and Kierkegaard's emphasis on interior conversion. Otto

---

[1] John Jay Hughes, "The Council and The Synod: A Tale of Two Popes," *St. Anthony Messenger* (October 1985), p. 17.

[2] Hughes, p. 18.

[3] Friedrich Schleiermacher, "Letter to Friedrich H. Jacobi," in *A Handbook of Christian Theologians*, Martin E. Marty and Dean G. Peerman, eds. (Nashville, Tenn.: Abingdon Press, 1984), p. 25.

[4] Søren Kierkegaard, "The Attack Upon Christendom," in Marty, p. 135.

was a Protestant mystic. For him, religion is a great mystery that "eludes complete conceptual analysis."[5]

Christianity must first be experienced, Otto said, before it can be believed. The Church is stagnant and sterile, he argued, because Christians are taught to believe things that are not part of their own inner experience.

Another look at **sola Scriptura**. Another major factor behind the Protestant thaw was the change in Protestant biblical scholarship. Within the very Protestant universities that had contributed to Protestant stagnation, thinkers began to take another look at the bedrock Protestant principle of *sola Scriptura*. What they concluded was this: The Bible was written over many centuries and in many different historical circumstances. In addition, there were many different styles of writing used in composing the Bible. Some parts of the Bible are history, some are poetry, some are exhortations and some are parables.

Protestant scholars developed certain research methods for studying the Bible. In using these methods, they concluded that Christians should read the Bible as the recorded experience of the people of God. In other words, the Bible is a book that has been filtered through the experience of the Jews and of the Church. It does not exist in a vacuum, outside of the context of the life of believers. The Church shaped the Bible as much as the Bible shaped the Church. With these conclusions, Protestant biblical scholarship moved closer to the Catholic position. In that position, both Scripture and tradition make up God's revelation.

The Church and the world. Protestant thinkers likewise grappled with the problem of Christianity's relevance to the modern world. Like Catholicism, Protestantism, too, had its fortress mentality. An American Protestant, Reinhold Niebuhr (d. 1971), addressed this problem in the early twentieth century. He called for the Protestant Church to face the problems caused by modern industrialization. He wanted the Church to explore, as he put it, "the meaning and significance of the gospel in the context of modern industrial society." As he saw it, the modern Church has "no vital influence upon the life of modern man." He called upon Protestants to take the gospel out into the marketplace. He wanted Christians to live with and serve the working classes.

Just as Catholics responded to *Rerum Novarum*, Protestants responded to ideas such as those advanced by Niebuhr. In both Catholicism and Protestantism the idea of the social gospel became popular. Christianity came to be thought of less as a system of *piety* and more as system of *service*. But this did not mean simply performing works of charity, as the Church always had done.

Rather, it meant transforming the very structures of society that create injustice and oppression. Sin came to be thought of, in both Protestant and Catholic circles, in terms of its effect on society. Previously sin had been

---

[5] Rudolf Otto, "The Idea of the Holy," in Marty, p. 18.

looked upon as the individual's transgression of divine law. Now sin was also seen as the means by which injustice and suffering are brought into the world. The *communal* dimension of sin was emphasized along with the *individual* dimension of sin.

This brief summary of trends within Protestantism shows that Protestants had paved the way for a change of attitude about Christianity. This changing attitude was to affect not only the Protestant Church, but the Catholic Church as well. The changing religious climate had an enormous impact on the path taken by the Catholic Church at Vatican II.

THE SECOND VATICAN COUNCIL

An ecumenical council. Vatican II was convened in four sessions from 1962 to 1965. It was unique among all the councils that have met in the Church's history. It was truly an *ecumenical* council at which the Church throughout the world was represented. At Vatican I, most of the delegates had been European—and principally Italian. Pio Nono's Italian perspective on the Church was thus assured of success right from the start. At Vatican II, however, Italians comprised only one-fifth of the total delegates. The Italian delegation still was the largest, but now more voices from other parts of the world could be heard.

In addition, at Vatican II non-Catholics and Orthodox Christians were present as non-voting "observers." Even lay people were in attendance—as non-voting "hearers" of the debate at the council. At Vatican I, Pio Nono had drawn up the agenda and handed it to the bishops for rubber-stamping. At Vatican II, the delegates worked with Pope John's advisors in preparing the agenda.

The documents. The work of the council was published in documents—four "Constitutions," nine "Decrees" and three "Declarations." There is a hierarchy of authority in the documents. The Constitutions are most authoritative. They define unalterable Catholic *doctrine*. The decrees come next. They recommend *renewal* of life within the Church in nine major areas. Finally, the Declarations are *policy statements*, as it were, on three critical issues for Christians.

On the Church. We could not possibly do justice to the teaching of Vatican II here. We can only offer a brief overview. We will start with the Constitution *Lumen Gentium* ("Dogmatic Constitution on the Church"). The future Pope John Paul II (elected 1978), when he was still a bishop in Poland, said that this Constitution was "the key to the whole of the Council's thought."[6] In it, the Council updated the Church's self-image.

---

[6] Karol Wojtyla, *Sources of Renewal: The Implementation of Vatican II* (New York: Harper and Row, 1980), 35.

The Council moved away from the static conception of the Church that had dominated Catholic thought for fifteen centuries. No longer was the Church to be thought of as an "it," but as an "us." The Church is a community. It is the "people of God." As John Paul II wrote in a book on the subject, "The Church is ourselves."[7] We the Church are not an institution of men at the top of a pyramid with everybody else at the bottom. Rather, we the Church are a communion of lay and ordained, male and female. The pyramid of the Middle Ages could perhaps be thought of as having changed to a circle where all hold hands and serve each other.

All in the circle are essential to the Church's self-definition and to its mission to proclaim the Kingdom of God. Some in the circle are called to serve as leaders. In that sense, there is still a distinction between hierarchy and laity. But in terms of participation in the life of the Church, there is no longer a "hierarchy of worth" as in the Vatican I Church. As the Council put it, "All are called to sanctity and have obtained an equal privilege of faith... [There thus remains] a true equality between all with regard to the dignity and the activity which is common to all the faithful in the building up of the Body of Christ."[8] We will look at three impulses in the life of the post-Vatican II Church in Chapter Twenty-One, within this framework of equality.

On life in the modern world. Leaving behind the fearful pessimism of Vatican I, the Council promulgated the Constitution *Gaudium et Spes*, Latin for "Joy and Hope." In this "Pastoral Constitution on the Church in the Modern World," the Council defined what it means to be a Catholic in the modern age. Far from opposing Catholicism to modernity, the Council declared, "Christians ought to be convinced that the achievements of the human race are a sign of God's greatness and the fulfillment of his mysterious design...."[9] Instead of retreating from the world, the Council assured men and women that "they can rightly look upon their work as a prolongation of the work of the Creator."[10] In other words, Christians are called not to segregate themselves from the world. Rather, they are called to bring the gospel into the world through their worldly work.

On relationship with non-Catholics. The Church of Vatican I, largely through Pio Nono's own proclamations, perpetuated the misconception that only Catholics are saved. Vatican II spoke of Catholics as being "*fully* incorporated into the Church."[11] Other Christians, the Council said, are "in some real way joined to us in the Holy Spirit." Henceforth, then, it would

---

[7] Wojtyla, p. 38.
[8] *Lumen Gentium*, 32. All quotations from the Vatican documents are taken from *Vatican Council II: The Conciliar and Postconciliar Documents*, Austin Flannery, O.P., gen. ed. (Costello Publishing Co., 1975; rev. ed., 1996).
[9] *Gaudium et Spes*, 34.
[10] *Gaudium et Spes,* 34.
[11] *Lumen Gentium*, 14.

be inaccurate to speak of "the Church" as if that phrase referred only to Catholics. Protestant, Orthodox and Catholic Christians comprise the Church.

THE ROAD AHEAD

For some Catholics, Vatican II raised more questions than it answered. After an initial burst of optimism, it soon became clear that Catholics were not agreed on what Vatican II meant. Catholics used the documents of Vatican II to argue for opposing positions on the same issue. One thing was certain. The Catholic Church would never be the same after Vatican II. The road ahead was marked by twists and turns yet to be negotiated, but it was at least a road *ahead*.

FOCUS 37

PIERRE TEILHARD DE CHARDIN: WAS HE AN UNSEEN PRESENCE AT VATICAN II?

Many Catholics contributed to Vatican II besides the delegates in attendance at the council. For example, the German theologian Karl Rahner, S.J. (1904-1984), served as an advisor to the bishops at the council. Likewise, the American Jesuit John Courtney Murray (1905-67), made enormous contributions when it came to the council's drafting of the declaration on religious liberty. But many think there was a strong "unseen presence" dominating the council—that of the French Jesuit, Pierre Teilhard de Chardin (1881-1955).

Teilhard's writings had been suppressed during his lifetime. But between the time of his death and the time of the council, many Catholics, including future bishops at the council, eagerly read Teilhard's works. Pope Paul VI would say of him, "Teilhard is indispensable for our times. His apologetic is necessary." Pope John Paul II's secretary of state would write that Teilhard anticipated John Paul's appeal: "Do not be afraid; open wide the doors to Christ, the immense fields of culture, civilization and development."

Teilhard had a unique vision. He was both a priest and a scientist, a world-renowned paleontologist. He saw the Holy Spirit at work in all creation, bringing that creation into harmony with God. He likewise professed a spirituality in which the Christian's work in the world contributes to the process by which life evolves toward fulfillment in God. He was frustrated by the Christian attitude which saw the world as opposed to Christian life. For him, human life in the world, through God's grace, was progressing toward perfection in Christ. Thus, for Teilhard, Christianity can only succeed if it looks upon the world as the place where the Holy Spirit brings creation to fulfillment. "By virtue of the incarnation," Teilhard once wrote, "*nothing* here below is profane for those who know how to see."

Teilhard's spirit influenced much of what the council accomplished, particularly the constitution *Gaudium et Spes*, ("Joy and Hope"). It was an appropriate title by which to summarize Teilhard's writings. He was a prophet of hope who found joy in exploring the world that God had created.

FOCUS 38

VATICAN II'S CHALLENGE: 'CHURCH, GROW UP!'

Many Catholics did not find Vatican II to their liking. In fact, some Catholics were opposed to the council's achievement and resisted change. Why was this? There are numerous answers, too complex to go into here. Let's consider just one possible reason for Vatican II's rocky reception. Much has been said about the new *prerogatives* for lay people in the post-Vatican II Church. Not as much has been said about the laity's new *responsibilities* after Vatican II. The council, in effect, called upon the laity to grow up spiritually. Perhaps some Catholics did not want to do this.

The council did not make some facile proclamation that all was right between Christianity and the world. Instead, the council called on Christians to relate to the world in such a way as to *convert* the world to gospel values. The council did not glibly pronounce the world's values to be compatible with Christianity. Instead, the council urged Christians "to *integrate* human, domestic, professional, scientific and technical enterprises with *religious values*." Thus for example, running an abortion clinic, making nuclear bombs, or working hard simply to accumulate money and power, would not be a proper way for Christians to relate to the world. In making peace with modern times, the council did not absolve Christians from acting responsibly in the modern world.

Nor did the council absolve lay Catholics from taking responsibility to carry out the Church's mission in the world. No longer could lay Catholics, for example, assume that it was the job of priests and sisters to bring the gospel into the world. Lay Catholics were urged to integrate their work with their faith in such a way as to evangelize the world through their work. In the council's new conception of Church, the laity had equal dignity, but also equal *responsibility* for promoting the Kingdom of God.

Perhaps this call to take responsibility as adult Christians for their lives in the world startled some Catholics. It was much more comfortable to be an "old style" Catholic, in which the prevailing attitude was, "let Father do it." Vatican II called upon the laity to abandon this attitude. It called upon Catholics to be visible, active Christians in the world—and not just in church on Sunday morning. This was quite a challenge, and we human beings don't take to challenges easily. For too long, Catholics had been content to be children resting in the bosom of Holy Mother Church. Vatican II, in a sense, told Catholics, "It's time to leave home, get a job and make your mark on the world."

CHAPTER TWENTY

THE POST-VATICAN II CHURCH

VATICAN II DID MUCH TO HELP the Catholic Church reassess its identity and redefine its mission. Yet, Catholic identity and Catholic mission are not concepts upon which all Catholics agree. There is a wide spectrum of opinion over Vatican II, even today—especially today—over a quarter-century after the Council's conclusion.

In the minds of some Catholics, Vatican II was the beginning of a process by which the Church was "Protestantized." As an example of this school of thought, consider Catholics who affiliated with dissident Archbishop Marcel Lefebvre. He was a French bishop who broke with Rome after Vatican II. Many Catholics joined him, and he ordained priests who adhere to his pre-Vatican II version of Catholicism.

At the other end of the spectrum are those who think Vatican II did not go far enough. Among other things, such Catholics call for increased participation by all Catholics in the governance of the Church. Perhaps their position is best represented by a joke that circulated after Vatican II: "At Vatican III, the bishops will bring their wives. At Vatican IV, they will bring their husbands!"

Some questions... Aside from the extremes of opinion, what has been the response of the Catholic Church to Vatican II? Where have we the Church moved since the Council? Where are we the Church likely to move in the days ahead? These are the questions the Church tries to answer today, as we the Church continue to assess our identity.

...And an observation. But first, an observation is in order. The turmoil over Vatican II has been mild compared to the turmoil that has followed other Church councils. After the Council of Nicea in 325, for example, the Church experienced tumultuous problems. For fifty years it was doubtful that the council would be accepted. Various regions of the Roman Empire swung back and forth between acceptance and rejection. Bishops were ousted physically from their sees. At one point, a Roman Emperor repudiated the council and reinstated Arianism. Whether or not Vatican II is to be accepted is a moot issue.

The bishops who met at the Extraordinary Synod in Rome in 1985 to evaluate the Council's achievement went on record as completely affirming the Council and all that it stood for. They said, "[T]he Second Vatican Council is a gift of God to the Church and to the world. In full adherence to the Council, we see in it a wellspring offered by the Holy Spirit to the Church, for the present and the future..."[1]

Thus, unlike the situation after other Church councils, the issue is not one of acceptance or rejection of Vatican II. Instead, the focus of discussion now is on the implications of Vatican II for the future. To discuss those implications in detail would be to depart from the realm of history and to enter the realm of prediction. But to tie together the past with the future in a tentative way, let's look at just two issues. The issues of *social justice* and *Church authority* seem to foreshadow most clearly the shape of the Church that is to come. The resolution of these two issues are important to the future understanding of Catholic identity.

THE CALL FOR SOCIAL JUSTICE

It would be inaccurate to say that Vatican II turned Catholics' attention from the altar to the world. Perhaps a more accurate way to put it would be this: Vatican II directed Catholics' attention *to* the world *through* the altar.

Vatican II emphatically taught that the Church's mission is to lead humanity into the Kingdom of God. In the person of Jesus, that kingdom has already begun to be realized. But its full realization lies beyond the confines of this world. Yet, Vatican II stressed that a spirituality that ignores the world is not sufficient.

In *Gaudium et Spes*, the bishops at Vatican II emphasized the modern Christian's duty to promote social justice. There the bishops said, "[I]t is a duty for the whole people of God, under the teaching and example of the bishops, to alleviate the hardships of our times."[2] In the post-Vatican II Church, Catholics' eyes were not to be turned only to heaven. They were to look toward the earth as well.

The popes on social justice. All the post-Vatican II popes, Paul VI, John Paul I and John Paul II, stressed the need for Catholics to work for justice if they are truly to consider themselves Catholic. Paul VI described "the growing gap between rich and poor" as "a scandal and a contradiction to Christian existence." At an address given before the United Nations General Assembly on how to establish peace, he proclaimed, "If you want peace, work for justice."

In his encyclical *Redemptor Hominis* (1979), Pope John Paul II condemned a consumer civilization that attends only to its own affluence while

---

[1] "Message to the People of God," in *Our Sunday Visitor* (December 7, 1985).
[2] *Gaudium et Spes*, 88, in Flannery.

ignoring the suffering of the poor. In *Laborem Exercens* (1981), John Paul updated the Church's teaching on justice for the working classes as first proclaimed by Leo XIII in *Rerum Novarum* and Pius XI in *Quadragesimo Anno*. John Paul called upon both capitalist and socialist systems to subordinate their goals to the welfare of the workers. He supported the right of workers to co-own and co-manage the industries for which they work.

Liberation theology. Popes were not alone in proclaiming social justice. Catholic theologians, particularly in Latin America, were developing theologies that collectively came to be known as liberation theology. Although there are different versions of this theology, there are several common themes. Perhaps the most important is this: the poor teach the gospel to the rich, and not the other way around. In other words, the gospel must be learned in the context of a life of deprivation and sacrifice. It is not learned in air-conditioned seminary classrooms. Only those who know poverty can truly preach the gospel.

Another important theme of liberation theology has to do with the nature of sin. Sin in liberation theology is principally social in nature. Sin brings about oppression. The actions of millions of wealthy Christians furthering their own wealth and affluence may mean that millions of poor persons do not have enough to eat. To overcome sin and its effects, profound structural changes must be made in society. Only governments can bring about such changes. Thus liberation theology calls for Christians to take an active part in the political process.

The bishops of Latin America, while not sanctioning any one school of liberation theology, strongly advocated the goal of liberation theology—a more just society. At a conference in Puebla, Mexico, in 1979, the bishops announced their "preferential option for the poor." They said, "Poverty is not a passing phase. Instead, it is a product of economic, social, and political situations and structures..." They called upon Catholics, particularly in the wealthy countries, to work to change structures that create and sustain poverty.

Pope John Paul II echoed this challenge when he visited America in 1979. In a homily delivered at Yankee Stadium in New York City, the Pope said, "The poor of the United States and of the world are your brothers and sisters in Christ. You must never be content to leave them just the crumbs from the feast. You must take of your substance, and not just of your abundance, in order to help them."

SHARING CHURCH AUTHORITY

Another major revision in Catholic thinking since Vatican II concerns the issue of Church authority. This issue does not merely involve the question, "Who runs the Church?" Rather, it involves principally the question, "How are we members of the Church to relate to one another?"

Issues of Church authority after Vatican II thus involve more than just the day-to-day operation of the institutional Church. The question of authority is primarily involved with the Church as "sign to the world." For, to the extent that we the Church relate to each other in love, compassion and justice, we legitimately can proclaim love, compassion and justice to the world.

In our relationships with one another, do we the Church proclaim the gospel, or do we proclaim power? In essence, this is a core question the Church has always had to answer for itself. How is the post-Vatican II Church answering that question?

Priests and laity. Vatican II described priests as "brothers among brothers." Presumably it meant "among sisters" as well. At the same time, the Council called priests "fathers and pastors." It has not always been easy for either priests or the laity to know how their post-Vatican II relationship was to be lived. In some parishes, pastors and parishioners have been on a first-name basis. They have shared administrative responsibilities on virtually an equal footing. In other parishes, the relationship is still very much one of "Father" relating to children.

Despite this variance from place to place, one thing has become clear since the close of Vatican II. The Church as an institution cannot be administered without the active involvement of lay persons. The American Catholic bishops have written, "[T]he laity are making an indispensable contribution to the experience of the People of God and...the full import of their contribution is still in a beginning form in the post-Vatican II Church."[3]

The laity are now serving the Church in many roles that were formerly reserved to priests and religious. As this process has taken place, the rigid separation of priests and religious from the laity has been replaced by a more collegial, cooperative relationship.

Ordination for whom? An issue that has arisen for many married lay persons involves the degree to which their gifts can be incorporated fully into the Church's mission. Such questions as the following are frequently heard today. Should a married man be denied the full exercise of his gifts to the Church simply because he is married? Or, shouldn't a woman who is performing nearly all functions previously reserved to priests, be ordained herself?

Such questions have been asked repeatedly since Vatican II. At present, Rome has resisted all attempts to allow married persons and women to be ordained. Pope John Paul II is not ready to allow either, except for individual cases of ministers coming to the Catholic Church from Protestant churches. He has not allowed individual women to be ordained; he doesn't think that he can. He has declared the issue closed and no longer open to discussion for Catholics. Yet, the numbers of single men presenting themselves for ordination continues to dimin-

---

[3] National Conference of Catholic Bishops, *Called and Gifted: The American Catholic Laity* (November 13, 1980), p. 9.

ish. In 1964, 47,500 men were studying for the priesthood in the United States. In 1984, this number had dropped to 12,000. The same period saw the closing of 241 seminaries in the United States alone.

The priest shortage appears to be a permanent reality in the Church. Because of this reality, the Church will be challenged in the years ahead to open the priesthood to Catholics other than unmarried males.

Rome and the national bishops' conferences. Vatican II emphasized the collegiality of bishops and pope. It called for a permanent Synod of Bishops to advise the pope. The Council stressed that pope and bishops acting together form the hierarchy. It is not as if the pope is at the top, followed by the cardinals and the Curia and then the bishops, as in medieval thinking. Rather, the pope serves the Church with his brother bishops.

Pope Paul VI took steps to foster this collegial relationship by encouraging the formation of national bishops' conferences in each country. At the same time, however, Rome has made it clear that the local bishop is not independent in his own diocese.

The bishops lead the way. The national bishops' conferences have done extraordinary work in implementing the reforms of Vatican II. In the Vatican I Church, it was usually Catholics other than bishops who tried to make the Church relevant to modern times. Today, especially in the United States, the reverse is often true. The American bishops are often miles ahead of the laity. The bishops, especially in their pastoral letters, have given Catholics a clear vision of what it means to be an American Catholic in the modern world. Often, in contrast to the Vatican I situation, it is conservative Catholics who complain today about the bishops' stance on important issues.

We could not do justice here to all the statements made by the bishops in their pastoral letters. They have written on a wide variety of issues: among others, feeding the hungry, providing alternatives to abortion for pregnant women, providing decent housing to the homeless, the importance of Catholic participation in the electoral process, the relation between Catholic social teaching and the United States economy.

Perhaps the most controversial of their letters was "The Challenge of Peace: God's Promise and Our Response" (1983). In it the bishops said, "Offensive war of any kind is not morally justifiable."[4] They condemned the arms race as "an act of aggression against the poor, and a folly which does not provide the security it promises."[5] The bishops called upon Catholics to become peacemakers. "Peacemaking is not an optional commitment," they said. "It is a requirement of our faith."[6]

---

[4] National Conference of Catholic Bishops, *The Challenge of Peace: God's Promise and Our Response* (May 3, 1983).
[5] "Challenge of Peace."

Such pronouncements have been criticized by some Catholics as "politicking." These critics say that the bishops should take care of religion and not interfere in an area that does not concern them. Yet, a close reading of the Documents of Vatican II suggests the opposite. The bishops meeting in synod in Rome in 1971 affirmed: "Action on behalf of justice and participation in the transformation of the world appear to us a constitutive dimension of the preaching of the gospel."

Rome and dissident theologians. One controversial issue involving authority in the post-Vatican II Church pertains to the teaching of theology. Here Rome has repeatedly warned theologians to align themselves with official Church teaching on issues such as papal infallibility, abortion and birth control, spirituality, seminary education, liturgical innovations, the role of women in the Church and so on.

The first major crisis after Vatican II involving Rome's teaching authority followed upon Pope Paul VI's encyclical, *Humanae Vitae* ("On the Regulation of Birth"), in 1968. The pope reaffirmed the traditional Catholic position that "direct interruption of the generative process already begun...[is] to be absolutely excluded as licit means of regulating birth."

The pope arrived at this position in spite of the recommendation by a papal commission. The commission advised the pope that artificial birth control is contrary to neither Scripture nor tradition. The encyclical met with a storm of protest and dissent. Studies conducted in 1970 showed that ninety percent of American Catholics rejected the pope's teaching. Recent statistics confirm that birth control practice among Catholic women is virtually the same as for non-Catholic women.

Following the furor over *Humanae Vitae*, Catholics have frequently disagreed openly with papal teachings. Theologians at Catholic universities in particular have departed from traditional teaching on many issues. Rome has often moved to suppress dissent among these theologians. Perhaps the most notable example took place in 1979, when Rome censored the German theologian, Hans Küng. The German bishops then revoked Küng's license to teach as a Catholic theologian at the University of Tübingen.

The most suspect area for a Catholic theologian involves teaching on sexuality. This was made clear in 1986 when theologian Charles Curran of Catholic University in Washington, D.C., was censored for his teaching on sexuality. He was prohibited from teaching certain courses on this subject. Curran filed suit in federal court seeking reversal of Rome's decision, but lost.

In recent years, Rome has sought to strengthen its control over Catholics who teach in Catholic colleges, seminaries and universities. It has said that theologians may not publicly express dissent from Catholic doctrine.

---

[6] "Challenge of Peace."

IMPLICATIONS FOR THE FUTURE

The debate over Rome's exercise of authority raises questions for the future. Many Catholics express the fear that Rome is undoing the work achieved by Vatican II. They have said that a full-scale conservative reaction is under way in Rome. By this view, Rome is now acting as arbitrarily and rigidly as it did in the days of Pio Nono. Other Catholics say that Rome's actions are necessary. This school of thought believes that incorrect interpretations of Vatican II have led to confusion among Catholics. By this view, Rome must take a strong stand to restore authentic Catholic teaching in the face of dissent.

The struggle to define authority in the post-Vatican II Church is still very much in progress. The historian cannot safely predict how the struggle will end. The historian can only point to the past and suggest parallels. By doing this we can observe the following. The Church has often stumbled when it insists on enforcing its teachings through the exercise of raw ecclesiastical power. The challenge for the Church in the years ahead is to preserve the apostolic faith. Yet, it must do this in such a way that the Spirit who makes all things new is not stifled. This is not a new challenge, but an ancient one. In effect, it is the story behind Church history.

FOCUS 39

TWO CATHOLICS WHO CAUGHT THE SPIRIT OF VATICAN II

If we were going to select someone as a model for Catholic life in today's world, we probably would base our selection on several criteria. It would be helpful to have someone who lived in the pre-Vatican II Church and who loved that Church. Continuity is important, especially in the life of the Church, where so much depends on tradition. Also, we would want someone whose faith was tested in the fires of sacrifice and struggle. No "sunshine Christians" would do. Finally, we would not want people unbalanced in their practice of the faith. We wouldn't select, for example, a hermit who didn't understand the real world. Nor would we want an activist gadfly who had never experienced the inner world of the Spirit.

By these criteria, whom should we select? Fortunately, we have not one but two candidates who meet the above criteria: Thomas Merton (d. 1968) and Dorothy Day (d. 1980). Merton was a Trappist monk whose life was dedicated to prayer and contemplation. Yet, from his monk's cell in Gethsemane, Kentucky, Merton knew and wrote more about Christianity in the modern world than most "active" Catholics. He was a champion of civil rights and a spokesman for peace and nuclear disarmament. He was an ecumenist and a leader in the dialogue between Christians and members of Eastern religions. In his writings, he taught that at the deep level of the human spirit God is one and the human family is integrally united.

Dorothy Day lived her faith in the workaday world. Like Merton, she was a contemplative. If Merton was an "active contemplative," then Day was a "contemplative activist." She showed how a Christian is to attend to the work of social justice. She was no shrill ideologue spouting slogans and condemning everything in sight. Instead, she persisted in working for justice through a quiet determination based on a life of prayer. When Vatican II was convened, she dropped her many busy activities on behalf of the poor and traveled to Rome. There, she locked herself in a room near the Vatican and prayed and fasted for the success of the council.

At the same time, Day was a strong and effective champion of the poor. Her Catholic Worker movement, co-founded with Peter Maurin in 1933, served thousands of disadvantaged people all over the United States. Her writings in the *Catholic Worker* newspaper showed her to be an outspoken advocate for justice and a devout Catholic at the same time.

If we had to pick one gift that Merton and Day shared equally it would be this. For all its faults, they loved the Catholic Church. They dedicated their lives to bringing all that was right with Catholicism into the modern world. They were Vatican II Catholics *par excellence.*

FOCUS 40

SUMMING UP:
THE 'BIG EVENTS'
OF CHURCH HISTORY

How did we get from the age of the apostles to today's Church? What follows is a list of important stages through which the Church has passed in reaching the present day.

Date	Event	Significance
64	Emperor Nero blames Christians for burning Rome	Beginning of age of persecution.
100	Emperor Trajan makes it illegal to be a Christian	Persecution intensified.
286	Roman Empire divided into East and West	Foundation laid for separate Byzantine and Roman Churches.
313	Emperor Constantine makes Christianity a legal religion in Roman Empire	Church becomes entangled with politics of Empire; beginnings of Church/state conflict.
325	Council of Nicaea	Nicene Creed refutes Arianism.
451	Council of Chalcedon	Jesus declared "one person in two natures"; Church's christology formally established.
525	Saint Benedict founds Monte Cassino	Beginnings of Benedictine movement in West.
756	Donation of Pepin	Establishes Frankish kings as rivals of popes.
994	Cluniac Reform	Monasteries associated with Cluny reform Church abuses.
1054	Schism between Rome and Constantinople	Division of Catholic and Orthodox Churches.
1095	First Crusade	Launches era of crusades, promotion of idea of Christianity as sovereign universal religion.
1209	Francis of Assisi founds Franciscan Order	Poverty as Christian ideal returns to Church.
1305	"Babylonian Captivity" of papacy begins	Scandal of papal corruption lessens credibility of popes as sole spokesmen for universal Church.

1378	Western Schism begins	Rival candidates for papal office further diminish papacy's credibility.
1443	Council of Florence ends	End of conciliar movement; many lose hope for reform of Church from within.
1517	Martin Luther posts his *Ninety-five Theses*	Protestant Reformation begins.
1534	Ignatius Loyola founds Society of Jesus	Catholic reforming, teaching and missionary order will stem tide of Protestant Reformation
1545	Council of Trent begins	Catholic Church clarifies its doctrine against Protestants and reforms Catholic abuses.
1648	Thirty Years' War	Wars of religion end with Europe devastated and Christians disillusioned.
1751	French *Encyclopédie* published	Enlightenment ideology replaces Christianity among many intellectuals
1832	Pope Gregory XVI's encyclical *Mirari Vos*	Papacy condemns democracy and modern thought.
1854	Doctrine of Immaculate Conception promulgated by Pius IX	First dogmatic proclamation by a pope without consultation of bishops in council.
1870	Vatican I declares doctrine of papal infallibility	Medieval notion of Church becomes official model of Church authority.
1891	Pope Leo XIII issues encyclical *Rerum Novarum*	Beginning of Church's modern social teaching.
1943	Pope Pius XII issues encyclical *Divino Afflante Spiritu*	Church accepts the application of modern scholarship to biblical research.
1962	Vatican II opens in Rome	Church redefines Catholicism in terms of modern life.
1968	Pope Paul VI issues encyclical *Humanae Vitae*	Beginning of large-scale dissent by Catholics from papal teaching.
1978	John Paul II elected	Integration of traditional hierarchical authority with principles of Vatican II.

CHAPTER TWENTY-ONE

VISIONS AND BOUNDARIES

THE FINAL CHAPTER in a book about history—the history of any-thing, much less the Church—is always the riskiest. As a history comes to a close, the author turns from being an historian toward becoming an analyst of the present scene and a prophet of the future. Historians who write a book dealing with the twentieth century must take a deep breath (or a stiff drink) for the courage to finish their works. They know that people such as myself scour the racks for their books and begin by reading the last chapter first in order to see how good they were at evaluating things.

To ease the anxiety of starting this chapter, I'll start with three droll remarks made to me on separate occasions by three separate priests of the diocese in which I was living in the heady days a decade or so after the conclusion of Vatican II. The first priest observed that, "When the nuns took their habits off after Vatican II, their brains fell out." The second priest, perhaps a more astute observer of the psychosomatic forces at play, noted that "Diarrhea is not a cure for constipation." Finally, the third, a practitioner of *realpolitik*, told me, "I do everything I can to thwart the implementation of Vatican II in my parish."

Addressing the post-conciliar confusion a bit more eloquently, and speaking twenty years after the Council, Cardinal Joseph Ratzinger, Prefect of the Congregation for the Doctrine of the Faith,[1] opined:

> [T]o defend the true tradition of the Church today means to defend the Council. It is also our fault if we have at times provided a pretext (to the "right" and "left" alike) to view Vatican II as a "break" and an abandon-ment of the tradition. There is, instead, a continuity that allows neither a return to the past nor a flight forward, neither anachronistic longings nor unjustified impatience. We must remain faithful to the *today* of the Church, not the *yesterday* or *tomorrow*. And this today of the Church is the documents of Vatican II, without *reservations* that amputate them and without *arbitrariness* that distorts them.[2]

---

[1] The Congregation for the Doctrine of the Faith was originally called the "Congregation of the Roman and Universal Inquisition," and then later, the "Holy Office."

[2] J. Ratzinger, with Vittorio Messori, *The Ratzinger Report* (San Francisco: Ignatius Press, 1985), p. 31 (empha-sis original).

These four statements—the Cardinal's and the three priests'—all have something in common. They represent an attempt to reassert *boundaries* which they hope will restrain *visions* that have grown out of Vatican II and which seem to be proliferating wildly out of control and growing in all directions at once.

VISIONARIES AND BOUNDARY-SETTERS

It is important to recognize and honor this boundary-setting function in the Church, just as it is essential to honor the visions that are given to us by our prophets. Without visions and dreams, we become sterile, moribund, static. These qualities are antithetical to the power and life of the Holy Spirit which must always animate the Church if it is truly to be Church. At the same time, however, visions must be tested against the overall sense of the Spirit which the Church has discerned through the centuries.

It is this long, venerable tradition of reflecting on and discerning what the Spirit is saying to the Church that makes Catholicism what it is. Along with the Roman Catholic Church, only the Greek Orthodox Church can lay claim to the centuries-old continuity between past and present that is essential to seeing the big picture of the Spirit's call to the Church. Catholicism means "universal" in more than one sense: In addition to being universal geographically ("horizontally," we could say), Catholicism is also universal temporally (or "vertically").

By this I mean that Catholicism by its very nature stands for the proposition that past and present are integrated into one continuous whole. Much like our belief in the Real Presence in the Mass, where the past of Calvary is not simply remembered or memorialized, but made present in the now of our lives, so, too, Catholic tradition, as exemplified in its doctrine and its actions throughout history are made fully alive in the Church's identity and mission today. We are a Pilgrim People, always seeking a better home, but as true pilgrims, we bring with us the baggage, traditions, memories, sorrows and joys of the past as we trudge along slowly toward our new destination. Pilgrims do not discard their past; they use it to make something new.

From the pontificate of Pope John XXIII (1958-1963) through that of Pope John Paul II (elected 1978) we have witnessed the tension between the vision-boundary dichotomy being played out in the life of the Church, often in a dramatic way. Pope John XXIII was a visionary. He dreamt the dream and tapped into the vision of a Church more in touch with (not necessarily in harmony with) the means that the world offered to assist the Church in spreading the gospel and advancing the Kingdom of God. Pope John Paul II, who, as a theorist at the Council[3] while Archbishop of Krakow, Poland, was a

---

[3] Archbishop Karol Wojtyla (the pope's given name) was a member of the Preparatory Commission of the Council, attended all four sessions, served on various post-conciliar commissions and from 1971 was a permanent member of the Council of the Synod of Bishops.

leading visionary at the Council. As well as any other person on earth, he fully caught and transmitted in his teachings the vision that the Spirit had transmitted to the Church through the Council.

Yet, when he became pope, John Paul II began to assert the boundary-setter dimension of his personality. In his statements and actions since 1978, we can see perhaps better than anywhere the vision-boundary dichotomy. Always calling the Church to move ahead to claim its heritage as the People of God, revived and stimulated by Vatican II, the pope nevertheless has had to "rein in" many visionaries whom he has felt are too far in advance of the *today* of the Church" as Cardinal Ratzinger characterized it. The struggle within the Church today by our visionaries—to push the edge of our boundaries ever outward in our pilgrimage—is constrained in many cases by our boundary-setters—the pope and his allies in the hierarchy who are seeking to make sure that we stay on the right road as we cross the desert toward the Promised Land.

This struggle is a necessary one if we are to be a vibrant and dynamic, Spirit-empowered people. The visionaries among us need to keep pricking and goading us, telling us, "Get a move on! There's more to do yet. Miles to go before we sleep." The boundary-setters pause for reflection. It's as if they say, "Wait a minute. Some of this strikes me as authentic, and some not so authentic." If you are a visionary, this analogy will perhaps strike you as old-fashioned and restrictive. If you tend to be more of a boundary-setter, you may feel that it's time to tell the visionaries to get lost. But, however annoying we are to each other, we're all in this together.

Let's take a look at how this vision-boundary tension has been playing out since Vatican II and what it might foreshadow. We'll reconsider some issues discussed in the previous chapter, but look at them under a different guise, that of equality.

EQUALITY IN THE LIFE OF THE CHURCH

Equality is a word that strikes some boundary-setters as absolutely irrelevant in Church usage. Their favorite refrain is, "The Church is not a democracy." No one could argue with that. The Church is definitely not a democracy, and never has been. Yet, while *democracy* may not be an adequate word to describe the relationship between Catholics, it is clear that Vatican II was pointing us toward a different relationship with one another than the traditional feudal, hierarchical model developed in the Middle Ages. The word that has best summarized that is *equality*—which does not mean *sameness*.

In the "Dogmatic Constitution on the Church" (*Lumen Gentium*), the Council stressed that "[A]ll share a true equality with regard to the dignity and to the activity common to all the faithful for the building up of the Body of Christ."[4] The visionaries have taken Vatican II at its word.

Thus visionaries, for example, have called for the work of the Church to be shared equally. Many parishes today are effectively administered by staffs that are made up entirely of laypersons. In his encyclical, *Christifideles Laici* (1989), Pope John Paul II tried to restore boundaries to what he saw as a merging of responsibilities and callings. For the pope, the laity's field of activity is the world, their families, their work, earning a living. It is there, according to the pope, that the laity bring the gospel to bear on the world, not in the halls of the rectory or parish center.

Visionaries respond by asking, "But who is going to do the work in the parishes if not the laity? There aren't enough priests and religious. Why not laypersons who have academic or other training similar to that attained by priests and religious?" As we look at the horizon, the visionaries seem to be winning on this one. It would simply be impossible to administer parishes today without lay staff and lay ministers.[5]

Nor can priests and religious provide everything that laypersons are seeking spiritually. Laypersons lead Bible study groups, prayer and meditation groups, social justice groups, youth retreat groups, and on and on, in nearly every parish. This blurring of distinctions between priest and religious on the one hand, and laity on the other, is unquestionably here to stay for the foreseeable future. This causes understandable anxiety in young persons considering the call to priesthood or religious life. For example, a young man considering the priesthood might wonder just how a priest is distinct from a layman who administers the parish, teaches Scripture, takes Communion to the sick, gives an occasional sermon—other than in the priest's role as celebrant at the Eucharist, confessor and presider over weddings and funerals.

The Catholic bishops in the United States have weighed in on this issue—clearly on the side of the visionaries:

> Over the past fifteen years, we have seen great numbers of lay people
> become involved in the liturgy as cantors and music directors, readers,
> eucharistic ministers, and altar servers. Furthermore, in some places laity
> are responsible for leading Sunday worship in the absence of a priest.
> Men and women of all ages engage in these ministries, which in turn can
> be a means of spiritual and religious formation for them.... All these
> actions, when performed in the name of Jesus and enacted under the aegis
> of the Church, are forms of ministry. Recent research indicates that at
> least half of our parishes have lay people or vowed religious in pastoral
> staff positions.... The Church's mission is being carried forward and far
> by all these lay ministers who tirelessly serve the Church and God's peo-

---

[4] *Lumen Gentium*, 32, in Flannery.

[5] It rankles many in the Church even to use the word "ministry" when applied to the laity. John Paul II sees the word as inapplicable to the laity's work in the world and would restrict it solely to "church work." It is clear that even there, however, he prefers that the laity's work not be called "ministry."

ple. We join pastors and parishioners in expressing gratitude for this development.[6]

A second equality issue involves social justice. Here, however, the equality that is sought to be established is not an equality of responsibility between clergy and laity, as just discussed, but instead the equality between the poor and the rich. In proclaiming at Vatican II, as quoted above, that "[A]ll share a true equality with regard to the dignity and to the activity common to all the faithful for the building up of the Body of Christ," we cannot pretend that people who struggle under grinding poverty day in and day out truly share in the common dignity promised to all.

Both visionaries and boundary-setters are acutely aware of this conflict between Church teaching and the actual situation, and both have moved to address it. In fact, insofar as social justice is concerned, it is sometimes difficult to know who is more visionary, the popes and bishops, or persons typically thought of as being more radical, such as Latin American liberation theologians.

John Paul II has established himself, like his predecessor Pope Paul VI (1963-78), as a social justice pope. Aside from making an obvious and visible effort to visit with the poor and speak on their behalf during his many visits to third-world countries, the pope has put the Church's official teaching at work in the service of the poor. In *Laborem Exercens* ("On Human Work," 1981), John Paul II spoke of the priority of workers and their labor over capital in economic and political systems—whether capitalist or socialist. Using a term that was close to his own Polish experience, the pope called for workers and the poor to live in *solidarity*[7] with one another in resisting attempts by either capitalists or Communists to control their lives through the manipulation of either capital or state-controlled economic systems.

In *Sollicitudo rei socialis* ("Social Concerns," 1987), John Paul II placed the Church's mission squarely on the side of the poor in developing countries, and especially on the side of the poverty-stricken South (southern hemisphere) as opposed to the rich North (developed northern hemisphere countries). Contrasting the Northern culture of weapons production and material prosperity with the culture of hunger and deprivation in the South, the pope warned that civilization as a whole was choosing death rather than life. He criticized both capitalism and Communism in their then present states, and called on countries dominated by either economic system to incorporate humane elements in order to protect and serve the poor. He did not say that one system as opposed to another—capitalism versus socialism—was inherently more in keeping with the gospel's values.

---

[6] National Conference of Catholic Bishops/United States Catholic Conference, *Called and Gifted for the Third Millennium*, 16-17 (1997).

[7] In the Polish experience, the word is charged with the connotation of resistance to oppression, as it was used by the underground and then successfully independent labor union *Solidarnösc* (*Solidarity*) in standing up to the Communist regime in Poland. Out of *Solidarnösc* a new, independent Poland arose.

In the third encyclical of his social justice trilogy, *Centesimus Annus* ("The Hundredth Year," 1991), written to commemorate the hundredth anniversary of Pope Leo XIII's *Rerum Novarum*, John Paul called for the dismantling of superpower military machines, criticized Marxism for ignoring the spiritual dimension to human nature, and called on predominant capitalism[8] not to exploit the poor in favor of ever greater wealth for the wealthy. Capitalism, he wrote, is a system in which things matter more than people and in which a compulsive consumerism quests for more and more things at the cost of true human freedom and happiness.

John Paul II's social justice encyclicals were bold, daring and radical. Never before had a pope put the Church on the side of workers and the poor as a class over against those who manage the means of production—whether capitalists or supervisors of a State-run socialism. In the plainest language, John Paul II was saying that to be a Christian is to be in solidarity with those who are poor and own nothing but their labor. For a boundary-setter like John Paul II, these were indeed challenging documents. But visionaries, who wanted to go even farther than the pope had gone, often ran afoul of the pope when they attempted to push his boundaries to what they saw as their logical extension.

In particular, advocates and practitioners of liberation theology (discussed in the previous chapter) came in for frequent censure from Rome. In 1984, Cardinal Ratzinger's Congregation for the Doctrine of the Faith issued an "Instruction," entitled "Certain Aspects of the Theology of Liberation," in which proponents of liberation theology were warned against an uncritical use of Marxist thought and method. In 1985, the Congregation ordered Brazilian Franciscan Leonardo Boff to discontinue teaching and preaching the ideas advanced in his book, *Church: Charism and Power*, wherein Boff criticized the institutional Church itself as the source of much of the oppression that creates a world climate of domination of the poor.[9]

Boff had described Christian base communities[10] (in Spanish, *communidades de base*) as the model for the post-Vatican II Christian community—as opposed to the parish, which he criticized as hierarchical, feudal, medieval and atavistic. In 1986, the Congregation for the Doctrine of the Faith issued another Instruction, "On Christian Freedom and Liberation," which supported the concept of base communities, but conceptualized them as part of the overall parish structure, rather than as separate from that structure. For Rome, the

---

[8] The encyclical was written after the collapse of the Communist regimes in the former Soviet Union and Eastern Europe, which prompted the pope to praise capitalism insofar as it nurtured human freedom and dignity.

[9] After an on-again, off-again attempt at reconciliation with Rome, Boff finally left the priesthood in 1992, comparing the Vatican to a bat that is afraid of the light, and characterizing his twenty-year vocation as a priest and Franciscan as a life dominated by oppression and censorship.

[10] Base communities are small, consensually run bodies of believers where priests and other leaders are called by the community rather than appointed from above, and who live with, serve and *are* the poor. The liturgy is usually celebrated in homes, factories or other places where the poor live and work instead of in traditional church buildings.

parish was still the basic community forming the society of the Church.

Yet, in something of a dramatic reversal, John Paul II wrote a personal letter to the bishops of Brazil in 1986 in which he spoke of base communities as the normal way to structure Church life in Brazil. He went even farther by speaking of liberation theology, rightly understood and in conformity to the two Instructions spoken of above, as being helpful and essential to the life of the Brazilian Church.

Brazil, which has the largest number of bishops in the world, and at least nominally, the largest number of Catholics, is thus something of a bellwether on the subject of the tension between visionaries and boundary-setters on the issues of social justice and liberation theology. As with the issue of equal responsibility between priests and laity, here, too, the visionaries—whether a social-justice pope or Brazilian bishops—seem to be setting the agenda.

Finally, we look at the third major equality issue before the Church today, namely, the role of women in the life and leadership of the Church. If we accepted the secular media's characterization of this issue, all the visionaries would be enlightened feminists, and all the boundary-setters would be men (usually portrayed as frightened, power-hungry men with sinister intentions). Yet, the actual situation seems to be typical of most issues that lie along a spectrum of opinion—one finds men and women of all stripes as both visionaries and boundary-setters.

What do the visionaries want? As with liberation theology,[11] there probably are as many answers as there are visionaries. I remember my baptism by fire into the intricacies of what I suppose could be called the "women's movement" within the Catholic Church. In 1978 or so, I attended a workshop in San Antonio, Texas, led by Sister Joan Chittister, O.S.B., entitled "Vision of Church and Ministry." Five or six other males and I (including one bishop) and some four or five hundred women listened to Sister Chittister launch into "consciousness-raising" presentations in which she laid out in unsparing detail the Church's many sins against women throughout the centuries and into the present. The line I best remember was her quotation of Saint Clement of Alexandria's (A.D. 150-215) dictum to the effect that "Woman is a she-ass over a cesspool."[12]

This remark stirred the sentiment in the gymnasium in such a fashion that I decided to take note of where the fire exits were and to make sure that my running shoes were laced tightly.

I suppose one could characterize that era as the "Anger Phase" of the Church's women's movement. Since then, it would seem that, similar to the situation with liberation theology, some women have given up on the Church's

---

[11] There are so many different versions of liberation theology that it is more accurate to refer to liberation *theologies*.

[12] I offer my apologies to both Sister Joan and Saint Clement if I have not remembered this quotation exactly, but these words seem to summarize the general drift of Saint Clement's views on women as represented by Sister Joan.

ever changing and have left the Church, while others keep working in their own ways to be both Catholic and women, painfully aware of the contradiction in their own lives of Vatican II's call to equal dignity for all Catholics.

Perhaps the example of one of my cousins is typical of what a Catholic laywoman might have gone through during the early days of the post-Vatican II Church. Sometime during the 1970's, my cousin left her promising career with IBM to earn a degree in theology at one of the same schools of theology to which the Church sends its brightest prospects for ordination to the priesthood. She sat in the same classroom with these men, befriended and was befriended by them, got the same training and received the same terminal degree that they did. Yet, when she returned to her home diocese and offered her talents and training to the Church, she was told, in essence, "No women need apply." Today she's engaged in a second career at a major university, and continues her spiritual quest in her own quiet way, without anger or bitterness over the rejection of her gifts, but with those gifts unwanted and unused nonetheless.

Other women have linked the Church's unwillingness to accept them on an equal footing with men to the larger issue of patriarchy versus feminism that occupies secular society. These women locate the Church's rigid attitude toward women in the patriarchal world view which they see built into the very foundation of Judeo-Christian thought and tradition. They do not see "fixes," such as permitting women to be ordained, as accomplishing anything unless the entire mind-set of the patriarchal tradition is eliminated and replaced with the feminist mind-set.[13] While there are various shades of opinion represented among women who take this position, the more radical among them call for a complete overhaul of the traditional conceptualization of a sexist male God and redeemer.[14]

BEFORE WE CLOSE, A WORD OF CAUTION

Sometimes it's difficult for those of us who grew up in the Vatican I Church to remember that at the start of the third millennium the majority of Catholics (most of whom are under the age of forty) don't think in terms of "The Vatican II Church"—simply because they have known no other Church. For them, today's Church is just the Church. That is why understanding Church history is especially crucial today. Without understanding how we the Church have grown, evolved and changed as a people throughout our two-millennium existence, we can't understand our place in the today of the Church. In that

---

[13] See, for example, Gerda Lerner, *The Creation of Patriarchy* (Oxford: Oxford University Press, 1986); Elizabeth Schüssler Fiorenza, *In Memory of Her* (New York: Crossroad, 1984); Rosemary Radford Ruether, *Women-Church: Theology and Practice of Feminist Liturgical Communities* (San Francisco: Harper & Row, 1985).

[14] See generally, Mary Daly, *Beyond God the Father: Toward a Philosophy of Women's Liberation* (Boston: Beacon Press, 1973); *Gyn/Ecology: The Metaethics of Radical Feminism* (Boston: Beacon Press, 1978); and *Pure Lust: Elemental Feminist Philosophy* (Boston: Beacon Press, 1984).

regard, it is often taken for granted today that everyone forty and under has the same grounding in the faith that we over-forty's got growing up in the pre-Vatican II Church. If you want quickly to be disabused of this fallacy, I suggest that you volunteer to teach CCD classes in your local parish to today's Catholic young people (or re-read Mary Ann Donaldson's experience at the start of Chapter Two).

Younger Catholics today are radically cut off in many cases from their Catholic tradition; they have little or no sense of the continuity with the past that is essential to understanding what makes Catholicism unique. Nor do they have the same preparation in Catholicism as a form of spirituality that we post-forty's received. While today's under-forty generation is (thank God) much more grounded in social action and community-building than we ever were, this *broadening* of awareness tends to overlook a *deepening* of awareness. Catholicism today tends to be understood by many as just one more way to improve the world, save the environment, promote justice, make sure no one's feelings are hurt and ensure that people are better off materially. I would say that all of these are "benefits" that come from living according to the gospel, but they are not the gospel itself.

The gospel is first and foremost a call to personal transformation in Christ. Jesus was not a social worker; he was a man who showed us that the human person is deeply flawed in its separation from God. He showed us that to overcome that separation the human person must grow in awareness of what it means to be saved and redeemed by the God-man. And more than showing us such things, he accomplished this salvation and redemption. Jesus became for us the sacrament of our encounter with God, the means by which we not only become God-conscious, but God-transformed. Jesus taught us what it means to be fully human, and through the Spirit he sent to his Church, he made it possible for us to *become* fully human.

The concern for equality in the Church that I have discussed above is authentically an attempt to empower us to become more fully human as Jesus wanted us to be—to have "life to the full" as he promised. Everything that the Church is doing to promote equality as discussed above is a means to promote life to the full in the gospel sense. Yet, if only the external dimension of promoting life to the full is presented to Catholics, with the internal dimension of personal transformation in Christ ignored, then Catholic life can quickly become stunted.

We seem awfully certain at times that making one another feel good (a disease we have picked up from secular society) is the same thing as the gospel, which it is not. In addition to listening to our visionaries of equality, we need also to listen to our visionaries of the inner life of transformation and conversion. And in addition to honoring boundary-setters who urge us to be a little more prudent as we constantly push for change in our relationships with one another, we likewise need to honor boundary-setters who tell us that not everything in life is good for us, that there is something called morality, which is more than just attempts by old fuddy-duddies in the Vatican to keep us from having fun.

This, of course, is a caricature of our situation in the Church today, but it does tend to make my point that Catholicism in the last analysis requires an integration of the inner and the outer dimensions to our lives. Vatican II has led to many reforms of the outer dimension to our lives. It likewise called us to reform the inner dimension, but that has not gotten as much attention, particularly as we have attempted to catechize the under-forty generation, many of whom would have trouble distinguishing Catholicism from the agenda of the left wing of the Democratic Party.

Our boundary-setter-in-chief has summarized this situation thusly:

> Christians today must be formed to live in a world which largely ignores God....To "hold on" in this world, to offer to all a "dialogue of salvation" in which each person feels respected in his or her most basic dignity, the dignity of one who is seeking God, we need a catechesis which trains the young people and adults of our communities to remain clear and consistent in their faith, to affirm serenely their Christian and Catholic identity, to "see him who is invisible" and to adhere so firmly to the absoluteness of God that they can be witnesses to him in a materialistic civilization that denies him.[15]

---

[15] John Paul II (Karol Wojtyla), *On Catechesis in Our Time* (Washington, D.C.: United States Catholic Conference, 1997), 75.

TIMELINE

	EMPERORS	HISTORY MAKERS	BISHOPS OF ROME (POPES)
A.D. 81	Domitian (81-96)		Clement (88-96)
A.D. 100	Trajan (98-117) Hadrian (117-138) Antoninus (138-161)	Ignatius of Antioch martyred (107) Polycarp of Smyrna martyred (c. 155)	Pius I (140-155) Victor (189-198)
A.D. 200	Septimus Severus (193-211) Decius (249-251) Valerian (253-260) Gallienus (260-268) Diocletian (284-305) in East and Maximian (286-305) in West	Irenaeus of Lyons (200) Clement of Alexandria (c. 215) Tertullian (225) Hippolytus (c. 236) Origen (c. 254) Dionysius of Alexandria (264) Dionysius of Rome (268)	Zephyrinus (199-217) Callistus (217-222) Stephen (254-257)
A.D. 300	Constantius (305-306) in West and Galerius (305-311) in East Constantine (306-324) in West and Licinius (311-324) in East Constantine (324-337) Constantine II (337-340) Constans (337-350), and Constantius II (337-361) Julian the Apostate (361-363) Valentinian (364-375) Gratian (375-383) Theodosius I (379-392) in East Theodosius I (392-395), both East and West	Alexander of Alexandria (328) Arius (c. 336) Eusebius of Caesarea (c. 340) Eusebius of Nicomedia (342) Hilary of Poitiers (c. 367) Athanasius of Alexandria (c. 373) Gregory of Nazianzus (389) Gregory of Nyssa (c. 395)	Miltiades (311-314) Sylvester I (314-335) Julius I (337-352) Damasus I (366-384) Siricius (384-399)

> *Single dates in parentheses indicate date of death; a span of dates indicates time in office.*

EVENTS

c. 95: **End of the Age of the Apostles**
Trajan makes it illegal to be a Christian

105: Ignatius of Antioch coins term "Catholic Church"
c. 140: **Ancient Roman symbol (R) in use; prototype of later Creeds**
140: Marcion founds his rival Church
144: Marcion is excommunicated
150: Hermas advances the rigorist position on forgiveness of post-baptismal sin:
Gnostic Valentinus gains a following
Writings of Justin Martyr (265), first classically educated apologist
c. 170: Athenagoras writes on Trinity
c. 178: Celsus' *True Discourse* (an anti-Christian polemic)

202: Becomes illegal to *convert* to Christianity
Sabellius promotes Modalist views in Rome
c. 220: *Didascalia* describes non-rigorist view toward post-baptismal penance
250: Everyone required to sacrifice to Roman gods
Cyprian of Carthage and Stephen of Rome debate validity of sacramental ministers
260: Gallienus's policy of toleration inaugurates 40-year era of peace
Term *homoousios* first introduced
286: Empire divided into East and West

300: "The Great Persecution"
c. 306: Synod of Elvira requires continence of all married clergy
311: Galerius issues an edict of toleration
312: Constantine's conversion: Christianity becomes "favored" religion
313: Constantine supports Synod of Arles and represses Donatists
321: Arius is excommunicated
324: Constantine becomes sole ruler of reunited Empire
325: Council and Creed of Nicea
328: Athanasius becomes Bishop of Alexandria
335: Synod of Tyre results in exile of Athanasius
337: Empire divided among Constantine's sons;
Donatists have become a major party in North Africa
350: Arian Constantine II becomes sole emperor
353: Synod of Arles condemns Athanasius
360: Synod of Constantinople ratifies *Homoian* Creed, nullifying Nicene Creed
373: Basil the Great refutes Pneumatomachians
374: Ambrose chosen as Bishop of Milan
378: Battle of Adrianople
380: Christianity as defended by Athanasius and Cappadocians decreed "official"
religion by Theodosius
381: Council and Creed of Constantinople
383: First monastery in the West
387: Augustine embraces Christianity

211

	EMPERORS	HISTORY MAKERS	BISHOPS OF ROME (POPES)
▶ A.D. 400			
	Honorius (395-423)	Jerome (420)	Innocent I (401-417)
	Theodosius II (408-450)	Augustine of Hippo (430)	Zosimus (417-418)
	Valentinian III (425-455)	Prosper of Aquitaine (c. 463)	Leo the Great (440-461)
	Marcian (450-457)	Theodoret of Cyrrhus (c. 466)	Gelasius I (492-496)
▶ A.D. 500			
	Justinian (527-565)	Boethius (c. 524)	Boniface II (530-532)
		Gregory of Tours (c. 594)	Gregory the Great (590-604)
▶ A.D. 600			
	SECULAR RULERS	Isidore of Seville (636)	Honorius I (625-638)
		Maximus the Confessor (662)	Severinus (640-640)
	Heraclius		John IV (640-642)
	(Byzantium; 610-641)		Martin I (649-655)
			Leo II (681-683)
▶ A.D. 700			
	Leo III	Venerable Bede (735)	Stephen II (752-757)
	(Byzantium; 717-741)	Boniface (754)	
	Constantine V		
	(Byzantium; 741-775)		
	Pepin the Short		
	(Franks; 751-768)		
	Charlemagne		
	(Franks; 768-814)		
▶ A.D. 800			
	Irene	Alcuin of York (804)	Leo III (795-816)
	(Byzantium; 797-802)	Benedict of Aniane (821)	Nicholas I (858-867)
	Louis I (the Pious;	Einhard (840)	Adrian II (867-872)
	Franks; 814-840)	Rabanus Maurus (856)	John VIII (872-882)
		Radbertus (865)	
		Ratramnus (868)	

TIMELINE

A.D. 400 ◀

405: Edict of Union which suppresses Donatists in North Africa;
Pelagius begins preaching in Rome
410: Alaric the Visigoth sacks Rome
411: Synod of Carthage outlaws Donatism
418: Synod of Carthage condemns Pelagius
430: Bishops Cyril and Nestorius feud over *Theotokos*
431: Council of Ephesus
433: Formula of Union
444: Hilary of Arles's submission to Pope Leo illustrates consolidation of
papal authority in the West
448: Synod of Constantinople condemns Eutyches's one-nature Christology
449: Ephesus II—"The Robbers' Synod"; *Tome* of Leo
451: Council and Creed of Chalcedon
457: Marcian's death triggers resurgence of Monophysitism
489: Ostrogoth Theodoric conquers Italy
By this point, term "Roman Empire" no longer pertains
Barbarians rule in the West; Byzantine Empire in the East

A.D. 500 ◀

525: Benedict founds Monte Cassino, writes *Rule*
529: Synod of Orange defends the core of Augustine's teaching
553: Second Council of Constantinople fails to reconcile Chalcedonians and
Monophysites
589: Third council of Toledo
Private penance in the West spreads from Ireland to continent

A.D. 600 ◀

600: Apostles' Creed in use in the West
Beginning of feudalism
612: Muhammad establishes religion of Islam
681: Council of Constantinople condemns Monotheletism

A.D. 700 ◀

c. 726: Byzantines begin policy of iconoclasm
732: Charles Martel repels Muslim invasion of Europe
756: Donation of Pepin establishes Papal States
787: Second Council of Nicaea condemns iconoclasm
794: Synod of Frankfort condemns Spanish Adoptionism
796: Synod of Frejus defends use of *filioque*

A.D. 800 ◀

800: Charlemagne "Roman Emperor"
843: Holy Roman Empire divided among three of Louis I's sons;
Byzantines restore use of icons
853: Gottschalk's positions on the Trinity and predestination are condemned

SECULAR RULERS	HISTORY MAKERS	BISHOPS OF ROME (POPES)
▶ A.D. 900		
Otto I (Germany; 963-973)	Odo of Cluny (942)	John XII (955-964) Benedict VI (973-974)
Otto II (Germany; 973-983)		John XIV (983-984) Boniface VII (984-985) John XVI (anti-pope; 997-998) Gregory V (996-999)
▶ A.D. 1000		
Otto III (Germany; 983-1002)	Avicenna (1037) Peter Damian (1072)	Benedict VIII (1012-1024)
Henry II (Germany; 1002-1024)	Anselm of Canterbury (1109)	John XIX (1024-1033)
Conrad II (Germany; 1024-1039)		Benedict IX (1033-1045)
Henry III (Germany; 1039-1056)		Sylvester III (1045-1045) Gregory VI (1045-1046)
William I (England; 1066-1087)		Clement II (1046-1047) Leo IX (1049-1054)
Henry IV (Germany; 1056-1106)		Victor II (1055-1057) Gregory VII (Hildebrand; 1073-1085) Clement III (anti-pope; 1080, 1084-1100) Urban II (1088-1099)
▶ A.D. 1100		
Alexius I (Byzantium; 1081-1118)	Peter Abelard (1142) Bernard of Clairvaux (1153)	Paschal II (1099-1118) Calixtus II (1119-1124)
Henry V (Germany; 1098-1125)	Peter Lombard (1160) Hildegarde of Hesse (1179)	Alexander III (1159-1181)
Louis VII (France; 1137-1180)	Baldwin of Canterbury (1190)	
Frederick I (Barbarossa; Germany; 1152-1190)		
Richard I (the Lionhearted; England; 1189-1199)		
▶ A.D. 1200		
Otto IV (Germany; 1198-1215)	Eleanor of Aquitaine (1204) Dominic Guzman (1221)	Innocent III (1198-1216) Honorius III (1216-1227)
Philip II (Augustus; France; 1180-1225)	Francis of Assisi (1226) Stephen Langton (1228)	Gregory IX (1227-1241) Innocent IV (1243-1254)
John (England; 1199-1216)	Bonaventure (1274) Thomas Aquinas (1274)	Urban IV (1261-1264) Clement IV (1265-1268)
Frederick II (Sicily and Germany; 1194-1250)	Siger of Brabant (1281) Albert the Great (1280)	Boniface VIII (1294-1303)
Louis IX (France; 1226-1270)	Roger Bacon (1292)	

	A.D. 900 ◄

910: Abbey of Cluny founded
962: Pope John XII crowns Otto I Holy Roman Emperor
994: Cluniac reform begins to spread across Europe

	A.D. 1000 ◄

1000: Feudalism has evolved into complex societal system
1022: Synod of Pavia decrees strict celibacy for all orders of the Church
1054: Schism between Eastern and Western Churches
1066: Battle of Hastings; William of Normandy becomes king of England
1076: Pope Gregory VII excommunicates Henry IV
1078: Investiture controversy begins
1095-1099: First Crusade
c. 1095: *Chanson de Roland*
1098: Cistercian Order founded

	A.D. 1100 ◄

1122: Concordat of Worms
1145: *The Sentences of Divinity* lists seven sacraments
1146-1147: Revolt of Arnold of Brescia
1150: Peter Lombard's *Sentences*
1147-1148: Second Crusade
1160: The *Cid*
1150-1250: Heyday of French troubadours
c. 1175: Peter Waldo begins preaching apostolic poverty
1178ff.: Albigensian heresy propagated
1140-1227: Goliardic poets flourish
1189-1192: Third Crusade

	A.D. 1200 ◄

1200: Feudalism is on the decline
1202-1204: Fourth Crusade
1208: Francis founds Friars Minor; papal interdict on London
1215: Magna Carta; Fourth Lateran Council;
         Order of Preachers founded by Dominic
1217: Fifth Crusade
1227: Beginning of papal Inquisition
1225: *Roman de la Rose* is begun
1204-1229: Albigensian Crusades
1274: Second Council of Lyons affirms doctrine of purgatory

	SECULAR RULERS	HISTORY MAKERS	BISHOPS OF ROME (POPES)
A.D. 1200			
	Rudolf (Germany; 1273-1291) Edward I (England; 1272-1307)		
A.D. 1300			
	Philip IV (the Fair; France; 1285-1314) Philip VI (France; 1328-1350) Edward III (England; 1327-1377)	John Duns Scotus (1308) Meister Eckhart (1327) Marsilius of Padua (1342) Ubertino of Casale (1341) William of Ockham (1347) Petrarch (1374) Catherine of Siena (1380) Gerard Groote (1384) John Wycliffe (1384)	Clement V (1305-1314) John XXII (1316-1334) Benedict XII (1334-1342) Clement VI (1342-1352) Innocent VI (1352-1362) Urban V (1362-1370) Gregory XI (1370-1378) Urban VI (1378-1389) Clement VII (anti-pope; 1378-1394) Boniface IX (1389-1404)
A.D. 1400			
		Julian of Norwich (1413) John Hus (1415) Nicholas of Cusa (1464) Thomas à Kempis (1471)	Innocent VII (1404-1406) Alexander V (anti-pope; 1409-1410) John XXIII (anti-pope; 1410-1415) Gregory XII (1406-1415) Benedict XIII (anti-pope; 1394-1423) Martin V (1417-1431) Eugene IV (1431-1447) Nicholas V (1447-1455) Alexander VI (1492-1503)
A.D. 1500			
	Henry VIII (England; 1509-1547) Francis I (France; 1515-1547) Charles V (Germany; 1519-1556) Henry II (France; 1547-1559) Edward VI (England; 1547-1553) Mary Tudor (England; 1553-1558) Ferdinand I (Germany; 1558-1564)	Thomas Munzer (1525) Ulrich Zwingli (1531) Thomas More (1535) Desiderius Erasmus (1536) Andreas Carlstadt (1541) Martin Luther (1546) Thomas Cranmer (1556) Ignatius Loyola (1556) Philip Melancthon (1560) John Calvin (1564) John Knox (1572) Teresa of Avila (182?) Charles Borromeo (1584) Mary Stuart, Queen of Scots (1587)	Julius II (1503-1513) Leo X (1513-1521) Adrian VI (1522-1523) Clement VII (1523-1534) Paul III (1534-1549) Paul IV (1555-1559) Pius IV (1560-1565) Sixtus (1585-1590) Clement VIII (1592-1605)

TIMELINE

1291: End of the Crusades
1295: Edward I's "Model Parliament"

1305: Beginning of the Babylonian captivity of the papacy
1337: Hundred Years' War begins
1347-1352: Black Death kills nearly a third of Europe
1377: Papacy returns to Rome
1378: Western Schism begins
1381: Peasants revolt in England

1415: Hus burned at the stake;
      Council of Constance condemns Wycliffe's doctrines
1431: Council of Basle; Joan of Arc burned at the stake
1438-1443: Council of Florence attempts to reunite Western and Eastern Churches
1453: Constantinople falls to Muslims;
      Hundred Years' War ends; Gutenberg's movable type
1464: Erasmus of Rotterdam born
1483: Martin Luther is born
1491: Ignatius Loyola born
1492: Spanish Inquisitor-General orders Jews to accept Christianity or be exiled

1500: Pope Alexander VI declares a crusade against the Turks
1501: Pope Alexander orders burning of books deemed threatening
      to Church authority
1503: Martin Luther enters Augustinians: John Knox born
1506: John Tetzel sells indulgences in Germany
1507: Luther ordained an Augustinian priest
1509: Henry VIII becomes king of England,
      marries Catherine of Aragon; John Calvin born
1517: Luther writes Ninety-five Theses, protests the sale of indulgences
1518: Luther refuses to recant Ninety-five Theses at Augsburg
1520: Thomas Munzer begins Anabaptist movement in Germany;
      Luther excommunicated by Pope Leo X
1521: Pope Leo declares King Henry VIII of England "Defender of
      the Faith" for his treatise condemning Luther;
      Luther, banned from Empire, retreats to Wartburg Castle and
      begins German translation of Bible

SECULAR RULERS	HISTORY MAKERS	BISHOPS OF ROME (POPES)

▶ A.D. 1500

Elizabeth I	Catherine de Medici (1589)	
(England; 1558-1603)	John of the Cross (1591)	
Francis II	Philip Neri (1595)	
(France; 1559-1560)	Peter Canisius (1597)	
Francis II		
(France; 1559-1560)		
Charles IX		
(France; 1560-1574)		
Henry III		
(France; 1574-1589)		
Henry IV		
(France; 1589-1610)		

▶ A.D. 1600

James I
(England; 1603-1625)
Charles I
(England; 1625-1649)
Louis XIV
(France; 1643-1715)

EVENTS

1524: Peasants revolt in southern Germany; Zwingli abolishes Mass in Zurich
1527: Imperial troops sack Rome; Lutheran reform reaches Sweden
1528: King Henry VIII seeks divorce; Protestant reform begins in Scotland
1529: Thomas More made Chancellor of England;
Luther and Zwingli debate the Eucharist at Marburg
1530: Philip Melancthon publishes *Confession of Augsburg*
1531: Zwingli killed in battle
1533: Henry VIII marries Anne Boleyn and is excommunicated
1534: Society of Jesus founded by Ignatius Loyola
1535: Thomas More executed by Henry VIII
1536: Catholic religious orders dissolved in England;
first edition of Calvin's *Institutes*
1541: Calvin returns to Geneva from exile;
John Knox assumes control of Reformation in Scotland
1542: Pope Paul III establishes papal Inquisition in Rome
1543: Pope Paul issues *Index of Forbidden Books*;
Protestants burned at the stake by Spanish Inquisition
1545: Council of Trent convenes
1546: Religious Civil War in Germany; Martin Luther dies
1554: Catholics have civil rights restored in England under "Bloody Mary"
1555: Religious Peace of Augsburg
1559: Expanded edition of the *Institutes*, now the "handbook of the Reformation"
1562: Third session of Council of Trent begins inaugurating real reform;
French Huguenots massacred at Vassey and French Wars of Religion begin;
Thirty-nine Articles published in England
1563: Council of Trent ends; Puritanism appears in England
1564: John Calvin dies; Philip Neri founds Oratorians in Rome
1567: Duke of Alba begins persecution of Protestants in Netherlands
1568: Jesuits establish mission in Japan
1572: St. Bartholomew's Day Massacre; John Knox dies
1573: Huguenots granted temporary amnesty in France
1577: *Book of Concord* prepared by Lutheran theologians
1579: John of the Cross writes "Dark Night of the Soul"
1580: Jesuit missionaries secretly arrive in England
1588: Pope Sixtus V founds Vatican Library
1593: King Henry IV declares, "Paris is worth a Mass," and becomes a Catholic
1594: Richard Hooker's popular spiritual works appear in England
1598: Edict of Nantes grants freedom of worship and press to
Protestants in France

1606: Guy Fawkes and Catholic coconspirators sentenced to death in England
1611: King James Bible published
1615: Jesuits number 13,112 members in 32 provinces
1618: Thirty Years' War begins
1622: King James I dissolves English Parliament
1623: Blaise Pascal born in France

SECULAR RULERS	HISTORY MAKERS	BISHOPS OF ROME (POPES)
▶ A.D. 1600		
Charles II (England; 1660-1685)	Francis de Sales (1622)	Urban VIII (1623-1644)
	Cornelis Jansen (1638)	Innocent X (1644-1655)
Peter the Great (Russia; 1682-1725)	Galileo Galilei (1642)	Innocent XI (1676-1689)
	Armand-Jean Cardinal Richelieu (1642)	
William and Mary (England; 1689-1702)	Richard Hooker (1647)	
	Oliver Cromwell (1658)	
	Vincent de Paul (1660)	
	Blaise Pascal (1662)	
	George Fox (1691)	
▶ A.D. 1700		
	Auguste Francke (1727)	Clement XIV (1769-1774)
	Jonathan Edwards (1758)	
	Voltaire (1778)	Pius VI (1775-1799)
	John Wesley (1791)	
▶ A.D. 1800		
	Bishop John Carroll (1815)	Pius VII (1800-1823)
	Joseph de Maistre (1821)	Leo XII (1823-1829)
	Cardinal Ercole Consalvi (1824)	Pius VIII (1829-1831)
	Friedrich Schlegel (1829)	Gregory XVI (1831-1846)
	Friedrich Schleiermacher (1834)	
	Count Louis Bonald (1840)	Pius IX (1846-1878)
	Bishop John England ((1842)	Leo XIII (1878-1903)
	Francois Chateaubriand (1848)	
	Felicite de Lammenais (1854)	
	Søren Kierkegaard (1855)	
	Robert Owen (1858)	
	Klemens von Metternich (1859)	
	Ferdinand Bauer (1860)	

EVENTS

1624: George Fox, founder of the Quakers, born in England;
    Cardinal Richelieu becomes first minister of France
1633: Inquisition forces Galileo to repudiate Copernican theories
1640: Jansen's *Augustinus* published posthumously
1642: English Civil War begins
1648: Peace of Westphalia ends Thirty Years' War
1649: King Charles I of England beheaded
1653: Cromwell becomes Lord Protector of England;
    Blaise Pascal joins Jansenist community at Port-Royal in France
1678: Catholics excluded from both houses of English Parliament
1682: King Louis XIV forces Huguenots in France to convert to Catholicism
1685: Louis XIV revokes Edict of Nantes (1598) and exiles French Protestants
1686: Pietist Auguste Francke organizes Bible study groups in Germany
1689: William and Mary become king and queen of England;
    Peter the Great becomes czar of Russia
1694: Voltaire born

1703: John Wesley born
1738: Wesley's Aldersgate experience
1741: Jonathan Edwards advances Calvinist theology in American colonies
1751: French *Encyclopédie* published
1761: Voltaire's collected works published
1773: Pope Clement XIV dissolves Jesuits
1778: Voltaire dies
1789: The French Revolution;
    French National Assembly nationalizes Church property
1790: John Carroll of Baltimore becomes first bishop of United States
1791: First Amendment to U.S. Constitution provides for
    separation of Church and State
1793: Robespierre outlaws Catholicism in France
1795: Catholicism is restored in France

1800: Napoleon Bonaparte become French "First Consul"
1801: Napoleon concludes concordat with Pius VII
1804: Napoleon named Emperor
1809: Napoleon annexes Papal States, takes Pius VII captive
1813: Simon Bolivar gains control of Venezuela; Mexico gains independence
1814: Pius VII returns to Rome
1815: Napoleon is defeated at Waterloo
1816: Pius VII issues *Etsi Longissimo*, urging Latin American bishops to
    support colonial governments
1822: Brazil becomes independent nation
1825: Aristocrats restored in France
1829: Catholic Emancipation Act permits British Catholics to hold public office
1830: July Revolution in Paris, Charles X abdicates;
    the Blessed Virgin is said to appear to Catherine Laboure

SECULAR RULERS	HISTORY MAKERS	BISHOPS OF ROME (POPES)
A.D. 1800		
	Archbishop Nicholas Wiseman (1865)	
	Joseph Prudhon (1865)	
	Rafael Carrera (1865)	
	Alphonse Lamartine (1869)	
	Rene Montalembert (1870)	
	Charles Dickens (1870)	
	Fredrick Maurice (1872)	
	Horace Bushnell (1876)	
	Cardinal Giacomo Antonelli (1876)	
	Bishop Felix Dupanloup (1878)	
	Frederic Le Play (1882)	
	Karl Marx (1883)	
	Victor Hugo (1885)	
	John Bosco (1888)	
	Isaac Hecker (1888)	
	Johann Döllinger (1890)	
	Cardinal John Henry Newman (1890)	
	Henry Manning (1892)	
	Otto von Bismarck (1898)	
A.D. 1900		
	Charles Perin (1905)	Pius X (1903-1914)
	George Tyrell (1909)	Benedict XV
	William James (1910)	(1914-1922)
	Cardinal James Gibbons (1921)	Pius XI (1922-1939)
	Louis Duchesne (1922)	Pius XII (1939-1958)
	Franz Schindler (1922)	John XXIII
	Baron Friedrich von Hugel (1925)	(1958-1963)
	Cardinal Desire Joseph Mercier (1926)	Paul VI (1963-1978)
	Adolf von Harnack 1930)	John Paul I
	Lucien Laberthonniere (1932)	(1978-1978)
	Henri Bremond (1933)	John Paul II (1978-)

TIMELINE

EVENTS

┤A.D. 1800◄

1832: Gregory XVI condemns freedom of religion and press in *Mirari Vos*;
Giuseppe Mazzini founds movement for Italian unification

1834: Pope Gregory condemns Lammenais in *Singulari Nos*

1837: Bishop John England of Charleston, South Carolina, proposes joint
lay-episcopal government of U.S. Catholic dioceses but is opposed by
other American bishops

1843: Queen Isabella II of Spain assumes throne

1846: The Blessed Virgin purportedly appears at La Salette

1848: Wave of revolution sweeps through Europe; Pius IX flees Rome
Marx and Engels publish *Communist Manifesto*

1849: Italian Nationalists declare Rome a republic;
nationalists are defeated and Pius IX returns

1851: Pius IX promulgates the "perpetual adoration" devotion

1854: Pius IX proclaims the doctrine of the Immaculate Conception

1856: "Know-Nothing" Party in America drafts anti-Catholic platform

1858: Bernadette Soubirous claims visions of Blessed Virgin at Lourdes
American priest Isaac Hecker founds Paulist Fathers

1859: John Bosco founds the Salesian Order

1860: Victor Emmanuel II becomes first "king of Italy"

1864: Pius IX publishes *Syllabus of Errors* condemning liberalism

1869: First Vatican council convenes

1870: Vatican I decrees pope infallible in matters of faith and morals;
revolution in Paris, establishment of the Third Republic;
Italian nationalists declare unification of Italy

1871: Italy grants papacy control of Vatican
Otto von Bismarck begins *Kulturkampf* against Catholic Church in Prussia

1879: French assembly passes anti-Catholic legislation

1890: Cardinal Charles de Lavigeie urges French Catholics to "rally" behind
the Third Republic

1891: Pope Leo XIII publishes *Rerum Novarum*

1893: Leo XIII issues *Providentissimus Deus* on the Bible

1894: The "Dreyfuss Affair" in France

1899: Leo XIII Condemns "Americanism"

┤A.D. 1900◄

1904: Anti-Catholic administration in France decrees separation of
Church and State

1907: Pius X condemns Modernism in *Pascendi Gregis*

1914: World War I begins

1918: Czar Nicholas and his family are murdered in Russia

1921: Adolf Hitler organizes storm troopers in Germany

1922: The U.S.S.R. is formally organized

1923: Teilhard de Chardin engages in paleological excavations in China

1924: Italian voters endorse Mussolini

1929: Italy and the Vatican conclude the Lateran Treaty

1931: Pius XI publishes *Quadragesimo Anno*

SECULAR RULERS	HISTORY MAKERS	BISHOPS OF ROME (POPES)
▶ A.D. 1900	Rudolf Otto (1937)	
	Alfred Loisy (1940)	
	Romolo Murri (1940)	
	Henri Bergson (1941)	
	Benito Mussolini (1945)	
	Adolf Hitler (1945)	
	Dietrich Bonhoeffer (1945)	
	Maurice de Wulf (1947)	
	Maurice Blondel (1949)	
	Joseph Stalin (1953)	
	Teilhard de Chardin (1955)	
	Paul Tillich (1965)	
	Karl Adam (1966)	
	Karl Barth (1968)	
	Thomas Merton (1968)	
	Reinhold Niebuhr (1971)	
	Jacques Maritain (1973)	
	C. H. Dodd (1973)	
	Rudolf Bultmann (1976)	
	Étienne Gilson (1978)	
	Dorothy Day (1980)	
	Jean-Paul Sartre (1980)	
	Karl Rahner (1984)	
	Edward Schillebeeckx	
	Jürgen Moltmann	
	Hans Küng	
	Gustavo Gutierrez	

Single dates in parentheses indicate date of death; a span of dates indicates time in office.

1933: Adolf Hitler becomes chancellor of Germany, and the first
     concentration camps are built by Nazis
     Dorothy Day and Peter Maurin found the Catholic Worker movement
1937: Pius XI issues the anti-Nazi encyclical *Mit Brennender Sorge*
1939: World War II begins
1941: Thomas Merton enters Trappist monastery of Gethsemani in Kentucky
1943: Information of the Holocaust begins to reach the Vatican
1943: Pius XII issues *Divino Afflante Spiritu*, encouraging modern biblical
     scholarship
1950: Pius XII declares the doctrine of the Assumption in *Munificentissimus Deus*
1962: Vatican II opens in Rome
1965: Second Vatican Council closes on December 8
1967: The Charismatic Renewal is begun at Duquesne University
1968: Paul VI publishes *Humanae Vitae* prohibiting artificial birth control
1973: U.S. Supreme Court legalizes abortion
1979: John Paul II publishes *Redeemer of Man;*
     Hans Küng's teachings are censored by the Vatican
     Latin American bishops at Puebla, Mexico, reaffirm the Church's
     "preferential option for the poor"
1980: Four American religious women are murdered in El Salvador
1983: U.S. bishops publish peace pastoral
1984: Number of U.S. seminarians has fallen from 47,500 in 1964 to 12,000
1985: Extraordinary Synod of Bishops in Rome reaffirms Church's dedication to
     the principles of Vatican II
1986: American theologian Charles Curran of the Catholic University is censored
     by the Vatican; U.S. Bishops publish economic pastoral
1986: Pope John Paul II writes personal letter to the bishops of Brazil, affirming
     the value of base Christian communities for the Church in Brazil.
1987: Pope John Paul II's Encyclical, "Social Concerns," places the Church's
     mission squarely on the side of the poor in developing countries, especially
     the poor in the southern hemisphere.
1989: Vatican promulgates standardized "Profession of Faith," a list of essential
     Catholic beliefs that all clergy and Catholic teachers of theology are required
     to follow, including reaffirmation of a ban on contraception and the marriage
     of priests.
1991: Pope John Paul II's Encyclical, "The Hundredth Year," calls for dismantling
     of superpower military machines, criticizes Marxism for ignoring the spiritu-
     al dimension to human life, and capitalism for exploiting the poor in favor of
     the wealthy.
1994: *Los Angeles Times* survey shows that nearly half of American priests believe
     that birth control is seldom or never wrong.
1995: Congregation for Doctrine of Faith states that the pope's prohibition of
     women's ordination is "infallibly taught."
1997: American Bishops publish "Called and Gifted for the Third Millennium,"
     reaffirm crucial role of laity in the church's life and ministry.

	SECULAR RULERS	HISTORY MAKERS	BISHOPS OF ROME (POPES)
A.D. 1900			
A.D. 2000			

EVENTS

1998: Pope John Paul II makes changes in canon law that would prevent debate within the Church on such issues as euthanasia and the ordination of women to the priesthood; publishes "To Defend the Faith," an apostolic letter upholding adherence to the traditional magisterium.
Georgetown University study shows that there are 10,000 fewer active priests in America than in 1975, that average age of diocesan priests is 58, and that nearly one-fourth are older than 70.

1999: Pope John Paul II travels to Mexico reaffirming society's moral imperative to help the weak by "expanding the circle of productivity and exchange."
Poll of young Catholics published in *Commonweal* shows that 52% of respondents did not think that "the necessity of having a pope" was essential to Catholicism, while 65% said that charity to the poor was essential.
University of Maryland Survey Research Center reports that two-thirds of Catholics say that when their conscience is at odds with the pope's teaching, they should follow their conscience.

2000: Church enters symbolic "third millennium" in participation of a world-wide Jubilee calling for prayer, fasting, repentance and a return to biblical piety.
In a service at St. Peter's Basilica in March, Pope John Paul II and several Cardinal-celebrants of a Mass of reconciliation ask forgiveness for sins against other religions, women and minority racial and ethnic groups.

GLOSSARY

Adoptionism A type of Monarchianism which taught that at some point in Jesus' life, such as his Baptism in the Jordan, God "adopted" Jesus by giving him divine power. This school of thought saw Christ as merely a man, but a man "permeated," as it were, with God's power. (Also known as Dynamic Monarchianism.)

aeons In Gnosticism, lesser dieties that produced material creation and inhabited and ruled their own realms of existence.

Apollinarism Extreme *logos-flesh* Christology advanced by Bishop Apollinaris of Laodicea which held that, while Christ had a human body, he had no human spirit. He was thus not truly a man.

apology From the Greek word *apologia*, referring to a written defense of one's beliefs or position.

archons (See **demiurge**.)

apostate One who renounced the faith in time of persecution.

Arianism A heresy preached by Arius toward the end of the third century and into the fourth which stressed that the Son (Jesus) is not of the same substance (*homoousios*) as the Father, but was created as a means for God to shape the world (a form of Platonism). The Arians could not conceive of a God in three persons who was at the same time the monotheistic God of Scripture, nor could they believe that the supreme, absolute God actually became human in Jesus. They referred to Jesus as a "lesser god." Arius said that the Son is not equal in divinity to the Father, a teaching which provided the impetus for the Council of Nicaea in 325.

canon From the Greek for "measuring rod"; has come to mean *norm* or *rule*.

catechumen A prospective convert to Christianity; the name given to a person seeking Baptism.

catechumenate A lengthy period of instruction required prior to Baptism.

Christology The study of Christ's person, focusing particularly on the union between his divine and human natures.

Christology, *logos-flesh* Supported the belief that the eternal Word (Logos) was united only to Jesus' flesh (or body), and not to his entire person—body and soul (which for the ancients was somewhat similar to our concept of mind). Thus Jesus was believed to be "a man in whom God's mind operated." When pushed to its extreme form this Christology denied that Jesus really grew and matured in wisdom and understanding or that he really suffered temptations or other human psychological conflicts. (See also **Apollinarism** and **Monophysitism**.)

Christology, *logos-man* Supported the belief that the divine Word (Logos) was united to a *man*, not just to "flesh." In extreme form this school tended to deemphasize the divinity of Jesus, seeing him as a "god-filled man," rather than as true God and true man. (See also **Nestorianism**.)

communicatio idiomatum Latin phrase meaning "communication of properties." A doctrine advanced especially by Bishop Cyril of Alexandria, maintaining that, because Christ's human and divine natures are united in the one person of Christ, what we can say about one nature can be likewise attributed to the other nature.

demiurge Used in Platonism to refer to an intermediary, lesser god that composed material creation (the "creator-god"). In Gnosticism the word refers to the evil god (creator of the material universe) which carried out the process by which the supreme God's fullness slipped away from him. In several Gnostic systems the demiurge is equated with the Jewish God, Yahweh, who created six vassal lords to serve him. These are called *archons* who, in turn, decided to "make man after *our* own image."

Didache Greek word for "teaching." An early second-century Christian writing describing important elements of worship and belief.

Didascalia A Syrian writing (c. 220) which, among other things, gives a detailed picture of the Eastern Church's requirements for post-baptismal penance.

Docetism From the Greek work for "appear," a heresy which stressed that Christ only *seemed* to have a human body and to suffer and die on the cross.

Donatism This was first proposed by Donatus (c. 311) in Northern Africa. It holds that the sanctity of the minister is essential for the valid administration of the sacraments. Donatus said that bishops who cooperated with the Romans during the persecutions had lost their baptismal holiness and thus could not validly administer the sacraments or validly ordain priests.

dualism A metaphysical system which held that God and the world are separate. Also, the Gnostic doctrine that the universe is under the dominion of two opposing principles, one of which is good and the other evil. (See also *monism*.)

Dynamic Monarchianism (See **Adoptionism**.)

ex opere operantis Latin phrase meaning "based on the person performing the action." Refers to the Donatist belief that the sacraments were only valid on the basis of the sacramental minister's personal holiness.

ex opere operato Latin phrase meaning "based on the action itself." Used to define the Catholic belief that the validity of a sacrament depends not on the minister, but on Christ himself who works through the minister.

filioque From Latin, meaning "and the Son." Refers to the formula added to the Creed of Constantinople (381) by the Western Church to express the belief in the "double procession" of the Holy Spirit from the Father and the Son, rather than from the Father only, as the Creed had originally stated.

Formula of Union A compromise statement drafted by Bishop Theodoret of Cyrrhus in 433 which temporarily ended the doctrinal quarrel between Alexandria and Antioch by declaring Christ to be "perfect man consisting of rational soul and body, of one substance with us in his manhood, so that there is a union of two natures; on which ground we confess Christ to be one, and Mary to be mother of God."

gnosis (See **Gnosticism**.)

Gnosticism A perverted version of Platonism based on the conviction that matter is evil and that salvation comes through gnosis (a secret "knowledge"). In the Gnostic system Christ was not the divine Son but a "messenger" who delivered the secret means to enlightenment.

heresy An opinion or doctrine contrary to orthodox Christian belief.

homoiousios "Of like substance." A term used to counter the suspicion that a similar Greek word, *homoousios* (see below), blurred the distinction between Father and Son.

homoousios Meaning "of the same substance," from the Greek words *homo* ("same") and *ousia* ("substance").

homoousios formula The doctrinal expression used by the Council of Nicaea to state the Son's equal divinity with the Father (theologically called "the *homoousion*"). In today's Creed it is translated "one in being with the Father."

hypostasis Greek word literally meaning "substance," but frequently understood also to mean "nature" or "essence." By the mid-fourth century it was being used for "person," so that a great deal of confusion resulted when writers applied the word to the three persons of the Trinity (Did the word connote that the Trinity was God in three persons or God in three substances?).

hypostatic union Term used to express the Christian belief that in the one person of Jesus Christ a human and divine nature (hypostasis) are inseparably joined together, or that there is a "substantial union" of the divine and human natures in the one person of Christ.

incarnation The Christian belief in the union of divinity with humanity in the one person Jesus Christ.

lapsi Latin for "the lapsed ones." The general name for those Christians who cooperated with Roman authorities during persecution. (See also **libellatici**, **sacrificati**.)

libellatici Latin nickname for those Christians who, under persecution, bribed Roman officials to sell them a libellus (see below; see also **lapsi**).

libellus Latin word referring to a certificate issued to an individual during the time of Christian persecution to certify that the person had offered sacrifice to the Roman gods.

logos Greek word for "word" or "reason." The Stoics used the word to refer to God as the controlling and creative principle within the universe. Christianity uses the word to refer to the second person of the Trinity, the eternally existing "Word of God."

Marcionism A heresy propagated by Marcion around 140, which taught that Jesus only *appeared* to be human and that the human body was evil. Marcion preached the existence of two Gods: the harsh creator-god Yahweh, and the Supreme One who sent Jesus into the world. Marcion considered love, or grace, the means of salvation, and law but a means of servitude to Yahweh.

Modalism A type of Monarchianism teaching that the one God exhibits different *modes* of behavior—one mode being represented by the Father, another by the Son and the third by the Holy Spirit. Any distinctions in the Trinity are dependent upon how God wants to operate at a given time. The heresy disbelieves in three divine persons in one God. (Also known as Modalistic Monarchianism or Sabellianism, after the most famous early Modalist, Sabellius. See also **Patripassianism**.)

Modalistic Monarchianism (See **Modalism**.)

Monarchianism From the word *monarchy*, a doctrine emphasizing the unity of God to the exclusion of his individualized personhood. (See also **Adoptionism** and **Modalism**.)

monism A metaphysical system adhered to by the Stoics which held that everything was part of one and the same ultimate substance: God. (By contrast, see also **dualism**.)

Monophysitism An extreme expression of *logos-flesh* Christology teaching that Christ possessed only one nature—a divine nature which fully absorbed his human nature.

Nestorianism An extreme expression of *logos-man* Christology preached by Nestorius and condemned by the Council of Ephesus in 431. Nestorianism held that the divine and human persons remained separate in the incarnate Christ. Following the Council of Ephesus, Nestorianism slowly began to emerge as the first separate Eastern Christian Church, centering in Persia and surviving today chiefly in Asia Minor.

Patripassianism Nickname given to a form of Modalism which stressed that the Father and Son were so completely united in the Godhead that it was accurate to speak of the Father as having died on the cross. The word literally refers to the belief that "the father suffers."

Pelagianism Pelagius believed that all the grace humanity ever needed was released into the world at creation. This "grace of creation" was available to anyone who asserted his or her free will in the direction of good. Thus, one's freely chosen decision unaided by God's grace is the first step toward salvation, and everyone has the capacity to take this step. Pelagianism was condemned when Pelagius denied that an unbaptized person who performed good works was excluded from heaven. (See also **Semi-Pelagianism**.)

Platonism The philosophy of Plato stressing especially that actual things are copies of transcendent ideas and that these ideas are the objects of true knowledge apprehended by reminiscence. Plato's philosophy greatly influenced early Christian thinking. Plato believed God and the world to be separate. God was the absolute and ultimate transcendent reality, above and beyond the world of the senses. In order to "arrange" the world (Plato did not believe in creation from nothing) and to sustain it, God employs a "craftsman" known as the demiurge, a "lesser-god." Platonism greatly influenced the heretical impulses within early Christian thinking which tried to keep God and his creation, spirit and matter, separate.

pleroma A Greek word in Gnosticism referring to God's divine fullness.

pneuma Greek for "spirit." In Gnosticism, the supreme God's divine spirit.

pneumatology The theology of the Holy Spirit.

Pneumatomachians Literally, "those who war against the Spirit." These heretics denied the divinity of the Holy Spirit. They were officially condemned at the Council of Constantinople in 381.

Rule of Faith This phrase refers to short summaries of the core Christian belief which began to develop early in the second century in response to heresy. Every Christian congregation possessed its own "rule of faith" by which it expressed the essential truths of Christianity in ordinary everyday language. These "rules of faith" were the forerunners of the great written Creeds.

Sabellianism (See **Modalism.**)

sacrificati Latin word used to refer to those Christians who actually sacrificed to the Roman gods during persecution. (See also **lapsi.**)

Semi-Pelagianism A school of thought founded by Abbot John Cassian which tried to steer a middle course between Augustine's emphasis on grace to the exclusion of free will and Pelagius's emphasis on free will to the exclusion of grace.

Stoicism A school of philosophy founded by Zeno of Citium about 300 B.C. holding that the wise person should be free from passion, unmoved by joy or grief, and submissive to natural law. This system of philosophy greatly influenced the Roman world and consequently Western civilization. For the Stoics the motivating force behind creation was the logos. This logos, which they defined as God the creator, was the actual "stuff" of God existing inside all matter. (See also **monism.**)

Subordinationism The belief that the Son (Jesus) was "less divine" than the Father (God).

Theotokos Greek for "God bearer." Used to define Mary as the "Mother of God" and accepted as an orthodox title for her at the Council of Ephesus in 431, as well as in the Formula of Union of 433 (see above).

traditor From Latin, referring to a Christian who "handed over" Church books to the Roman police during the persecutions, hence the English "traitor."

INDEX